DANNY BLANCHFLOWER

Dave Bowler is the author of *Shanks, the Authorized Biography of Bill Shankly, No Surrender, a Biography of Ian Botham* and *'Winning Isn't Everything . . .', a Biography of Sir Alf Ramsey.*

DAVE BOWLER

DANNY
BLANCHFLOWER

A Biography of a Visionary

VISTA

First published in Great Britain 1997
by Victor Gollancz

This Vista edition published 1998
Vista is an imprint of the Cassell Group
Wellington House, 125 Strand, London WC2R 0BB

The right of Dave Bowler to be identified as author
of this work has been asserted by him in accordance with
the Copyright, Designs and Patents Act, 1988.

The detail on page 18, from the May 1956 England v Brazil
programme, is reproduced by kind permission of Wembley
Stadium Ltd.

A catalogue record for this book is
available from the British Library.

ISBN 0 575 60238 4

Printed in Great Britain by
Cox & Wyman Ltd, Reading, Berks

98 99   10 9 8 7 6 5 4 3 2 1

To Mom and Dad
Everything I am and have done is thanks to you.
And for Denise
Though it's storming out . . .
Always
David

Contents

Acknowledgements

This is the thirteenth book that I've inflicted upon the world. A number of unlucky souls helped me put it together and I'd like to offer my thanks.

Without the assent of Jackie Blanchflower in the first place, nothing would have come of the idea. I'd also like to thank Cindy Blanchflower for her forbearance under difficult circumstances.

Many, many people have given their time to talk to me over the course of the last year and their contributions form a major part of the book. To you all, I am eternally grateful and I hope that you recognize the Danny Blanchflower you knew in the following pages. My thanks then to Ronald Murdock, Bertie Wright, Cecil Kelly, Bertie Peacock, Lord Mason, Steve Griffiths, Larry Canning, Tommy Thompson, Stan Lynn, Peter Aldis, Amos Moss, Dave Walsh, Peter McParland, Derek Dougan, Sir Walter Winterbottom, George Robb, Ron Reynolds, Cliff Jones, Maurice Norman, Sir Stanley Matthews, Johnny Haynes, Peter Osgood, Eamonn Bannon, Geoff Hurst, Pat Jennings and Pat Rice.

In addition to the interviews, many people wrote in response to assorted appeals for help, and the information they provided was invaluable: Margaret Morrow, Eric Wright, Hunter Davies, Clive Walker, David Goodyear, Mark Wilson, Mr Holland, Brian Woolley, Frank Slater, Peter Walton, Maurice Tomlins, Dennis Jackson, R. Jackson, Robert Linton, Glynn Lunn, Peter O'Dell, Billy Currie, Margaret Stevenson, Michael Haran, John Fulton, John Parkinson, Tony Larner, Neil Rioch, Steve Stride, Jim from Belfast, Wesley McCamley, Don O'Doherty, A. Griffin.

In addition, I'd like to recognize the assistance provided by Malcolm Boyden, Miles Barter and Radio WM, the *Belfast Telegraph* and the very generous people of Northern Ireland, the *Barnsley Chronicle*, the *Birmingham Evening Mail*, *Sunday Express*, *Daily Mail*, Lesley Lind and the University of St Andrews, Roy Miller and the Irish FA, and the following football clubs: Aston Villa, Stoke City,

Arsenal, Michael Spinks and Barnsley FC, Crystal Palace, P. R. Barnes and Tottenham Hotspur, Tranmere Rovers, Blackpool. The bibliography at the back of the book lists those books that were invaluable during my research – I'd like to thank all those authors for their unwitting assistance.

I'd like to thank John Roberts for his help early on with the book along with his regular words of encouragement – the *Independent* is always worthwhile for its tennis coverage alone!

At Gollancz, thanks to Caroline North, who commissioned the book, and Ian Preece, who has been extremely patient, refusing to complain once the initial deadline passed. His enthusiasm and faith in the whole project has been crucial. At the agency Tanja Howarth and Mark Hayward have looked after business with their customary style and vigour. Hackenbush would like to offer greetings to Bryan Dray. Thanks too to Carrie for her encouraging words – hope you enjoy the book.

As ever, Denise was a tower of strength as I put this all together, despite my frequent complaints.

Finally, thanks to Mom and Dad for buying the *Sunday Express* when I was young. Without you, this book would never have happened. So the rest of you know who to blame.

Introduction

Glory, Glory, Danny Blanchflower

Let's start in heretical vein. Football is not all about winning.

Dear God. There's a thought to conjure with as we pause briefly to watch one hundred merchant bankers, charged with the safe delivery of another football-club flotation, plunge to earth from a fourteenth-storey City window, driven to their unmourned deaths by the very idea that the game might be about a ball rather than a gilt-edged share option. You can hear the jaws dropping in board rooms the length and breadth of the Premiership, can't you? Why else would Liverpool, Arsenal or Manchester United exist if not to win the League or enter the European Champions League? Or, more accurately, if it wasn't to make money by winning the League or entering the Champions League? Just recently, Manchester United confirmed their position as the club everyone loves to hate when, on reaching the semi-finals of the European Cup, chief executive Martin Edwards could only complain that they'd lost £400,000 in prize money because of the fluctuations of the exchange rate. Would Sir Matt Busby, a canny manager who understood the vital importance of cold hard cash, ever have made such a crassly parsimonious statement when on the verge of European football's greatest prize? Was it prize money that took his Babes into Europe in the first place? Was it the thought of wealth untold that made him rebuild Manchester United from the ashes of the war and then from the ashes of Munich? Or was it the lure of competing with the best, of building a club of which he and the city, the country too, could be proud? Of course financial stability is crucial to a club and its future, but I've yet to see thousands queuing outside Stamford Bridge for a glimpse of the financial accountant, whatever his flair for the profit and loss account. The important thing is to retain perspective, achieve a balance between on- and off-the-field activities.

Dreams of glory are a far more enduring currency than any that can be covered by a mere chequebook or a balance sheet. Men like Roy Evans, Alex Ferguson, Ruud Gullit and Arsene Wenger understand this, but are still forced to labour within fiscal timetables towards strategic goals.

Football *isn't* just about financial reward, winning teams, change strips, executive boxes and whirling cash registers. It's about Brighton supporters desperately clinging on to their club in the face of calamity. It's about kids going to watch Bromsgrove Rovers or Blackburn Rovers with their parents, listening to tales of the past, dreaming about the heroes of the present and of emulating them in the future; about waiting to watch your latest visitors, be they Inter Milan or Inter Cardiff. It's about remembering Matthews, Wright, Edwards, Haynes, Moore, Finney, Best, Giles, Astle, Lineker, Shilton, the very thought of them and what they could do, the recall of their and your own youth warm to the touch, lighting up a cold winter evening. It's about emotional contact not financial conquest.

When we reflect on recent seasons, the abiding memory of Aston Villa, for example, won't be the premium on their shares. It will be Dwight Yorke's delightful chipped penalty that knocked Sheffield United out of the FA Cup. The most glorious acts of 1995–96 were performed in the black and white stripes of Newcastle United, Kevin Keegan's side driven on by the thrilling belief that attacking football could bring in the rewards, that the means were every bit as important as the ends, maybe more so. Perhaps under Kenny Dalglish, in these new PC (Post Cantona) years, Sir John Hall will finally get his hands on the Premiership trophy he craves, but Newcastle may not be everyone's favourite other team for much longer. There are even reports of disquiet among the Toon Army at this early stage. Under Dalglish, inspiration will be sacrificed for efficiency, Ginola for an engine, Asprilla for an artisan. The ends are now all-important. Look at the undignified scramble that brought George Graham back into the game, back to his rightful place at Leeds United, the club stigmatized by Revie's 1960s win-at-all-costs philosophy and Wilkinson's love affair with the efficient, the dull and the banal. And yet even they can't kill the real fire that burns within the game itself.

When the hype has died down, we're left with the truth that football is only a game (sorry, Mr Shankly). In fact, it's at its best when it is only a game. Football was the game we played in the park as kids, the sport that entertained the working man on his day off, the game that has helped countless players avoid the harsh necessity of growing up. We all want to see footballers take their profession seriously, to see them behave with maturity and dignity off the field, and to perform better on it as a result. We all like to see our team win but, most of all, we want to see them playing bright, incisive football; we want to watch the players having fun, see them expressing themselves intelligently and joyously so that we too can enjoy it to the full. That's why we shell out our hard-earned cash on season tickets that many of us can't really afford. It's really quite simple. Football is a game. *The* game. The greatest game on earth. As one footballer once said, 'The game's about glory. It's about doing things in a style, with a flourish. It's about going out and beating the other lot, not waiting for them to die of boredom.'

That footballer was Danny Blanchflower, his name one of the most evocative in the footballing canon. Blanchflower was no innocent of course – no one who won 56 international caps, played in a World Cup Finals and led a side to the League and FA Cup Double could be that. He wanted to win, to succeed, to claim the medals and trophies as much as anyone else, writing, 'I think that a team should fight to its utmost within the rules and have a most enthusiastic desire to win, but there's a lot of difference between that and being a bad loser. A side which continually passes the buck isn't stopping to think, "Why did we lose? Was our method good enough? What can we learn from our mistakes?"' Addicted to the beauty of sport, he knew that the full realization of his vision came only in winning in the grand manner rather than in falling gloriously at the final fence, but he still felt it was far better to lose in style than gain a wholly pragmatic triumph, if triumph it be; in Blanchflower's dictionary, the words pragmatic and triumph were antipathetic. In a crushing critique of Helenio Herrera's ultra-defensive Inter Milan in the *Sunday Express*, following the Italians' European Cup win over Real Madrid in 1964, Blanchflower expounded his whole philosophy on the game in a few sentences. 'You cannot begrudge them respect as a polished professional team who carry out a cold, predictable plan to destroy the opposition. But you cannot entertain thoughts of them with the same warmth and affection as you could with Real Madrid. It was Di Stefano and Puskas and the other players who made Real Madrid grand. With Inter Milan, it is the defensive style of Italian soccer plus the guidance and discipline of Herrera that seem important to them. It is the coach rather than the great players who dominates the game. When that happens the game becomes a thing of more interest to the coach than to the players and the fans.'

Then there's Blanchflower's own view of the 1961 FA Cup Final, when Spurs beat Leicester amid the grandeur of Wembley Stadium to become the first side this century to attain the foot-balling Grail, the Double: 'I felt that we deserved to win but there was nothing convincing about it. It meant we had achieved the Double and that was a wonderful thing but the last day at Wembley had not been grand enough to finish it off. Against Burnley the following year we played better. It was a better Final and there was more satisfaction in winning it.' Although Blanchflower never managed a European Cup winner's medal in his time at Spurs, it was clear that he'd rather miss out altogether than capture one under methods similar to Herrera's.

Yet Blanchflower himself could be equally dogmatic in his view of the game; bloody-minded to a fault. His reputation is secured by virtue of the fact that he sided with the doves rather than the hawks, promoting the balletic grace of Pele or Eusebio at the expense of the industry of Ramsey's World Cup winners in 1966, for example. Nor would his repugnance for the over-coached and the furrowed-brow types disguise the fact that he was always looking forward. He was not trapped in a time warp, carping at every innovation. Back in the 1950s, Blanchflower was a proponent of floodlit matches when clubs balked at the expense. He argued that teams should begin to film themselves and, if possible, opposition sides to help improve the quality of their own game. Shackled by the traditional British way of playing with two full-backs, three half-backs and five forwards, Blanchflower tried to convince Aston Villa that a 3–3–4 or 4–2–4 formation might pay dividends, even before the Hungarians and Brazilians showed that this was the way forward. He railed against the maximum wage and the restraint placed upon players by their professional contracts, arguing that the clubs might pay players' wages but that they didn't own them and nor did their financial hold on their staff entitle them to treat them like slaves. He looked forward to the days when there might be a Super League involving English and Scottish clubs. The European Champions League would seem sensible to him, though he would protest in the most vociferous terms about the illogicality of admitting runners-up to that competition, and would be appalled by UEFA's financially motivated agenda. In short, Blanchflower wanted to improve the spectacle, not mortgage the soul – what would he have thought of Tottenham chairman Alan Sugar's recent comment that 'football will remain our core activity'?

He wasn't always right, though – his support for Luton's chairman David Evans in the 1980s or for a Great British international team illustrated that – but his motivation was always sincere. He wanted to improve the game, no more, no less, and for that he should be remembered fondly. Indeed, it's true to say that he is remembered with a greater degree of affection than that which was sometimes bestowed upon him during his life. Such was his utter belief in himself and his methods, he found it easy to stir up ill feeling wherever he went, berating and ridiculing those he saw as ruining football. For all the short-sightedness of authority and of some of his team-mates, he rarely offered them the benefit of the doubt, sometimes seeing them as malevolent rather than myopic. Dogmatic in his views, he had little patience for those who could not grasp his progressive ideas. Ironically, for one who was to become such an elegant and eloquent columnist in the national press, he did not always communicate his ideas with sufficient clarity. Some of his statements sounded surprisingly oblique; just as Cantona confused many with his remarks about the seagulls following the trawler in search of sardines, Danny's flights of fancy could also perplex. As Chelsea manager, his insistence on repetitive training in search of perfection confounded young players with a short attention span and an instinctive need for variety. Patience was a virtue that sometimes eluded him too, having little time for those he would dismiss as thoughtless traditionalists. As such, he was a man who divided opinion. Those who agreed with him, who understood him and his philosophy, as was overwhelmingly the case at Tottenham, loved him. Those who disagreed felt he was a bolshie troublemaker, an agent provocateur. Visionaries rarely have an easy passage.

And whatever else might be said, Danny Blanchflower was a visionary. Throughout the research for this book one comment was made time and again: Blanchflower was twenty or thirty years ahead of his time. Cursed with a lack of pace, a disability that would have destroyed many another career, he turned that drawback to his advantage. Instead of concentrating on the physicality of the game, he looked instead at its intellectual dimension. Unable to sprint his way out of trouble, he used a keen brain to ensure that he didn't find himself under pressure in the first place – his positional sense was quite remarkable. Incapable of darting past three or four defenders by sheer speed alone, he got other players – Gavin Smith at Barnsley, Cliff Jones at Spurs – to do his running for him, breaching the defence with a precisely delivered pass directly into their paths, eliminating four or five opponents from play. At Barnsley and then, to a lesser degree, with Aston Villa he toiled under managers who tolerated rather than celebrated his presence, a pattern that continued through the early years at Tottenham once Arthur Rowe had succumbed to the pressures of management. It was not until he came to an understanding with Bill Nicholson in the final few years of his career that he was fully appreciated, unshackled to play creatively, captain responsibly, lead authoritatively. At the head of a team of all the talents – the destructive Mackay, solid Norman, rumbustious Smith, mercurial White, dazzling Jones – Blanchflower finally flourished in all his glory, confirming himself as perhaps the finest captain the British game has seen.

Arthur Rowe spotted Danny's talent early on, recognizing his 'tremendous ego', the prerequisite for a great captain. Every great team has its own rhythm, its own pace, its own tempo. Its character and personality stems from the man who provides its pulse, its heartbeat – these are not just great technical footballers, but great men who command respect and set the tone. Remember the role of Cruyff with the Dutch and Beckenbauer with West Germany in 1974, Michel Platini directing the French side of the early 1980s, Ruud Gullit driving Holland to the European Championship in 1988? These were teams controlled by mighty egos, men of purpose, ideas and integrity, giants who pulled the strings on the field. Blanchflower had such a role with the Double side at Tottenham; he was a man convinced of his worth, determined to apply his principles and utterly confident of the outcome.

On and off the field, he had the bearing of a leader, a commanding presence which radiated from within, drawn from a complete confidence that he could be the master of any situation. Hunter Davies, author of *The Glory Game*, that celebrated study of the Tottenham side of the late 1960s, met Danny briefly, but the encounter was typical: 'I was sent one year by the *Sunday Times* to cover Le Mans, which was daft, as I knew nothing whatsoever about motor racing. I arrived late with no press passes or tickets, and in a little queue outside one of the offices I saw Danny, recognized that crinkly face at once, knew him from his walk, as all true fans can always do. He was working for the *Sunday Express* at the time. I asked him if he could help me, what the form was, how you got in, and he led me to the right people, the right places. I only discovered later that he had arrived only ten minutes before me, knowing just as little as I did, but he was willing to waste his valuable time helping a rival.'

But Danny Blanchflower was no saint. Any man who married three times can lay claim to his fair share of faults, so there's no point in running away with the idea that he was a paragon of virtue; his eye for the ladies shows just how seductive he found the twin ideals of romance and new experience. But this is a book about football, unashamedly and unapologetically so. Whatever the ramifications and confusions of his romantic life, they are the concerns of the family alone and they have suffered sufficient intrusion from the press over the years. Danny Blanchflower was, after all, the first person to tell Eamon Andrews just what he could do with his big red book on *This Is Your Life*. He believed his private life was his own. It's a view that commands respect. His personal life was no different to that of thousands of people all over this country, all over the world. Blanchflower became an icon because of his footballing qualities, and it is those which make him a figure worthy of study.

Unlike lesser mortals, Danny was not afraid to fall on his face, for he was a devout believer in the principle that failure was the friend of the intelligently ambitious. Defeats were not the end of the road, but milestones, staging posts along the way to a final triumph. Where others would scowl at the spectre of defeat, fall apart under the pressure of failure, Danny would be sifting through the game, analysing what had gone wrong, how it might be countered, ensuring that his stock of knowledge grew still further. Although he was supremely confident in his own abilities, he was never arrogant enough to assume that he knew it all. Each day, each game, provided the chance to learn a little more. Few would agree with such a philosophical stance. For many, defeat was a disaster rectifiable only by more hard work, which often translated (and still does) as running an extra mile in training the following week. Forty years ago the idea that the necessary hard graft could be done by your brain alone, and might yet yield better answers, was anathema.

The tales of Danny having arguments with managers over the training schedule are legion. To a modern audience they are unbelievable for they often stemmed from managers refusing to allow the team to work with a ball during the week! Thankfully, things have progressed, but British football still stands accused of an astonishing insularity, an arrogance that says our way is the only way. Yet in comparison with the stance taken in the 1950s, we are living in enlightened times. Such was the parochial nature of the game then, few were in any doubt that England possessed the finest side in world football. Even after the Hungarians had demonstrated that this was palpably not the case, few coaches were willing to tinker with the traditional 'WM' formation that had served them well on the domestic front over many years.

That WM formation has become lost in the mists of time, but in order to understand just what Danny was rebelling against, it's important to grasp the rudiments of that system. The actual line-up followed this pattern:

PLAN OF THE FIELD OF PLAY

ENGLAND

(White Shirts, Dark Blue Shorts)

Goal
R. MATTHEWS
(Coventry City)

2		3
Right Back		*Left Back*
J. HALL		**R. BYRNE**
(Birmingham City)		(Manchester United)

4	5	6
Right Half	*Centre Half*	*Left Half*
R. CLAYTON	**W. WRIGHT** (Capt.)	**D. EDWARDS**
(Blackburn Rovers)	(Wolverhampton Wanderers)	(Manchester United)

8		10
Inside Right		*Inside Left*
J. ATYEO		**J. HAYNES**
(Bristol City)		(Fulham)

7	9	11
Outside Right	*Centre Forward*	*Outside Left*
S. MATTHEWS	**T. TAYLOR**	**C. GRAINGER**
(Blackpool)	(Manchester United)	(Sheffield United)

With those positions established, within most teams there was little straying from your allotted place. Larry Canning, Danny's colleague at Aston Villa, explains that, 'It was very straightforward. The full-backs defended, the half-backs, especially the wing-halves, divided their time between winning the ball, collecting it from the full-backs and playing it through to the forwards. The forwards created and scored the goals. Very basic, but it allowed people to do their job, rather than midfielders being expected to score twelve goals a season, as they are now.' The fact that teams played five forwards and just a couple of out and out defenders explains why so many teams, even those who were rooted to the bottom of their division, managed to score at least seventy or eighty goals a season and why 5–4 scorelines were not uncommon. On a domestic level, virtually every team played this formation, so home success depended on employing it better than your opponents. More inquisitive minds turned to different ideas, however. If you could confront a WM side with a 3–3–4 formation, then you would blunt their attacks more successfully by having the extra defender, while you would still retain four forwards to threaten their two full-backs. Other systems might also have inherent advantages and the hungry intellect of Blanchflower was soon keen to test them. Men of like minds understood that to survive, you must adapt, must broaden your horizons and experience.

That all seems very obvious, but it must be remembered that Danny played most of his football in the immediate post-war period, when the very idea that we might have something to learn from the 'Continentals' – the very word carried pejorative undertones – was deemed ludicrous. We'd just won the war, after all. It seems idiotic now, but this was the prevailing attitude in spite of our poor performances at World Cup level, a competition England didn't even enter until 1950, a mistake further compounded by our refusal to enter the early European club competitions. Those with a more expansive view of the world game, people like Ron Greenwood, Matt Busby and Walter Winterbottom, all attempted to adopt new styles and more modern methods, to prepare properly and to expose the British game to European and South American influences, but they were voices in the dark. The English method was to run round in circles during the week to build up your strength before running on to the field on a Saturday, where this strange leather sphere became your object of desire. Small wonder that so many teams were dislocated, incapable of the flowing inter-passing that characterized the peerless Hungarians who trounced England at Wembley in 1953. That defeat alone should have turned English football inside out, but it didn't. Larry Canning asks the question: 'What did we learn from that game? What influence did it have? They were the best team I ever saw, we all went down to see that game at Wembley, Danny too, and it was an exhibition. Although they all had the individual ability to beat anybody on their own, they didn't. They always went two against one – the forward would approach the defender, give it to his mate, go past the defender and get the ball back, and England were then a man short. Do that at speed and the other side are soon half a dozen men short. This was beautiful football, and what did we take from it? Newcastle United wore the same vertical stocking tops the following year. That was all we learned. Danny was disgusted, he knew how to play, he'd seen them do it, wanted us to do it, but nobody else would take any notice.'

The core of Danny's philosophy was that football should be a spectacle, that supporters should be treated to an entertainment as much as a sporting event. He regularly commented, 'You can win ugly and you can win decently. I would rather play well and lose than win by playing tough.' Perhaps that's why his brush with management, at club level at least, was doomed to fail. With every passing year, it becomes more and more important to win. If you're not a winner, you're out of work. On the Monday following the 1997 FA Cup Final, the holding company behind Chelsea saw their share price rise because they had taken the trophy and had found a route into potentially lucrative European competition. On the same day, Manchester United's share price tumbled on the departure of the talismanic Cantona. It seems as if the FT Index is the league table that counts now, but for how long can that last? The competition that exists between Manchester United and Newcastle United is not the same as that between Tesco and Asda. In the latter example, both can win, both can become yet more profitable. But between the Uniteds of Manchester and Newcastle, there can be only one winner – there's only one Premiership trophy.

Perhaps it's time to re-evaluate Danny Blanchflower's credo for the good of the game. The vast majority of our clubs have got to accept that, barring a freak aberration, in the foreseeable future the League will only be won by one of three or four teams. Once the City realizes that Everton, Tottenham, Wimbledon, Coventry, Southampton et al haven't a hope of winning the Premiership, what happens then? The very nature of sport means that they cannot all lift the glittering prizes, while some must inevitably suffer relegation. Southampton may have more money to spend now than at any time in their past, but alongside the spending power of Arsenal, Liverpool or Newcastle, it's still peanuts. The real difference now is that the management is not only beholden to the supporters but to people and institutions who actually have a financial stake in the club and want to see a return on their investment. To succeed in the future, clubs will need to see themselves as winners of a different kind. They need to pack their grounds week in, week out by playing attractive, intelligent and constructive football, both in victory and defeat. How can Leeds United justify the enormous cost of a season ticket when even the most ardent supporter knows that he or she is very likely to sit comatose through 0−0 draw after 0−0 draw? When a team has no chance of competing for the top prize, the very least it can do is put on a show, give the fans some glorious, memorable drama for their money.

Danny Blanchflower was innovative, an original thinker, an enigma who was much misunderstood, though that was often at his own instigation, for he was never averse to provoking discussion for its own sake. Using his own frame of reference, Danny would smile at the confusion aroused when he discussed his latest theory in the *Sunday Express* through the medium of Lewis Carroll's Mad Hatter and the March Hare, his bizarre use of Wonderland encapsulating the surreal machinations of the Football Association. As his brother Jackie points out: 'Danny was a one-off, very interested in the theory and the tactics of the game, and he had his own way of expressing it. He'd never stop talking football, even when you might want to be off doing something else. You didn't have to talk to Danny, you'd just listen to him!' The intricacies of the game consumed him, as did golf later on in his life. These were not mere physical recreations, but intellectual stimulants too. It was his belief that it was always better by far to do things your own way and in style than to knuckle down and accede to the blank conformity that continues to blight the face of football. Commentating in America on an early incarnation of the NASL in the 1960s, he soon ran into trouble with the TV moguls by remarking: 'These teams can't play.' Told by a producer to accentuate 'positive truths rather than negative truths', Danny returned to tell the watching audience, 'I'm positive these teams can't play.' No mere maverick, Danny Blanchflower had all the credentials to back up his theories. While he was with Tottenham, he was once asked: 'Do you like your life, Danny?'

'Well, I have to,' he replied. 'It's the only one I have. But I'd like it better and I'd like football better if you didn't have to win.'

Danny Blanchflower was a winner, but more important, he was a football man. This is his story.

1 Belfast Childhood

Belfast is a city that inspires more conflicting opinions than perhaps any other in the United Kingdom. For a start, a sizeable minority of its own citizenry don't even believe that it should be a part of that Union, a view which automatically polarizes opinion both there and in the rest of the UK. But to define a city as diverse, interesting and attractive merely in terms of the bloody and painful conflicts of the last thirty years is lazy, inadequate and hopelessly misleading. Having seen the thousands of television and newspaper pictures over the last three decades, you'd be forgiven for thinking that everyone in Belfast is at one another's throat, all day, every day. On the mainland, attitudes have hardened over the years, the prevailing mood being one of weary uninterest in the trials and tribulations of Northern Ireland. Such a state of mind is decidedly unfortunate and does not do justice to the genuine warmth of a community that could be forgiven for becoming stone-hearted. Distasteful as it is to lump an entire population into a homogeneous mass, it's true to say that there are no friendlier, no warmer, no more helpful people in the whole of the UK than those who live in Northern Ireland.

Today such a statement might be met with cynicism by those who have not experienced the extraordinary hospitality of Belfast. Television has led us to expect a city filled with religious and political bigots with no time for anyone who does not share their views. Nothing could be further from the truth: Belfast is a city of music, sport, fun and passion. It has always been so, but these are truths that have long been hidden by the inevitably selective nature of journalism, which must dwell on the sensational. Yet the civil unrest of these past years is not the only example of Belfast finding itself under siege during this century. It took its fair share of blows from the depression of the 1930s, and its docks and surrounding environs in the east of the city were picked out for especially heavy attack from the Luftwaffe during the last war.

Yet nothing has been able to prevent the generous city life from continuing. As my own father, who was stationed in Belfast during the war, puts it: 'We were in a pub on the night of the Irish Cup Final, just having a quiet drink. Some supporters from the winning side came in and insisted on buying us drinks. We didn't have to buy another all night long, couldn't stop them buying drinks for us. We were awash with the stuff.' All this in a city under regular and heavy bombardment. In essence, Belfast is still what it always has been, a unique city with a community that does its own thing, in its own way, in its own time. More than anything else, it's a city that believes in itself, has pride in itself and possesses a powerful, indomitable, unbreakable spirit.

That spirit certainly found its way into the soul of Robert Dennis Blanchflower, born in Dunraven Park, in the Bloomfield district to the east of the city on 10 February 1926. The first of five children – three boys, two girls – Danny, as he was soon known, was born into a typical working-class Presbyterian household. His parents, John and Selina, had married two years earlier and lived with Selina's parents, the Ellisons, before moving into their own home; the first of several moves for the infant Blanchflower. The Ellisons, Robert and Rachel, had a rural background in Board-mills, County Down. Selina's parents moved into the expanding city of Belfast once they'd married, maintaining the family by running a dairy service in addition to the income Robert generated by driving a delivery van for a local bakery. Both died in the mid-1930s, leaving Danny amazed that 'they lived their whole lives in that small cycle of events and places in the heart of Ulster'. This was early confirmation that their grandchild had wider horizons and would not be tied down to the city of his birth. Danny clearly had his eyes on an altogether more exciting existence, the more so since he saw his father toiling day after day as a craftsman in the shipyards, working long, gruelling hours for comparatively meagre rewards.

John Blanchflower must also have had a little of the wanderlust spirit about him. When Danny was still just three years old, he sold their first family home in Grace Avenue with the intention of emigrating to America in the hope of making a new life for his new family. This was a big step for anyone to take, albeit one on a path well worn by his fellow countrymen. In the event, a bureaucratic error prevented the Blanchflowers from making the long journey across the Atlantic. Danny, and his yet unborn brother, Jackie, were saved for the world of football. John was obviously a spirited individual with an abiding interest in the United States, for before he was married he was greatly taken by the jazz sound which had begun to capture the hearts of music lovers on this side of the ocean. In the early 1920s, in the aftermath of partition, there were regular civil disturbances on the streets of Belfast. A curfew existed from ten in the evening until six the following morning. To circumvent this, Curfew Dances were set up, opening just before ten and continuing right throughout the night. According to Jackie, his father played an integral part in the entertainment: 'When the jazz dances were springing up, he'd black his face like a minstrel and play with a banjo band. He had a very good voice.' Danny described his father as a 'simple man of sincere convictions, a good father, considerate and generous'. He could also be quite intense when the mood was upon him, reflecting a consistency of purpose and of intent that his son inherited. Though he had no formal training, John was interested in radio sets and by simple, solid perseverance could often repair broken sets. In this too he had a powerful influence on Danny, who later found work as an apprentice electrician.

If the legacy of his father could be seen in Danny's determination and his dogged application of logical principles to any problem that confronted him, it was from his mother Selina that he took his love of sporting competition, especially football. Unusually, perhaps, she was a talented player herself. She regularly turned out for the Roebucks, a powerful ladies' team in Belfast, playing as an inside-forward. She fostered Danny's own keen interest in the game and offered him a stable home environment with the minimum of fuss. Indeed, Danny was moved to point out that his parents 'did their best to guide me without nagging advice and cramping instructions'. In short, they encouraged him to tread his own path in life, stimulating his enquiring mind, supporting his own natural inclination to go his own way.

Danny's upbringing was restricted to the streets of east Belfast, though he developed a penchant for getting lost, wandering off on his own if ever he heard the sound of a street musician. For all the support he received from his parents as he grew up, times weren't easy – had his father not tried to take them away from all that and off to the promised land, the New World to the west? As the 1930s wore on, Belfast felt the oppressive weight of the depression, as did everywhere else. Its shipyards were hit just as hard as those on Tyneside or Clydeside, the impact just as devastating. Danny's schoolboy friend Ronald Murdock recalls that 'Belfast could be a very dull place for the majority of the people in those days. There wasn't much money around and any kind of work was scarce. It's hard to believe, but even through all that, I think people were much happier than they are today. They were much kinder to one another too.'

If anything, Danny's drab surroundings, and the knowledge that work could be taken away from his family at any moment, must have hardened the child's resolve to escape the realities of working-class life. Not one to wax lyrical about the solidarity brought about by the deprivations suffered by the working class, never sentimental about the difficulties of bringing up a family on an ordinary working man's wage, Danny felt that he'd do better to escape the potential poverty trap altogether, rather than simply rail against it. The possibility of making something special of his life certainly existed – from the very outset he was an intelligent boy. His curiosity was a huge natural advantage, of course: any student who actually wants to learn has a start on those who would rather be elsewhere. Equally, he had a healthy regard for the work ethic, even as a child. Another friend from school, Margaret Morrow, nee Lowry, points out that, 'Like most of us, Danny was from a normal working-class background where hard work was the order of the day. We all knew we had to work hard to get anywhere and accepted this as the norm.'

Danny's formative schooling came at Ravenscroft Public Elementary School. A small school, it offered the distinct advantage of small class sizes, allowing each pupil the maximum amount of a teacher's time. Danny flourished in this environment, Ronald Murdock remembering, 'He was an excellent pupil, certainly well above average.' Writing for the *Birmingham Evening Mail* some twenty years later, Danny explained: 'It has always been my policy to learn the hard way and above all to aim at consistency, which I believe is the true yardstick of knowledge and skill.' Understandably, this marked him out from his colleagues at school, for Danny proved to be an earnest and intense young lad, keen to make the most of any educational opportunities that came his way. Certainly

Ronald Murdock felt that Danny 'was a lonesome character, even as a boy. He didn't have too many schoolboy friends, but I liked him and we got on very well. Reserved isn't quite the correct word for him, but he just didn't join in with his peers like most of the boys did. That doesn't mean he was reticent in any way, because he wasn't, he was very forthright in his opinions. But I also found him to be very pleasant, very droll.'

School was a pretty serious business for Danny, but as soon as the classroom was exchanged for the sports field, he came into his element. Quite simply, he loved football and lived for the game. His first exposure to the organized game came with the 19th Belfast Wolf Cub XI, playing for a representative Belfast Cubs side against the Dublin Cubs in 1937 as a consequence. Wherever and whenever he could, he was playing, Ronald Murdock recalling that, 'He learned his football from his mother and from kicking a ball, any sort of ball, from Ravenscroft school through the streets to where he lived in Bloomfield. He and I played football on the way home from school at lunch hour and then on the way back again. In the afternoons, my sister would make a hankie-ball and we'd play with that, having a shoot-in in the Melrose Avenue entry, where Margaret Lowry lived. We were very good friends and played in the same football team with other lads like Jackie Mitchell, Maurice Masters, who went on to play with Glenavon, and Jim Masters. It was a very good team that we had there.' In spite of the quality of the side, Danny recalled in his *Soccer Book* that they still took plenty of beatings. Naturally, that didn't dim his enthusiasm for football. If an activity fully engaged his mind and attention, that was reason enough to go on with it. It was its own reward.

Danny was clearly the leading player at the school and captain of the football team, something which helped his popularity with his fellow pupils, compensating for his rather aloof and self-contained demeanour. Margaret Lowry was his counterpart on the hockey side and remembers, 'Danny learned a lot about football from the sports master, Tommy O'Hara, who coached the hockey team too. Each year, we played a hockey match and, needless to say, they always won! Danny and I were good friends, though we always bantered each other about the results of our matches. He already had leadership skills in those days, he was an obvious school captain.' Essentially, any fondness Danny betrayed for his peers stemmed almost solely from a mutual appetite for sports. Those who enjoyed football had an immediate and healthy respect for a boy who was clearly so much better at the game than they were, while Danny himself could not be bothered with those for whom football was not a consuming passion.

Perhaps that's the best way of describing Danny's apparent lack of social skills at that early stage; he simply could not see the use of acquiring them or, more accurately, lavishing his considerable charm on those who did not interest or intrigue him in some way. It's reasonable to suggest that Danny was perfectly content within his own world, spending time on his education or lost in thoughts of football. That's not to say he was a dour child or one without humour, for he was perfectly happy to take part in various pranks. One friend, Robert Linton, recalls him 'showering a policeman on points duty with paper cuttings from the top deck of the bus. He had a great sense of humour and was full of tricks.' However, Danny kept his tricks up his sleeve, not wasting them but using them only when they would have just the right impact. Very methodical and deliberate in his ways from an early age, he knew the value of timing.

Equally, as a precocious boy, Danny may well have found the whole business of childhood and his days at school profoundly limiting, he might have found ordinary youthful activities juvenile and foolish. While not exactly a budding Einstein, he was very bright and quite advanced for his age, with a mature outlook that showed little interest in the fripperies of school life. Ronald Murdock makes the important point that 'he didn't suffer fools gladly, the more so as time went on' and consequently childish games may have grated. An impatient child, Danny looked forward to the end of his schooling so that he could get on with the real business of living, of making his mark on the world. Given his genuine astonishment that his grandparents could live their entire lives within the space of a few miles, perhaps he was equally impatient with life in the province, keen to see the rest of the world. Such an ambition would only have been heightened when his great hero, Peter Doherty, left Glentoran for England, to play for Blackpool and then Manchester City. Danny idolized Doherty, and understandably so, for he was a truly great player, one who ranks with the likes of George Best as the very finest Northern

Ireland has ever produced. For the youngsters of Belfast dreaming of footballing glory, Doherty was the man to emulate.

Belfast's youth could have had no better role model than the Irish inside-forward. On the field he had quick feet and a razor-sharp mind, able to play his way out of the tightest corners – no less an authority than Bill Shankly named Doherty as his most difficult opponent and, as recently as 1974, in the post-Best era, *Rothmans Football Yearbook* recorded that he was 'regarded by many judges as the greatest player Ireland has ever produced'. In addition to these considerable gifts, he had that star quality, making him a Gullit or Best kind of figure. A charismatic individual he inspired a fierce loyalty in those who were close to him, but this was not simply because he was such a fine footballer. What marked Doherty out was the way he conducted himself, his innate decency, his determination to uphold the ideals of the game, the responsibility he felt for playing football the way it should be played. Always looking to advance its theory and practice, Doherty was, like Blanchflower, ahead of his time.

During their daily games, the kids of the Bloomfield area tried to copy Doherty, with Danny always at the hub. Another school friend, Eric Wright, recalls, 'We played football every day between the lampposts and the garden railings in Ravenscroft Avenue – we had to play the tennis ball up the kerb and on to the pavement in order to score. There were usually twelve of us there. Danny and Billy Morgan, the best players, picked the teams; the standard was very good, because Billy went on to join Belfast Celtic and a couple of the others joined Distillery or Glenavon.' Danny had an insatiable appetite for the game, playing whenever he could and for whoever would have him. Once he demonstrated his command of the game, he was always in demand, writing later, 'When I was a boy we were always having a game, in the street with lampposts as goals or on wasteground with coats as goalposts. Our ammunition varied. Sometimes it was a rubber ball, or a cloth ball, maybe a paper ball and, very occasionally, a real caseball . . . we could always be found playing football. Why, I even remember playing three games on some Saturdays – for the school in the morning, the Boys Brigade in the afternoon and for the local team in the evening.'

The step up to the Boys Brigade provided the first big challenge for Danny, who recalled feeling out of his depth. Playing for the local side at the age of eleven, he was physically disadvantaged, for some of the other teams included lads who were three or four years older, a huge gap at that age. Unable to cope with the pace of the game, Danny was all at sea for a time; it was almost a case of a boy playing against men. If this taught him anything it was to place a premium on skill and swiftness of thought rather than simple brute strength. If he was to beat the swifter and stronger, he had to do so with intelligent running and incisive passing. Boys Brigade games certainly taught him to read the game, a knowledge that he brought back to the Ravenscroft side. Having started as an outside-right before moving inside, he ended his days at the school as 'a roving centre-half'. In addition, he began to bring his new tactical awareness to bear on the school team, as Ronald Murdock recalls: 'He thought of nothing but football, football, football. When it was time for a school game, before the school sports master had come round, Danny had put up on the blackboard all the different moves that you could make. The headmaster, Mr Rogers, asked the sports master, "Do you understand this?" And he said, "I don't understand one thing he has on that board!" Even then, as a boy, he was so far ahead. He was a very, very good footballer. You could see that this was his game, that his ideas were very clever. When he spoke about the game, which was often, his eyes lit up and he was very eloquent.'

By now Danny had a younger brother with whom he could enjoy a kickabout, often playing on a piece of wasteground on Castlereagh Road that was later to be graced by George Best, among others. Danny's brother Jackie was born on 7 March 1933, and as the decade came to a close, he found himself roped in with Danny's way of thinking: 'He'd get me up at six o'clock in the morning to go training with him, and by the time I was six he had me out helping him deliver newspapers on his own little news round!' The paper round had come into being to finance a new bike, which allowed him to travel further afield than his own little corner of Belfast. Pretty soon, he was offered far more scope for travel, when his age of innocence was rudely interrupted in September 1939 with the outbreak of war. Still just thirteen at the time, Danny remained at Ravenscroft, playing in some representative matches. As Ronald Murdock explains, schoolboy internationals were put on hold for the duration: 'We had inter-school matches in those days because of the war, because, of course, the English schoolboys couldn't come across. If you played in those, it was like an international cap! I was fortunate enough to play with him in a couple of those games, though never with the same skill that he had!'

Six months later, in March 1940, Danny left Ravenscroft, but his aptitude for all things academic was rewarded with the offer of a scholarship to the Belfast College of Technology to take a general education course. As he pointed out in his autobiography, there was no suggestion that this three-year course would lead him into a university education, as there was no way his father could afford to send him there. Danny really went to college to learn a trade so that he might pay his way at home. More to the point, with the war raging across Europe, he wanted to get involved and make his mark, and education took a back seat in his thoughts. As methodical as always in his preparation, he joined the Air Training Corps, an organization designed to give young-sters of pre-military age the chance to do training exercises and understand the rudiments of life in the services rather than being simply dropped in at the deep end when they enlisted or were conscripted. His reasoning was typical: 'Stimulated by the reported exploits of the RAF fighter-pilots I joined the Air Train-ing Corps with an eye on future glory.' Around the same time Danny left college too, realizing that without a hope of a university place at the end of it, further education was futile. An uncle found him a place as an apprentice electrician at Gallaher's tobacco factory, an employer renowned for the quality of its workforce.

By the spring of 1941 the war was having a massive impact on everyday life in Belfast, although, as Ronald Murdock says, 'Dur-ing that time there was a lovely spirit about the place, people were so helpful to one another in a way you'd never have dreamt of prior to that.' The docks were obviously a major target for Goering's forces, and the east of the city took a regular and appalling pounding. Had there not been an aircraft carrier berthed in the docks, enabling its crew to fight back with wither-ing anti-aircraft fire, the damage might have been far worse than it was, though it was still considerable. The Blanchflowers were among those who suffered the most, their house being destroyed along with many others, while John was away fighting in France. The family was briefly evacuated to the surrounding countryside, though Danny stayed on in the city and joined the ARP as a cycle messenger, a brief spell which reinforced his distaste for authority figures, many of whom he felt grew pompous with the trappings of office. The war's most intolerable imposition on him seemed to be the collapse of organized football, with most junior competitions suspended. As a result he found it very difficult to get a game of any quality beyond the normal kickabout at work during the lunch break.

Again, Danny seized the initiative when he was offered a set of football shirts for ten shillings. By the summer of 1941 he had set up his own club, Bloomfield United, named after his home district. In his autobiography, Danny states that the team was made up of fellow workers and those 'of my neighbourhood acquaintanceship', though one opponent, John Fulton, recalls that 'Danny's team consisted of Air Force cadets. We met in the East Belfast Summer League – I played for the 19th Boys Club – at the Grangefield Playing Fields.' That league was set up partly at Danny's instigation too, so that the teams might have some semblance of an organization on which to rely. Having a proper league structure to play in also meant that players took games more seriously and were more likely to give up their free time to play. Quickly, Danny made a reputation for himself and came to the attention of the local professional sides. It was Glentoran, home of Peter Doherty, who first approached Danny early in 1942, just before his sixteenth birthday. The team secretary Sammy Weir offered Danny the chance to sign amateur forms for the club, an offer he accepted with alacrity. However, this was not quite the opportunity he had dreamed of. Once again, he found himself in trouble, too small to compete with the powerful men who played for the Glens.

As he had with the Boys Brigade team, Danny soon drifted away from Glentoran, discouraged at the gulf which existed between him and the more mature footballers that surrounded him. Inevitably, he had been unable to break into the Glentoran side and found himself to be little more than a camp follower, helping out behind the scenes rather than playing on the field. He could not bear to miss out on playing the game and so returned to Bloomfield to continue his footballing education. To some, this may seem like a lack of ambition, even courage, but that's far from the case. While others might have chosen to carry on fighting against the odds, Danny's logical mind soon concluded that an unequal struggle was a pointless one. If he continued to follow Glentoran around he would lose valuable match practice – playing against senior professionals would mean him rarely seeing the ball and having still less time to dwell on it. For Danny, the story of David and Goliath was a fluke result and, as the small David, he was sensible enough to see that the odds were stacked in favour of the Goliaths. Underdogs might win every now and then but with nothing to even up the contest, it wasn't a likely outcome. He retreated to play with those who were his equal, learning far more about the game that way. This was not cowardice nor evidence of a lack of relish for a fight, but hard-headed realism – it was this line of thought that later led him to shy away from football management when again he realized that the odds would be too heavily set against him doing things his way.

Danny proved that he was always ready to fight his corner when he joined up, Jackie recalling that 'he forged his age to get into the RAF'. Given the need for men to help the war effort, the authorities were happy to turn a blind eye to such youthful ambition and so Danny found no difficulty in enlisting as a trainee navigator. Part of his training involved studying for and then taking a special RAF ATC examination covering English, mathematics, mechanics, physics and electricity. He passed through this course on 11 December 1943. In turn, this meant he won a scholarship to St Andrews University in Scotland, offering him the opportunity both to travel away from Northern Ireland and to further his education. He arrived in Scotland for yet another short course run by the university under the Air Ministry Training Scheme in April 1944. He remained there until his exams in September that year, with the proviso that he should return at the end of the war to complete his studies. He studied mathematics, mechanics, physics and electricity and applied kinematics, and while there he made an impression on those around him. His tutors made special reference to his being a 'steady worker who fully justified his special entry. Thoughtful and mature' was the considered verdict. Achieving above average marks once more, he was recommended for a Commission in the General Duties Branch of the Royal Air Force.

Naturally, it wasn't all work at St Andrews, for Danny was soon installed in the university football team and managed to make time to play a range of other sports such as rugby, hockey, squash, badminton and table tennis. In addition, swayed by the historical connotations of St Andrews, he took up golf and began a lifelong affair with a game for which he felt almost the same passion as football. The very nature of St Andrews and university life also made a great mark on him. He wrote later of 'the wearing of the scarlet gown, the adult approach, the pursuit of knowledge, the casually accepted respect for honoured customs – both riotous and hallowed . . . this cultured charm'. At last he found himself in the adult world he had craved for so long, putting behind him the irritations of childhood. This was the chance to enjoy stimulating conversation about issues of real import, to enjoy his sport, to feel independent. The very fact that he had lied about his age to get into the RAF shows just how keen he was to leave his youth behind him and embark on the adventures that might lie ahead. This is further underlined by the fact that there was no conscription in Northern Ireland and he could have sat the war out had he chosen to do so. His decision to join up was a brave and principled one which emphasized his yearning for glory, for the company of those who might teach him something of value and for the stimuli of new experiences.

After spending months travelling around the military training camps of England, Danny was finally posted overseas, to Canada, in the spring of 1945. He was based at the navigation school in Rivers but before he had completed basic training out there, the war was over. He and his unit were shipped home in August and saw out the year in Docking near King's Lynn, where he was berthed alongside Richard Burton. Essentially he and his colleagues were now killing time and Danny was able to play as much football as he liked, which was plenty. Coming home on leave for Christmas, the former Irish international Johnny Geary invited him to turn out for Glentoran. Danny quickly impressed during the course of a reserve game. The three years he'd had away from the club had allowed him to grow to manhood so that he could now compete for the ball. In addition, the intensive physical training schedule he had lived with in the RAF meant that he was now far stronger than the rather frail character that had first turned out for practice with the side in 1942. The change in his game was all for the good. He'd always been a talented ball player but he now had the necessary physique to back it up. After just one reserve outing, Danny was promoted to the first team and made his senior debut for Glentoran against Belfast Celtic, playing as an inside-forward.

Glentoran already had a long and glorious tradition as one of Northern Ireland's finest clubs. Founder members of the League in 1890–91, they'd taken the Championship on eight occasions and the Irish Cup six times before the war, losing in the Final three times in the war years. Despite that proud history, times were hard for the Cock'n Hens, as they were nicknamed. In May 1941, their home ground, the Oval, was destroyed by German bombers. Playing their home games at Distillery's ground, money was always an issue for Glentoran, as they tried to rebuild their old home. Even so, they were very keen to sign Danny, recognizing his potential, with perhaps one eye on any fee they might get for him from an English club a few years down the line.

Before returning home that Christmas, Danny had his sights firmly set on a return to St Andrews to continue his studies within the RAF. Nevertheless, after his success with Glentoran he suddenly had a glimpse of a different future, one where football, his greatest passion, could become his way of life. Frank Thompson was manager at Glentoran and, with the aid of other club officials, he set about persuading Danny to sign on with them. Offering him £50 as a signing fee and then £3 a game, their blandishments were too much to resist, the more so since he'd been playing for the club as an amateur. He signed without question until the end of the season, without looking into a contract that bound him to the club 'talents, body and soul', as he put it. Weeks later, he discovered that other players at Glentoran had received fees of up to £500 and wages of £10 per game. Although it was too late to do anything about it, having already signed up, Danny took this as evidence that football directors were not to be trusted. It was a belief he held, with increasing fervour and few exceptions, for the rest of his career.

As an Ulsterman, Danny found it easy to gain his release from the RAF. After Christmas he was assigned to a base in Plymouth, whereupon he began to seek a way out of the Force. As a volunteer from Northern Ireland, he could not be retained, unlike British servicemen. It soon became clear that there was no possibility of his returning to St Andrews in the near future – the initial places were given to those older students who returned from the war – and the prospect of kicking his heels waiting for the day when he might be permitted to return to Scotland was not an appealing one. Pending his release, Danny guested for Swindon Town for a time, mostly in their reserves, but in April 1946 he was free to return to Belfast and Glentoran.

Returning home, he encountered various friends from the past, who noticed a more relaxed manner about him. Robert Linton, who had played alongside him for Ravenscroft and who had also received a similar scholarship to the College of Technology, recalls meeting Danny 'at a dance at the Plaza in Chichester Street in Belfast. I collided with him when he was carrying a tray full of drinks that went up in the air, but there was no argument over it, he just laughed the incident off.' Even though he was now playing for Glentoran, he kept up his apprenticeship at Gallaher's. When he finally left their employ, Jackie recalls, 'He got a medal for good attendance, though I don't know how because he was hardly ever there!'

Nevertheless, it was as a footballer that Danny now saw himself. Reaching the Glentoran first team meant he had passed the first real milestone on the way to a career in the game. Many footballers had made their way from the Irish Leagues into English football. Indeed, according to James Walvin, in his book *The People's Game*, in the 1920s Arsenal's manager Leslie Knighton 'specifically searched for footballers in the drab streets of the Shankill and Falls Road areas'. Oddly, Danny could have left the club before he really started with them for, at the end of the 1945–46 season, his contract lapsed and, thanks to an administrative error following the departure of manager Frank Thompson, he was not invited to re-sign. A number of other clubs were suddenly rumoured to be interested in getting his signature on considerably better terms, some going so far as to approach him direct. Feeling some sense of loyalty to the Glens, Danny waited for them to get back to him. In addition, the chance of playing for Peter Doherty's club was a very significant factor in this decision. Danny idolized 'Peter The Great', adopting many of his mannerisms, such as always eating ice-cream before a game. For one so in love with the romance of the game, the chance to follow in his idol's footsteps held a very real allure, one that shouldn't be underestimated. So it was that when Glentoran eventually got back to him, with an improved offer of £3 per week rather than per game, Danny signed their contract.

In preparation for the 1946–47 season Glentoran had taken on new players, signing centre-half Con Martin for an allegedly exorbitant signing-on fee and top wages. If Danny was undermined by a generosity that had not been extended to him, he didn't show it. He performed impressively in the reserves, benefiting from the solitary hard work he'd put in during the summer running along the shoreline at Portrush. Circumstances at the club found Danny moving back from inside-right to right-half with the reserves, a position he took to with ease. Within weeks a spate of injuries saw him installed at right-half in the first team. Almost by accident, he had found his niche for he was always going to find it hard going up front, skilful ball player though he was. The greatest flaw in his game was his lack of pace. Bertie Wright was a team-mate at Glentoran, training alongside him. As Bertie explains, 'Danny wasn't the fastest player in the world. One night we were out running and he said, "Bertie, this is no good to me. I could do a few sprints, but you could give me fifty yards start in the hundred and still beat me. I'm going to ask for a ball." They were very reluctant to give us the ball, because training was usually just running round the pitch, but he went in to see the manager, and ten minutes later he came out with a football. He said, "I tell you how I worked it. I went in and said, 'Look, Frank, if I'm going to be a joiner, I need the tools to make me a joiner. If I'm going to be a footballer, I need the equipment I'm going to play with. If I don't get a ball to go out and practise with, I'm afraid I'm going to have to give it up. As regards putting any speed on to me, you might as well try to put it on a tortoise!' " Danny was never afraid to speak up!'

Danny's logic remains compelling, but back in the 1940s his ideas were radical in the extreme, for very few sides worked with a ball in training. Although the Glentoran officials tolerated his ideas, they weren't welcomed too warmly. Yet his threats to give up the game were not idle ones. He genuinely believed that if he was not given the chance and the encouragement to improve his game, there was little point in continuing. Once again he betrayed his impatience for what he saw as petty, small-minded stupidity, following the examples of the past without ever questioning their validity. To Danny, whose mind was always ticking over, looking for new wrinkles, innovations and ideas, this was lazy and unforgivable. The chance to work with a ball now that

37

he had moved back to a wing-half position was his salvation. In such a position, Danny could scheme and create. With the ball at his feet, he could see the whole game laid out before him. With his incisive, instinctive footballing intelligence, he could see what would be the most telling pass, where space might be available, what would create the most havoc in the opposing defence. Speed was not the imperative it might be in attack, thoughtful placement of the ball was. The only way to improve his already excellent distribution was hours of practice with the ball at his feet.

It's significant that Danny's first full season in the senior game was 1946–47, the first real post-war season. Crowds were good, as football offered one of the few affordable entertainments for the working people. And in that season of all seasons, that was the prerequisite: entertainment. Of course supporters wanted their side to win, but if they came away having watched an exhibition of skill and plenty of goals, they were happy enough with that. Football was not a war, after all – these people had just been through the real thing and knew the difference, unlike some of today's commentators and participants who see football as an extension of trench warfare. Back in 1947, football was fun first and competition second. In the same vein, the summer of 1947 was Denis Compton's glorious season, when he batted with a verve and vigour that few had seen before. Compton played his cricket as though he enjoyed it, egged on by enchanted crowds who wanted to forget the horrors of previous years and the deprivations of rationing. Glentoran's crowds, then of similar persuasion, had the same impact on Danny. Romanticizing his surroundings came naturally to him but he later wrote that 'football is the hard conflict that has grown from the rivalry of hamlets, it's the game of the working-class man, something in which he can become directly and immediately involved. He may be interested in politics, for instance, but he cannot go down to the House of Commons and cheer or boo the proceedings inside, even though they concern him.' In post-war Belfast he felt that sense of engagement with the supporters.

He was right to practise his ball skills assiduously, for the standard of football in Northern Ireland was impressive. Bertie Wright comments: 'During the war, and then in the seasons just afterwards, we had a lot of English players over here who were First

Division players at the time. I remember the Linfield side having seven Stoke City players on the staff at one point. We had quite a few good players as well – Ted Sagar, who played in goal for England, and a few who were maybe not regular first-team players but good ones nonetheless, like Albert Young from the Arsenal, Jimmy Woodburn from Newcastle United, players from Partick Thistle and Manchester City. As well as them, you had some excellent local players like Jimmy McAlinden, Con Martin, Bertie Peacock, Charlie Tully, Noel Kelly, Jimmy McIlroy, so the standard was pretty good all round.' In spite of the stiff competition, Glentoran had settled into some decent form in spite of playing at Distillery's Grosvenor Park which, according to Bertie Wright, didn't provide the 'best of pitches to play on, but we enjoyed it'. They enjoyed it so much that by February 1947 Blanchflower and Wright had won selection for the Irish League team to play the Football League at Goodison Park.

Such representative games were a feature of the footballing calendar at that time and there was a great sense of anticipation attending the games. The Football League side was an especially strong one that year, including players such as Stanley Matthews, Wilf Mannion, Billy Wright, Frank Swift and Tommy Lawton. Given that the final such game before the war had ended in an 8–2 defeat at home in Belfast, the young Irishmen could be forgiven for approaching the game with a degree of trepidation, especially such an inexperienced player as Danny. The Irish were always at a grave disadvantage in these games since many of their best players had moved to England to play and so were unavailable, but there was a good spirit among the players and determination to do well, not least because each realized that an excellent performance might be the passport to a move to the Football League itself.

'We travelled across on the boat to Liverpool on the Monday night for the game on Wednesday,' remembers Bertie Wright. 'And we stayed out at the Royal Birkdale Hotel. It had snowed for two or three days before the game and the conditions were absolutely atrocious. The night before the game, they cleared the snow off the pitch. Without the covering, it froze overnight and it was in a shocking state when we came to play on it.' Danny's memory of the game was surprisingly similar to his recollections of debut games for the Boys Brigade and then for Glentoran.

Conceding that the bumpy pitch acted as something of a leveller, he felt completely lost, writing, 'I knew in my heart I had not played very well. The way that Mannion, Hagan and Lawton had played the game had bewildered and fascinated me. They were faster and fitter. I could understand that. But the way they flitted and changed positions behind my back as I concentrated on the ball was strange to me ... in this out of focus mood I did not make much use of the ball when I did happen to stumble upon it.'

While Danny might have felt he was out of sorts, his colleagues were more generous. Bertie Wright argues that, 'Danny didn't have such a poor game. In fact, the game went very well for us. They scored a couple but we pulled one back, they went 3–1 ahead and then I scored a penalty, and we eventually lost 4–2, which was a very good result for us. Bearing in mind that that was our first representative match, Danny was already the anchor man and I thought he had a decent game in the circumstances.' Perhaps Danny's recollections of the match were clouded by the fact that no English scouts had made a beeline for his signature following the game. According to Bertie Wright the only player to attract that kind of attention was 'Tommy Thompson at outside-right, and he was telling them that he was only twenty-four when he was twenty-eight, because he wanted to get signed up!' Certainly for the Irish League to hold a very strong side to 4–2 was an excellent display and not one that could have been accomplished had they had any passengers on board. Danny's own performance must have been better than he imagined.

If Danny didn't suffer fools gladly, then he was equally hard on himself. He refused to make excuses for a poor performance but would grow angry at his perceived deficiencies. A perfectionist, his ability to read situations quickly meant that he could not hide behind bravado, talk of ill fortune or off days. While that can be of benefit, clarity forcing him to address his weaknesses, it's a quality that can also be demoralizing for it illustrates all too well the gulf between the great and the merely good. Certainly Danny was upset after the game, but after allowing himself a few days to work through the events of that Wednesday evening, his mood brightened: 'I took hope from the thought that Mannion and Hagan and Lawton were players of great experience and that

I was young in the game, just beginning to stumble upon its secrets. I soon realized that my failure had led me to the beginnings of a new understanding of the game while those who had played better seemed largely unaware of this.' This was a typical Blanchflower trait. Time and again throughout his career he would come back to this theme, one he echoed later in a column in the *Birmingham Evening Mail*: 'I think we are adopting the wrong attitude in concentrating on results all the time and not enough on the lessons to be learned.'

With that in mind, that first representative game was perhaps the most important he ever played. It opened his eyes to the greater glory of the game and lit the fires of ambition within him. Good though the standard of Irish football was, it was nothing like as good as that played in England. There were some fine players at home but no truly great ones. Nor was there any strength in depth. Mannion and his colleagues had given Danny a masterclass in positional play, in playing with speed and purpose, making the ball do the work for them – they did to Danny what the Hungarians were to do to England six years later. There were no players of that quality for him to take on week in, week out. Since Danny was such a perfectionist, becoming a mere journeyman footballer was not enough for him. He wanted to better himself, to play at the highest level, to maximize his abilities and to make a name for himself. As demonstrated on that wintry night in Liverpool, the difference between the Irish and English game was the difference between a black-and-white TV set and a colour one. If football had been a passion before this match, it quickly became an obsession afterwards. His brother Jackie notes: 'He was very keen to get into English football, which was always the attraction for young Irish players. There wasn't enough of a challenge in Northern Ireland for him.' Bertie Wright agrees that Danny didn't have 'a lot of interests other than football. He was quite determined by then that football was going to be his career, and he was devoting all his time to that in every way.'

Danny began to train harder, doing half an hour before work each day to build up his strength and stamina, but this in isolation wasn't enough. He needed to play against the best players on a regular basis but could not engineer a move at this early stage of his career. Although he was twenty-one when the representative fixture took place at Goodison, he'd only been playing senior football for a matter of months, the war years having robbed him of a season or two of valuable experience. Despite the disappointments of that day, 1946–47 was a good season for Danny, giving him a grounding in the basics of the game, helping him establish himself in a new position and turning him into the bulwark of the Glentoran side. They even reached the Final of the Irish Cup before losing to Belfast Celtic by the solitary goal of the game. When it came to signing up again for the following season, Danny had reason to expect a rise, bearing in mind the money paid out to others the previous season. 'He was always in dispute because he knew that Con Martin and Noel Kelly were getting far more money than him,' recalls Bertie Wright. Asking for a signing fee of £200 and £6 a week, he was dismayed to find that Glentoran quoted new League rules to him which stipulated a maximum signing fee of £20 and wages of £5 a week. Deciding that if those were the rules then he must abide by them, Danny took the directors at their word and signed only to find that some players received under-the-table payments of considerably more. Money was not the sole motivation behind the complaints; these were also provoked by the injustice that was being done. Although extra money would have been very useful in those years of austerity, Danny was not driven by the promise of cash. However, if players of similar stature were being well rewarded, he felt that he should receive the same remuneration, and rightly so. Once more, it didn't make him widely popular in the corridors of power.

Throughout that year Danny nursed his sense of grievance. It was a season of steady improvement in which he began to attract the attention of other teams. Nevertheless, if he was to stay in Northern Ireland, he wanted to re-sign for Glentoran. Again he was denied the money he wanted since he could not prove the club had made illegal payments in the previous year, and they refused to admit it. To circumvent the problem, they reached a novel solution, according to Bertie Wright: 'Danny was smart, so they found him some work in the office at the shipyards.' For that he received an additional £3 a week while having the mornings free to train. As Jackie explains, 'The job was as a time-keeper but he was never on time to be able to keep it!' He quickly tired of the arrangement. He had cherished hopes that at long last he would be able to train like a full-time professional, but there was no one to train with during the day, nor were there any facilities to use. In addition his job was soul-destroying and, to his mind, pointless. Rather than carrying on with this charade – which was an undeniably easy existence – he chose to take on more taxing work. He returned to his trade as an electrician in the Falls Road bus depot and adopted once again the regime of early morning exercise before work. The additional training proved to be beneficial according to a new team-mate, the future Northern Ireland international and team manager Bertie Peacock: 'I only had one season with him at Glentoran, in 1948–49. He was a leader on the field, a very important member of the team, but he was always looking to get away from the club and over to England.' His brush with that Football League side had only reinforced his desire to experience life, as well as football, somewhere other than in Northern Ireland. He loved his home city and his home nation, but his was too restless a mind to be contained within its small boundaries. Danny always had to be doing something worthwhile, had to be pushing himself. He was too familiar with, and too secure within, his homeland.

As the 1948–49 season was coming to its close there was the annual argument about money. The compromise thrashed out this time was in the form of a gentlemen's agreement with the directors, who promised that should he leave the club he would receive a third of the transfer fee. This was a widespread practice in Irish football at the time and one which kept wages down for the clubs as the players hoped for a financial bonanza in the future. With this in mind, Danny felt sure that his time would come and that he could afford to continue accepting Glentoran's terms. He even told Jackie, now a more than useful player in his own right, ' "I'll get over there to England and then I'll send for you." In the event I went to England with Manchester United a couple of weeks before he did!' Danny must have experienced a bittersweet mixture of pride in his brother's achievement and utter frustration that he was still marooned in the province at the quite advanced footballing age of twenty-three. Time was beginning to run out. Despite his immense self-confidence, Danny began to worry that he might waste his best years playing for Glentoran. Within a couple of weeks of Jackie's departure, those fears were allayed, though perhaps not in the grand manner to which he aspired. Dreams of the First Division had to be put on hold for, as Bertie Peacock points out, 'He wanted to get away, and the only way he could do that was to go to Barnsley.'

2   Going to Seed

At the risk of alienating every supporter of the Premiership's latest recruits, the first name to spring to the mind of an ambitious, footballing romantic keen to further his career in the game would not be Barnsley FC. Not now, and certainly not in the spring of 1949, when if Barnsley represented anything in football, it was quiet, competent mediocrity. In forty seasons since their election to Division Two of the Football League, they had spent thirty-seven of them in that Division, three in the Third Division (North). Third place in both 1914–15 and 1921–22 was the closest they had come to promotion to the top flight, missing out by 0.075 of a goal on the latter occasion, denied by goal average. Those few years either side of the Great War represented a golden age in Barnsley's football. They reached the FA Cup Final in 1910, losing 2–0 to Newcastle United in a replay at Goodison Park after a 1–1 draw at Crystal Palace. Two years later they were back at Crystal Palace to face West Bromwich Albion in the Final. After a goalless draw there, Barnsley's Harry Tufnell finally broke the deadlock in extra time at Bramall Lane to give the club the only trophy in their history. To a young man from Belfast, born almost fourteen years after this solitary triumph, the name Barnsley meant little in footballing terms. In his *Soccer Book* Danny wrote, 'All I knew about the club and place was what I had heard; that Barnsley was a dirty little mining town in the heart of the Yorkshire mining country; and the club, because they won the Cup in 1912 with a rugged team, had the reputation of being dour cup fighters.' Not the kind of promise to make a young man's heart race with anticipation, especially since Jackie had gone off to glamorous Manchester United, then the FA Cup holders. Nevertheless, Barnsley offered an escape from what Danny now saw as the stagnant waters of Irish League football. He'd done his apprenticeship there, but now needed a sterner test of his mettle. He hoped Barnsley and Second Division football in England would offer that.

The actual transfer itself was fraught with problems. As far as Danny was concerned, he had an agreement with Glentoran's directors that if he moved on he would receive a third of the fee. When he was summoned to the Grand Hotel in Belfast to meet Angus Seed, the manager of Barnsley, the two discussed Barnsley's prospects in the company of two Glentoran directors and Frank Grice, the club manager. Danny then committed the cardinal sin for any footballer in the 1940s. He used his brain. On his own initiative, he asked how much the fee would be. As Derek Dougan, his colleague in the Northern Irish team a decade later, and an influential figure in the PFA, states: 'Clubs just wanted you to sign your contract, stay quiet and not bother them. You weren't supposed to have any intelligence if you were a footballer.' There's little doubt that Glentoran wanted to keep the actual amount under wraps, and Danny knew why. He made it plain that he wanted to know the fee so that he could calculate the cut to which he was entitled but instead Glentoran made a final offer of £700, arguing that the deal Danny spoke of had been struck with a club official acting beyond his powers. Indeed, by offering £700, they were giving him a very generous settlement! While he was considering his next move, he was paged to take a phone call. As he made his way to the phone booth a man stepped out of the shadows as though from a spy novel. He assured Danny he was a scout for Arsenal and asked him not to sign anything until he had reported back to Highbury. He was sure that the manager, Tom Whittaker, would want Danny to join the Gunners.

Many would have been flattered by this cloak and dagger approach for Arsenal were one of the greatest powers in the land. Characteristically unpredictable, Danny, rather than being pleased, was furious that Arsenal should only now approach him when a deal had been all but struck with another club. He stalked off to return to his conversation with Angus Seed and the Glentoran directors. By this time he was growing tired of the whole protracted affair. He knew full well that he would be unable to get further money from the Glens, the directors trying to swell the coffers in the hope of returning the club to a rebuilt Oval. More than that, he was sickened by the cynical way in which his good faith had been exploited over the years. Though he had been argumentative when it came to agreeing terms, he had always settled amicably in the end when faced with the *fait accompli* of the League rules. He realized just how badly they had exploited him, how they had used his own ambition, love of the game and, worst of all, his own firmly held principles of fair play against him. As he wrote in his autobiography: 'I was quickly losing my respect for them. All their glad talk in previous years about wishing they could pay me more if League rules permitted was now meaningless.' Danny wanted to wash his hands of the whole sad affair and get on with the rest of his life. While some would have stayed at the club until they gave in, waited until Arsenal stepped into the breach, or sought an under-the-table settlement from Barnsley, Danny refused to stay around men he considered to be hypocrites, men who were bringing the game into disrepute. Again, he saw no point in fighting the inevitable, wasting valuable time and energy in attempting to shift the immovable; the sensible move was to beat a tactical retreat and move on to the next battle, one that might be won. Consequently, in a mood of anger as much as of ambition fulfilled, he agreed to leave Glentoran for Barnsley and accept the Irish side's paltry offer.

It was sad that Danny should leave Glentoran under such circumstances for they were always his team, ever since he had first seen them as a child. He had a good rapport with the supporters and played some excellent football there, learning much about the game. Even so, he did not feel particularly grateful to the club who had given him his chance. Although he conceded that he would not have signed professional forms for any other club back in 1946, he felt that Glentoran had had very good service out of him. His position in the team was due reward for his outstanding ability, not some favour they'd done for a local boy. Even so, he admitted that for the rest of his days he always looked out for Glentoran's results and remained proud of his association with them. But, at the time, the manner of his going left a sour taste.

It was not the most auspicious opening to his career with Barnsley. Although he did not bear a grudge (that was a waste of time), he could be forgiven for feeling disgruntled when he went to his new club, the more so since he felt that Angus Seed had sided with Glentoran on this sensitive issue. Seed had consistently refused to divulge the transfer fee and had maintained that Glentoran were acting in Danny's best interests, behaviour that roused his suspicions. If that hadn't endeared him to his new signing, things soon got worse. Making the journey across England to Barnsley, Danny finally arrived at the 'dirty, deserted station at Barnsley [which] did not impress me'. He stood on the station for fully half an hour waiting for someone to collect him before phoning Seed at the club offices. He had not expected Danny to arrive for another two days and dispatched someone to collect him. It was at this point that things finally began to fall into place. He took to the club instantly, writing, 'Oakwell was a grand little stadium, clean, solid, well cared for and a credit to the club.'

Danny had come to the club for £6000, a sizeable investment in those days. It illustrated just how much work needed to be done at Barnsley. Angus Seed saw Danny as the linchpin that would revive the side's ailing fortunes, for he was under no illusion as to the size of the task. Although this put pressure on the new boy, it was the kind of pressure he enjoyed. Danny rarely lacked confidence in himself and now, at twenty-three, he felt he was good enough to make a name in England. He exuded self-belief, even to a crowd who had yet to see him play. Supporter Michael Haran recalls, 'Our local team, Littleworth Youth Club, were in the Final of the *Chronicle* Cup and so all fifteen supporters set off for Oakwell, which held 40,000! We and their thirty supporters congregated beneath the directors' box for the match, but before the game there was an announcement that our new signing from Glentoran would hand out the Cup. All eyes turned to the box above and Danny gave a regal, majestic wave to us all below!'

He might not have been quite so sanguine had he paid much attention to the history books. The merest glance at Barnsley's record in the seasons since the war put the job ahead of him into stark perspective. The club had become the living embodiment of dull, middle of the table consistency in just those few years. In 1946–47, they took 42 points, 16 short of promotion, and came in tenth. In 1947–48, they managed just 40 points, again 16 short of promotion, finishing twelfth. As Danny joined in the closing days of 1948–49, Barnsley were to claim 40 points again and once more finish 16 points shy of a place in the First Division. To make matters worse, they had managed to win just one Cup tie in those three years, when they defeated Huddersfield 4–3 in January 1947. Subsequently they'd lost to Preston, Manchester City and Blackpool. Little to thrill the public there and little prospect of improvement from the players they had at the time. They had apparently recognized their limitations and had signalled their lack of ambition in January 1949, a couple of months before Danny arrived at Oakwell. Barnsley's post-war hero had been Chilean forward, George Robledo, who had registered forty-five goals in 105 games for the club, but they could not keep him, selling him to Newcastle United for a fee of around £20,000. There were other good players at the club too, including Scottish international outside-left Johnny Kelly and Northern Irish goal-keeper Pat Kelly, but the side was solid and unspectacular. Robledo had provided the verve and imagination from the forward line but now he'd gone. Investing a sizeable proportion of his fee in attracting Danny from Belfast made it clear that he was expected to be the source of their invention, their new main-spring from right-half. If Danny was not a positional replacement for Robledo – that onerous task fell largely to Alex Wright, who had joined the club in 1947 from Hibernian but had not yet won a regular first-team place – he was seen as the man who would make things happen on the field, the side's star player who could conjure openings from nothing.

Signed after the transfer deadline had passed, Danny had to kick his heels as the league season came to its close. He made his debut for the club in a Sheffield County Cup game against Rotherham and played again in that competition in a 1–0 win over Leeds. He may not have realized it at the time, but he was under surveillance, his performance closely monitored by Steve Griffiths, Barnsley's inside-right: 'I'd come to Barnsley to coach the second team and things were going along OK. When the wonder boy signed, it caused a stir. Six thousand pounds was quite something for a club like Barnsley. The first game I saw him play was in the second team against Leeds, and Angus Seed wanted me to give him a report on him, how he'd played and so on. When we got to the ground, Danny wasn't there and we had a reserve getting ready to play instead. Danny walked in with a few minutes to spare and proceeded to strip opposite me. When he took off his shoes I nearly fainted – he must have had feet as large as I had ever seen. My first thought was to wonder just how somebody could play football with feet that size, but I soon found out. Once Danny arrived, it changed my career at the club. I knew I had to get back in the first team because I couldn't be satisfied until I was partnering Danny. You don't often get the chance to play with such a great player. He was an attacking wing-half right from the off and I had the chance to play right in front of him. When I needed to push the ball away, he was always on the spot, easy to find, a superb player, always in spaces to get a team-mate out of trouble.'

The *Barnsley Chronicle* also went into raptures over the club's new signing: 'Blanchflower was always fighting for the ball and using it to great advantage, his passes being very precise ... Blanchflower and Griffiths did everything but score ... Blanchflower produced the finest half-back performance seen at the ground this season ... he is a footballer, and that's saying something in these rag-time days. For once, Barnsley's half-back line had a man in it who never tired of feeding his forwards. Pass after pass reached them with uncanny accuracy.' That was a lot to live up to, but this good press so early on helped him settle into his new surroundings. In the wake of such rave reviews, he was perhaps fortunate that the season was ending, so that the fans might have time to lower their expectations of him during the close season. Nevertheless, he did manage to fit in his first game in the English Second Division, Barnsley's final game of the season having no impact on the promotion or relegation issues. His career began at Oakwell as Barnsley were beaten by the only goal in a torpid encounter with Chesterfield.

Returning to Belfast for the summer, Danny was left to reflect on the changes of the previous few weeks. In spite of the traumas surrounding the transfer, he was pleased with the move to a football club that he hoped had some ambition. Certainly Angus Seed had impressed it upon him that he was not to be the last of his signings, but that he might be the most important. Equally, he realized that he owed Seed a debt, for he was the first English manager willing to take a chance and pluck him from the obscurity of the Irish League. Other clubs had had him watched, but all were worried that he would be too weak or slow to cope with the rigours of English football. Clearly Seed was not of that opinion. In addition, by buying a creative player such as Danny it was apparent that he wanted Barnsley to shed their tag as a rough, physical outfit who relied solely on aggression. The very fact that Danny was signed in order to replace one of Barnsley's folk heroes, Skinner Normanton, was evidence of that. The same age as Danny, Skinner had made his name as a fierce tackler after he'd joined the side from the Barnsley Main Colliery team. Rough, tough and combative, he lacked the finesse of Blanchflower but had been a mainstay of the side, refusing to allow the opposition past. When Danny arrived at the club, his days were effectively numbered – although some remember them as a prototype for the Blanchflower and Mackay partnership, Danny and Skinner were only on the same team on fourteen occasions. His more regular half-back partner was Arthur Glover, then in his thirties and entering the final phase of his career. His experience and his steadying influence was vital in helping Danny get to grips with the English style of play, impressing upon him the importance of his defensive duties.

This new teaming still lay ahead when he returned to Barnsley for pre-season training in July 1949. He had hoped that the transfer to England would see him moving in more cultured circles, at least so far as the football was concerned. Having been tortured by Mannion and company two years earlier, he felt sure that their skills sprang from advanced coaching and highly specialized systems of training and practice. He was disabused of that notion very quickly. Training consisted of running, followed by running, then some running with a little bit of running to finish off the day. There were more general exercises too, such as skipping and hurling a medicine ball around, but essentially the Barnsley lads got fit by lapping the pitch *ad infinitum*. Danny accepted that you needed to be fit and have reserves of stamina in order to play the game to your full potential, but he felt this was taking things to ludicrous extremes. He consoled himself with the thought that once they had achieved a good level of fitness, as the season approached they would move on to ball work and more intelligent exercises. Again, he was wrong. He was very disappointed, but as the new boy at the club he kept his own counsel, his morale maintained by the thought of the new season on the horizon. Even his first practice game could not dampen his spirits. Facing Skinner Normanton, who had the ball at his feet, Danny wondered how he might stop him. According to an interview with Michael Parkinson, Danny was sure that this product of the cerebral English game would have half a dozen tricks up his sleeve with which to bamboozle the Irish boy who'd come to take his place. Readying himself for a shimmy to the left or right, moments later Danny was picking himself up off the floor as Skinner, ball and all, had run right over the top of him on the way to goal. It was a rude introduction to the physicality of League football but an important one. As he was to recall later when accused of being too cultured for his own good, he replied, 'I know all about clogging. For goodness' sake, I spent two years at Barnsley!'

Not only was Danny playing in new surroundings, he was living in them too. Initially, he stayed with his Barnsley team-mate, Steve Griffiths: 'He lived with us for quite a while when he first came to the club. It was hard to find a house then and it was a time when household goods were just as hard to acquire. Danny had some friends back home and when he left they gave him a chit so that he could buy what he needed from a store in Halifax. Danny asked my wife and I to go with him to show him where it was and so on. We were only too pleased to help out, but to our surprise we came home with double of everything. Danny wanted to kit our house out too! He certainly made us happy – many's the time we cleaned them and said, "Well played, Dan!" He was very generous with his friends but he could be pretty forthright too.'

In addition to preparing himself for the new season, Danny set about preparing himself for life after football. With a trade as an electrician behind him, he wanted to stretch his mind in other directions and enrolled at Barnsley Mining and Technical College, where he met Roy Mason, who was to become the Labour MP for the town and subsequently a Labour peer: 'We actually shared a desk. I was studying economic theory at that time while he followed accountancy. He was a very sensible, outgoing, friendly sort of chap at that time, with the intelligence to add another string to his bow for when he finished playing football.' Once again, as Danny achieved further vindication, he emerged from his shell just a little more, to become more relaxed and at ease with himself. Football remained the consuming passion but he was increasingly confident away from the game, allowing his natural, easy charm to come to the fore.

With the start of the season came the first real tests for Danny, and he came through them comfortably enough. With season tickets priced in the positively scandalous range of £2 to £5, the supporters demanded value for their money and Danny was determined to provide it. Clearly a cultured footballer, he was a cut above the average player in the Second Division from the outset. Michael Parkinson, then a young boy watching his local side, felt as if every game was Danny's swan-song, that he might be spirited away to the First Division at any moment, so apparent was his gift for the game. The *Barnsley Chronicle* was happy to boast about the club's wonderful new signing, revelling in his talent. After a draw in the derby game with Sheffield United their reporter, Socaro (virtually all local papers at the time carried reports under peculiar pseudonyms), wrote, 'Blanchflower is cast in the mould of the soccer giants . . . the girth of his skill is immense . . . his total effort was to blunt the spearhead of the visitors' attack . . . he also fed most of the forward movements.' That Danny should be so industrious in defence nails the myth that he could only go forward. He could tackle as well as any; good tackling is a question of timing, not brute force. Equally, his calm self-possession meant that he would often force forwards into error, make them commit themselves too early, goading them into a rash move, shepherding them away from the danger area.

Danny maintained this impressive form, and after just ten games in Barnsley's first team he was selected to play for Northern Ireland against Scotland at Windsor Park in Belfast on 1 October 1949. He might have wished that the selectors had held back that honour a little longer – certainly his Barnsley team-mate, goalkeeper Pat Kelly, did. Both made their debut in a crushing 8–2 defeat. True to form, Danny was depressed with his first game on the greater stage, considering himself 'one of the miserable failures of a weak Irish team. I wandered around that field in a trance . . . my innocence of top-class football led me to bewilderment and confusion . . . I slipped furtively away from Windsor Park feeling sure that my international career had ended the day it had begun.' That was Danny Blanchflower: a contradictory mix. He had powerful self-belief, yet he could easily be crushed, however temporarily, by failure. However much he professed to relish defeat as part of a learning curve, he seemed to find it terribly hard to deal with at first hand. Age, success and experience combined to take the edge off such dejection in the future but at the time he was laid low by what he saw as an unacceptably poor performance, though he at least conceded that nerves had played a part, noting later that 'I could not sleep much before the game'.

He may have been nervous, but that did not stop him taking in his surroundings. Once more, he was displeased with what he found: 'I was young but I was not impressed by the preparation of the team. It was a terrible team, losing by large margins, hopeless and abandoned. There was no leadership, no plan, not much to look forward to.' This is not the kind of talk that finds favour with administrators, but it came from the heart. As a proud representative of Northern Ireland, he was upset to find that the players weren't given a fair chance to make an impression. He was of the opinion that international football seemed to be run for the benefit of the committee men rather than the players and supporters. It was an impression he'd begun to form at his very first representative game against the Football League two and a half years earlier. Here, he recalled 'borrowing and buying clothing coupons for a new suit to fit the occasion. The boat was loaded with officials. It was my first encounter with them and it was a bit of a disillusionment. The foolish among them far outnumbered the wise. Forever more after that, the news of my selection for any team was reduced in terms of pride and satisfaction by the thought of the selectors and what they represented. There is an awful lot of nonsense talked about the honour of playing for one's country. Does that not depend on what the national team stands for? Where is the honour in playing for a shambles, an outfit that stands for nothing save waste, inefficiency and hypocrisy?'

These were pretty strong feelings, but ones that were prevalent in the game. Remember that in the 1940s and 1950s, even into the 1960s, many team managers did not have the final say over team selection or policy. The 1962 film *The Saturday Men* focuses on the day-to-day workings of West Bromwich Albion, then one of the top clubs in the country. The most telling part of the thirty-minute documentary is a board meeting where manager Archie Macaulay is treated like a second-class citizen, merely allowed to recommend that the directors select the team he wanted. This was not an isolated incident, but an accurate picture of the way almost every club was run. Consequently, many of the more forward-thinking players and managers had to rebel against the iniquities of the system. Danny was not alone in his condemnation of it all; think of the work done by Jimmy Hill and Cliff Lloyd at the PFA with regard to freedom of contract and the maximum wage; of Len Shackleton's attitude to the directors in his autobiography; of Matt Busby manipulating the make-up of the boardroom at Old Trafford to get his own way; of Bill Shankly's bust-ups with directors at every club he went to; of Brian Clough's constant brushes with authority. Indeed, if anything underlined Danny Blanchflower's comments on the stupidity of the footballing authorities it was the failure of the FA to make Clough the England manager. The likes of Danny and Cloughie were despised in the corridors of power because they spoke the truth. On the terraces they were lionized for their honesty. As both would agree, how can you improve the game if the powers that be want to root it in the last century?

More than anything else in the game, Danny railed against what he saw as injustice. Throughout the years in his newspaper columns he would point to the absurdities perpetrated by the FA, by club directors and officials. He already felt he'd been swindled by Glentoran and now he felt the public was being cheated by the Irish FA. Crucially, he felt that the international side was doomed to failure because no one would take responsibility, nobody wanted the blame when the inevitable mauling had come to pass. Training was virtually non-existent, so that no one could suffer injury, while trainer Gerry Morgan was little more than a kit-man at that point. It was left to Jack Vernon, the captain, to give a team talk, simply giving each man a few instructions. Danny was told not to be adventurous, to stay close to Vernon himself at centre-half and to let nothing pass, hardly the reason he'd been selected in the first place. Danny felt the side was preparing itself for defeat before a ball had been kicked. Although Northern Ireland had a small pool from which to select, surely they could play with greater verve and ambition rather than gripped by negativity?

On his return to Oakwell, he managed just two games before he broke his foot in a heavy tackle at Leicester City. Hobbling through much of the game, the *Barnsley Chronicle* still commended him on his 'near perfect display of close and accurate dispossessing tactics'. His injury meant he could not be considered for Northern Ireland's next match, against England at Maine Road three weeks later. This time, the men in green were humbled by 9–2, further proof of the huge gulf that existed between their football and the rest of the home nations. Now out of the international picture, Danny felt frustrated that Northern Ireland simply offered themselves up as sacrificial lambs. Certainly England had a better team – any side that included Tom Finney, Neil Franklin, Billy Wright and Stan Mortensen was too strong for many international opponents – but there was no reason to go into the game already beaten. When the Irish met up, why were they not practising together in five-a-side games? Why did they not try to play together to strike up a rapport on the field? Why did they not work on free-kicks and corners? If they were to lose, at least do so with honour not in abject surrender.

Impatient to a fault with anything he saw as thoughtless stupidity, Danny was already tiring of life with Barnsley too, the more so as he sat kicking his heels on the sidelines, waiting for his foot to heal. Able to watch training but not participate, he was struck by the wasteful nature of the exercises, perplexed by the pointless repetition of activities that had nothing to do with what happened on a Saturday afternoon. Roy Mason remembers that his mind was constantly working on new ideas to improve the team. 'We were very good friends, we visited one another at home and so on – Danny lived in Darfield in a club bungalow. Danny lived the game, talked the game, breathed the game. I remember walking through Barnsley one day, through the bus station, and Danny stopped me. He pulled out a piece of chalk and started drawing on the wall, mapping out his tactics. He was demonstrating how if Lindsay, our right-back, would only do what Danny was telling him, he'd go on to play for Scotland!'

Returning to the team in November, Danny found a side that had lost its sense of purpose, its momentum. Having picked up seventeen of the first twenty-six points available, they had then embarked on a run from November to the end of the year which saw them grab just six out of twenty-four to leave them floundering in mid-table. Danny was slowly finding his form again, reporter, Conn, commenting in the local press after a defeat at home to Sheffield Wednesday that 'he seldom put a foot wrong and fed the forwards with fine accuracy'. When the side lost to Stockport County in the third round of the FA Cup, the alarm bells began to sound and there was talk of relegation. Although Danny had been an influential signing, the loss of Robledo the previous year meant Barnsley lacked a cutting edge. Well though Danny might feed the forwards, there was no razor-sharp striker to capitalize. Hard though they tried, the three main forwards were not prolific marksmen – Griffiths was the most successful, scoring fifteen goals in his injury-truncated season of twenty-seven matches, Baxter scored the same number and Alex Wright managed seventeen, the last two being virtual ever-presents. In contemporary terms these are very respectable performances, but this was an era where most successful teams would expect to have one forward nudging thirty goals and a couple of others weighing in with twenty or more; top scorer in Division Two that season was Grimsby's Tommy Briggs with thirty-five, and they finished just one point ahead of Danny's club. So comparatively short of firepower were Barnsley, there was talk of using Danny at inside-forward. But then who would make the bullets for him to fire? He could not be creator and finisher.

He remained at right-half, playing as the chief tactician on the field, though he was not the captain. This inevitably caused friction behind the scenes. Steve Griffiths recalls, 'He was always talking tactics. It didn't go down too well with one or two who were in charge at Oakwell.' Nevertheless, such was Barnsley's plight as a small club of limited resources, they could not take any action against their star player. Even in defeat, Danny could be outstanding. As they went down 4–0 at Swansea, the *Barnsley Chronicle* noted that 'Blanchflower alone of the visitors' middle line displayed that constant calm so necessary to defenders under pressure'. A few weeks later, they remarked on his 'ice-cool defence-splitting constructions'.

Having missed Northern Ireland's game against England through injury Danny wasn't surprised to be left out of the team to play Wales at Wrexham in early March, even though the side had taken such a merciless hammering in his absence. As they assembled it became apparent that Jack Vernon would not be fit for the game. As the nearest available player, Danny got the call to replace him. This was doubly fortunate. Knocked out of bed at six on the morning of the game, Danny hadn't time for the nerves that had kept him awake prior to his debut. Secondly, the opposition were Wales, the least threatening of the other three home countries, offering him the opportunity to atone for his poor performance against the Scots. The game, a goalless draw, went well for Danny, the Belfast press pushing his name forward for further international recognition. Just as significant was the fact that this was the final game in which FIFA allowed players from the Republic of Ireland to play for both Irish national sides, thereby reducing the already tiny pool of players on whom Northern Ireland could call – Tommy Aherne, Con Martin, Dave Walsh and Paddy Ryan were all excluded from the team in future. Clearly this made it easier to win international caps.

With renewed vigour and confidence in himself, Danny saw out the season with Barnsley, playing some of his finest football to date. Where he had always excelled going forward, his defensive game was now improving. In a game against Hull he came up against Raich Carter. The *Barnsley Chronicle* reported: 'This was a shadow of the real Raich Carter, the Hull player-manager. The man who made the magic in the master's foot look miserable mediocrity was Blanchflower. When he was not checking a raid by Carter and company, he was prompting his forwards with a series of passes that travelled as smooth as the waters of Lough Neagh near his native Belfast.' As the season petered out in disappointment, Barnsley registered their regulation thirty-nine points to finish thirteenth, their away form simply dismal. In the close season Angus Seed acted to remove their weaknesses, bringing in Cecil McCormack from non-League Chelmsford and Eddie McMorran, the Irish international, from Leeds United, with Alex Wright leaving for Spurs. With this new formation up front there was some hope that the goalscoring drought might be at an end and that the team could progress.

It wouldn't have been the close season had there not been a contractual dispute for Danny to fret over. In an attempt to make a unified stand against the standard League contract the players' union advised players not to re-sign for the 1950–51 season. When the union retracted its threat, Danny missed the union meeting and wasn't advised of the change of policy. As a result he had a flaming row with Angus Seed, who threatened to report him to the FA as a troublemaker. Danny's response was, 'Don't threaten me or I shall take the next boat back to Ireland and you'll not see me again.' Later on, when he discovered that there had been a misunderstanding, Danny returned to the manager's office and signed with good grace, but his principled stand had been indicative of his character. He had put his entire career on the line – had he gone home, Barnsley would have kept his registration and prevented him playing in England again – to do what he saw as the right thing. Although matters were smoothed over, this argument was the beginning of the end for Danny and Barnsley.

However bitter the disagreement, however seminal it was in his decision to move on, this was not the root of his disenchantment with the club. That stemmed from Barnsley's archaic training methods. As his brother Jackie notes, 'He wasn't too pleased with life there. Whenever we met up, he used to say, "Do you have a ball at Manchester?" I'd tell him, "Yeah, we've twenty or thirty balls." And he'd tell me that Barnsley trained without a ball. He was stubborn like that, he had his idea about how a thing should be done, and if he disagreed he wouldn't back down. He was looking for a move because he couldn't agree with the tactics or the system they had there. He always wanted to do better.'

Danny wrote 'this was my second year of full-time training and it was beginning to seem a grim monotonous grind to me'. As an Irishman coming into the English game, it's true to say that he looked at its methods with a clarity that those brought up in its traditions might have lacked. He pointed out in his autobiography that the English 'make-up compels the idea that a man must go through hell and high water to get anywhere. It doesn't matter whether he is going in the right direction or not – so long as he is suffering . . . playing with the ball was something we enjoyed; and enjoying something was out.' Small wonder that so many players spent so much time on the golf course or in the snooker hall, escaping the tedium of these mindless sessions. As an iconoclast, Danny came to training with a desire to tear down dull conformity and introduce new ideas, if only to keep himself interested – he already realized that Barnsley were going nowhere and so looked to make his own entertainment to keep his fertile mind occupied. Danny was also something of a footballing schizophrenic, driven on in equal parts by an egotistical ambition to win fame and fortune for himself and a selfless desire to improve the game as a spectacle. Yet he did not pay mere lip service to the idea of football as an entertainment for the public. He genuinely believed that unveiling a thrilling product was a crucial component in creating a successful team. The root of his challenge to accepted practices was sensible enough – if training and play did not evolve and develop, if teams stuck with the tried and tested for ever and a day, they would inevitably fall behind those who tried to change. Even if not every new innovation worked, some would. That would leave the opposition in the same state of confusion that Danny felt after that Football League game in 1947, unable to understand the fluidity of the other team's play.

With the start of the 1950–51 season it was clear that Barnsley had found a better balance. Cecil McCormack went off like a rocket, scoring twenty-six goals in the first twenty games of the season, including five in the 6–1 demolition of Luton. Nevertheless, as the *Barnsley Chronicle* reported, 'The pleasing feature about the team's form at the moment is the classy work of Danny Blanchflower . . . he has played the role of chief schemer . . . and has supplied a stream of judicious passes to the front line.' In recognition of this form, Danny was chosen for Northern Ireland again, lining up against England at Windsor Park. Playing poorly once more the team went down 4–1, with Danny unable to put his game together. Even so, the very fact that he was an international meant that his name was becoming better known across the country. First Division sides began to take note of his progress and it became apparent that he might be able to move into the big league. His form at Barnsley was inspirational, with a reporter in the *Chronicle* raving after the team thumped promotion favourites Preston, Tom Finney and all, by four goals to one: 'That present day prince of half-backs Danny Blanchflower just could not be faulted. His tackles and interceptions were perfect and his accurate "on the carpet" passes up the middle and down the wings made me wonder is there a better wing-half playing in the country today?'

Emboldened by his form, Danny began to make ever-increasing demands on the Barnsley side. Michael Parkinson has written of the glorious impact Danny had on Gavin Smith's game, for example. The outside-right was astonishingly quick but a fairly ordinary player. Parkinson wrote that, 'Danny would point, Gavin would gallop and at the precise moment he most wanted the ball, it would arrive in his path, perfectly weighted and so inviting it should have been edged in gilt.' Unsurprisingly, Smith was one of the converts to the Blanchflower way, along with Steve Griffiths. 'When he'd moved into his own house, we continued to discuss the game at training with Gavin. Then one morning, the trainer came and asked what we were doing. Danny was our spokesman and tried to put him in the picture, but the coaching manuals were very negative and outside his way of thinking at that time. Angus Seed had informed me I was to take up a position as coach, trying to get me to toe the line, but I remarked that what Danny was trying to do was correct, even though our results were good at the time. We had a discussion and Danny walked back to the changing rooms and refused to take any part. When they asked him where he thought he was going, he said, "Somewhere, anywhere where I can progress." '

These were the opening salvos in a war with Seed that lasted for several months. Danny wanted to practise with the ball in the afternoon but the management refused to sanction it, saying he'd have no energy left for Saturdays. ' "If you get the ball, the others will want it," had been one of the arguments Mr Seed had used – as if such a thought was the horrible end,' Danny wrote later. The bad feeling continued to fester, the more so as Barnsley's form met with its inevitable mid-season slump. A tricky third-round Cup tie ended in defeat at Northampton, the immediate repercussions faintly farcical. According to Danny, 'Angus Seed ran a pub in which he lived and he was reluctant to return home before his pub closed. So he took us on a very long coach tour and we all fell asleep on the way home.' Things were rapidly going downhill. Letters in the local press complained that the players weren't trained to their previous pitch and that there was a lack of discipline at the club, a fault that might have been laid partly at Danny's door since he found it impossible to bite his tongue in training. Danny's response to another session of lapping the field was to ask for a ball; Seed's was to impose himself on the club by refusing. The arguments became ever more rancorous. If Danny asked for a ball, Seed replied that if he didn't see one during the week, he'd be more desperate to have possession on a Saturday, whereupon Danny would argue that if he didn't have the ball in the week, he wouldn't recognize it on Saturday. Such arguments could not continue for long. Seed settled the dispute by saying, 'The trouble with you is that you think this club is not good enough for you.' Danny filed a transfer request in retaliation. He was put on the list since the club didn't want unhappy players. Given that Danny was an international – he'd made his fourth appearance in a 6–1 drubbing against Scotland in November 1950 – they must have had an eye on the profit they could make out of him too.

Just as with Glentoran, Danny was sad to be leaving for he was popular in the town. One young supporter, Glynn Lunn, recalls: 'My brother Roy and I were nine and ten at the time and we used to wait for Danny on match days in Barnsley Bus Station. He was always wearing a tweed overcoat with his boots in a brown paper bag. We accompanied him to the ground and at the end of the match he'd always go into the other dressing room to get the autographs of the visiting team for us.' Even so, it suited Danny to be on his way. Barnsley were not going to get anywhere near promotion, they were stifling his instincts and his desire to progress and, as such, they were no longer of any use to him. His international prospects, or lack thereof, must have helped him arrive at the decision to move. Playing in that game against Scotland in November, he was again out of sorts and found himself dropped for the next match the following March. He realized that playing in the Second Division was not adequate preparation for these games. In this League he might come across a great player like Tom Finney two or three times in a season. If he was to improve he must tackle them week after week. Not only did he need a club with greater ambition and a more modern outlook than that of Barnsley, he needed one that was secure in the top flight. Although that match at Hampden Park had exposed his shortcomings, it had allowed him to fulfil a childhood dream when he lined up with Peter Doherty in what was to be the latter's final game for his country. Even in the twilight of his career, Doherty was still a quality player and a great man, doing everything that a top-class footballer should, playing well, encouraging the youngsters, cajoling the senior players to a greater effort. Danny was inspired by this encounter and resolved to emulate his hero. He knew that to do so, he had to get away from Barnsley.

The transfer quickly descended into black farce. The club responded to Danny's requests for information by saying that no one was interested in him. That might have gone on for months had he not been at college with a youngster who worked in the local telephone exchange. He was interested in the goings-on at Barnsley and, by virtue of his unique position, was able to monitor the calls into the club, the details of which he relayed to Danny. There were enquiries about him his classmate confirmed, but when Danny would ask at the club the next day, there was still no official news. This was sadly typical of the way players were treated. Danny was close to despair. Barnsley owned his registration and that was an end to it. Finally, after Barnsley had been beaten 7–0 by League leaders Preston in mid-March, club chairman J. P. Richards asked him if he still wanted a move. When Danny said he did, Richards told him to be ready at ten the following morning, but wouldn't even tell him where they were going!

The mechanics of the transfer itself show just how players were little more than slaves. The whole affair was an affront to Danny's dignity. On the way to the Midlands, Richards asked him a host of questions relating to his background, education, family and so on. It was only later that Danny realized that he was taking notes so that he might give a character reference to his next employers, presumably so that he could advise them that this heathen Irishman wouldn't steal the family silver. The only surprise was that he wasn't led into the hotel where the deal was done in chains with a lead round his neck; he was, though, forced to eat in the kitchens of the hotel while Richards disappeared to do the deal with this mystery club in the proper dining room!

A deal done, Richards returned to tell Danny that he had arranged to transfer him to Aston Villa and that he should now meet their chairman, F. H. Normansell, and team manager George Martin, and that he'd given Danny 'a good character', a phrase which perplexed him. Was Richards so pompous as to think he 'could give and take away other people's characters?' Apparently so. There was no sense that Danny might want to make up his own mind about the move. What was there to decide? He was a footballer, Villa were a bigger club, he'd move on the same terms that he'd 'enjoyed' at Barnsley, thanks to the maximum wage. What was there for him to consider? It never occurred to Richards that Danny might not like Villa's style, might not get on with the manager, might not want to go to Birmingham, might prefer to wait for other offers.

In fact, Danny was charmed by Martin's visions of glory as well as the evocative name of Aston Villa. Once he confirmed that he would be allowed to train with the ball, he was sure that the move would be a good one. The slave was sold to the Villa Park plantation for £15,000.

3   A Prophet Without Honour

Back in 1951 it was a big jump from Barnsley to Aston Villa. The clubs operated in different spheres, at separate levels of the game. Compared with the homely environment which existed at Barnsley, Aston Villa was a sprawling monolith. If Oakwell could be likened to a cosy terraced house, Villa Park was a mansion. As Villa's Larry Canning explains: 'There were planets between Villa and Barnsley at that time. And players wanted to come to the club because they looked after the players – we were always being asked how you got a transfer to the Villa.' (Jackie Blanchflower had an answer to that particular poser: 'Whenever Manchester United went down there, you'd have to stand on a bench to hang your coat up and our old trainer used to say that was the way Villa picked their players. If you could hang your coat up while standing on the floor you were in, because they just wanted powerful six-footers and they played an old-fashioned style that didn't change.' Given that there was an element of belittling the opposition before a game in that statement, it was also true that Villa were a strong, physical side and had been for a number of years.)

Danny hardly fitted into that bracket. He was ostensibly brought into the side as a symbol of a proposed changing of the guard at Villa Park, following in the footsteps of Tommy Thompson and Dave Walsh, who had been transferred in, and Peter Aldis who made his debut in that same 1950–51 season. Nevertheless, the backbone of the side was made up of Villa stalwarts such as Harry Parkes, Frank Moss and Dickie Dorsett, each of whom were into their thirties when Danny arrived. As members of a team that had gradually fallen off in performance in the post-war seasons, it seemed that the time had come to ring the changes, a difficult period for all concerned. Every player reaches the end of the road at some stage, but it should be recalled that in the early 1950s this was a much more sensitive issue. The players were not bid a fond farewell with a lucrative testimonial game, though they might receive a benefit of around £750 if they were lucky. If the players were well paid in comparison with the average worker, they certainly were not in the super income brackets of today's top performers – they could not hang up their boots and go into complete retirement, materially secure for the rest of their lives. Yet more emotive was the fact that these were the players who lost many of their best years to the war. Admittedly they were the lucky ones simply by virtue of having survived intact, but their professional lives were wrecked. A player such as Frank Moss, whose father had also been a major figure at Villa Park, winning five England caps in the 1920s, was part of the furniture at the club. He eventually amassed 296 League games for Villa – had it not been for the war, that figure would have been nearer 550. Half his career, and perhaps representative honours too, were snatched from him. It was no easy job nudging such players out of the game.

Even so, there was a gradual realization at the club that change had to be made. Having finished reasonably, if unexcitingly, placed in the first two seasons after the war, 1949–50 saw the start of a decline. George Martin replaced Alex Massie as manager in December 1950 in an attempt to arrest the club's fall from grace, but despite his early efforts, and by the time Danny Blanchflower got to the club in March 1951, Villa were precariously placed one off the bottom of the First Division, with 20 points from 31 games. Below them sat Sheffield Wednesday with the same points from an extra game, while above were Chelsea with 21 from 30 and Huddersfield with 23 from 32. With the club lacking star names among its solid but ageing playing staff, the omens for survival were not good.

George Martin's appointment seemed, on first glance, a good one. He'd taken Newcastle United to promotion and had established them as a strong unit in the top flight. Interestingly, it was Martin who signed George Robledo from Barnsley prior to Danny's arrival at Oakwell. With a good scouting network established in Yorkshire, he had already made note of Danny's talents when he was with the Magpies. On his move to Villa, it transpired that neighbours Wolves had been in the hunt for Danny's signature, but the move had broken down when Barnsley demanded cash rather than a player exchange. One Wolves director then gave the Villa chairman a tip about Danny's qualities, information which Martin backed up. Had Martin remained at Newcastle, Danny might well have lined up alongside the likes of Jackie Milburn in the strong teams that fared so well in the FA Cup throughout the 1950s. As it was, Martin left Newcastle for Villa in an attempt to escape from bitter behind-the-scenes wrangling, with which he could not cope. Given that Villa required a single-minded man with a clear sense of purpose and the determination to overcome whatever obstacle was put in his way, this hardly made him the ideal choice as manager, unless you happened to be in favour of the status quo, as the directors were.

Aston Villa was a club crying out to be taken into the new century. Larry Canning described it as a 'mausoleum'. In some respects, the very splendour of Villa Park, that huge Victorian edifice, gave it a palatial grandeur that rooted the club in a different age; even the name spoke of the last century. Visiting Villa Park, coming up to its front doors is an experience unlike that which you will encounter at any other club. Where other clubs may be humble, modern, run down or go-ahead, that frontispiece turns Villa Park into a stately home. The surroundings produce an atmosphere and an environment redolent of the nineteenth century that is tremendously difficult to shake off, even as we enter the twenty-first. Today, Villa have a proud record of seven Championships and seven FA Cup wins. But six of each were seized by 1920. In the intervening three-quarters of a century, they've managed one of each to go with the European Cup, which represents their finest hour. This is poor fare for a club of its stature, achievements emulated or surpassed on the domestic scene by far smaller clubs such as Ipswich Town, Nottingham Forest, Derby County, Portsmouth, Huddersfield Town and Leeds United. Those who determined the club's future laboured under the misapprehension that just because the club was called Aston Villa it was automatically the best. Today things have been modernized behind the scenes and restored to order on the field by Brian Little. One could hardly call a side that now regularly qualifies for European competition a sleeping giant, but Aston Villa continue to doze fitfully. Since it's rarely been out of the top division for long, it's a club that hasn't had to ask itself the hard questions that others such as Blackburn, Newcastle or Chelsea have had to pose. Only two men of iron will have been able to interrupt the flow at the club, namely Ron Saunders and now, Brian Little.

They, in their differing ways, turned the club inside out. Even so, a perceived lack of major signings has long frustrated the Villa faithful. For a club that regularly drew crowds of forty or even fifty thousand when they were in the Third Division in the early seventies, and have more or less finished in a respectable position in the top flight since, how often have Villa really been in the running to sign the big names? With all due respect, Sasa Curcic, Savo Milosevic, Mark Draper and Gary Charles do not come from the very top drawer. When push comes to shove in the hunt for the likes of Shearer or Ravanelli, Bergkamp, Zola or Overmars, Villa are conspicuous by their absence – even their record signing Stan Collymore is a maverick, having had an unsettling and dis-apointing spell at Liverpool only to move on rather quickly. Every club has to be run along businesslike lines these days and big spending cannot guarantee success, but until Villa follow the lead of clubs such as Blackburn, Chelsea and Newcastle who have gone for broke, can they realistically challenge for the top prizes? To outsiders it can seem that this club which plays its football in such grand surroundings is more interested in retaining its place in the top flight. Status is, and always has been, all. As Dave Walsh remembers: 'We all got a fortnight's holiday in the Netherlands just because we got out of trouble the season Danny came!'

That desperate urge to cling on was the prevailing *raison d'etre* when Danny arrived to play his first game for them, on St Patrick's Day in 1951. With relegation staring them in the face, it was imperative that Villa grabbed some points, and quickly. Danny was a professional and so he understood the merit of that. Having just promoted himself from the Second Division, he certainly didn't want to go back down there within a matter of weeks. Even so, as he applied himself to the task, it was with a sense of mount-ing foreboding. If he had entertained ideas that Villa might be his club for life, those hopes were soon to be dashed.

On entering the ground his first impression was that 'it stood as an edifice to feats of glory long since achieved, and that nothing very much that could happen now, or ever again, would arouse in it the same feelings of excitement it must have known in those great Villa days ... inside there was the same half-haunted air. These were not unpleasant offices but the march of time was gradually leaving them behind ... everything was old and solid and neglected.' A friend of Danny's when he was at Villa, Maurice

Tomlins, recalls that, 'He used to say, "You walk into the dressing room at Villa Park and you just felt you could never live up to the standards and the history of the place. It was oppressive." '

That's not to suggest that there was a bad atmosphere at the club, nor that the players did not get on. As his colleague Amos Moss, Frank's brother, recalls: 'There was a good spirit at the club, I always thought, though it did live in the past a little, especially for someone like Danny, who was very forward thinking.' Indeed, it was that spirit that did most to stave off relegation in Danny's first season. He made his debut in a home fixture against Burnley. Villa claimed the points with a 3–2 win, ending a losing streak of five games – indeed, it was only their second win in fourteen matches. The *Birmingham Evening Mail* remarked that 'Blanchflower was prominent with good constructive work'. Even so, a defeat the following Saturday at Middlesbrough left them in deep trouble. With back-to-back games against Wolves to come over the Easter period, relegation began to look a foregone conclusion. To usher it in, the players held an impromptu 'celebration' at their hotel, dispelling much of the tension that had surrounded their recent play in the process. Having accepted the unacceptable, it no longer held any fears. Villa did the double over Wolves, embarking on a run of nine games without defeat, which saw them soar to mid-table respectability with points to spare.

In his eleven games prior to the end of the campaign, Danny managed to make quite an impact on the supporters with his elegant passing and calm distribution, though many felt his all-round game needed to be tightened. In his excellent history of the club, Peter Morris wrote that 'at first, his obvious liking for attack and corresponding deficiencies in defence earned him criticism at Villa Park. But once Blanchflower found his feet in First Division football and curbed his gay sallies upfield, his natural ability bloomed into positive brilliance. His intelligent positional play which, paradoxically, took him away from his opposing inside-forward instead of close marking, as was normal for a wing-half, made him a difficult man to dominate. Inside-men in fact found themselves trying to mark Blanchflower instead of Blanchflower marking them!' This was a perfect example of Danny's philosophy on the game, that attack really was the best form of defence and not just some dullard cliche. Danny insisted on playing his game, on imposing himself and his skills on each match, attempting to nullify the opponents' skills by simply overwhelming them with his own. Naturally he was sometimes caught out, for, good player though he was, the First Division still represented a considerable step up in quality. His limited international experience had been some preparation, but it still took time to settle into the new surroundings.

He adapted quickly. As he pointed out, First Division players were quicker, but mainly in terms of thought rather than pure physical speed. In that regard, the higher grade of football was made for him. Larry Canning remarked: 'He was a bit of a plodder, but he was a good tackler. He'd make players go the way he wanted them to go so that he was always in position to nip the ball off them. His speed was in the way he thought and how he could size up a situation very quickly. The nearest to Danny nowadays is someone like David Batty. He knows what's on and can do it quickly and if he gets caught, he can get out of jail. That was what Danny did so well. Batty's a bit harder, Danny was more fluid, but a softer version of David Batty is the closest I can see to Danny.' Amos Moss confirms that impression: 'He was a tremendously good player. He wasn't very quick and he wasn't especially strong, but he had an indefinable way of getting into the right place at the right time. You can't teach that – you look at someone like Paul McGrath now, bad knees, can't train, but he's always in the right place to break up a move – it's a sixth sense, you can't coach that. Danny was a far better player but I don't think even he could tell you how he did it. The ball would just naturally come to him, like a magnet. His best position was right-half, though I think he'd have liked a free-roving commission, but that was against the tactics of the day.'

Comparisons with McGrath and Batty may shock a number of observers today, but they shouldn't. Since his move to Newcastle and particularly since Glenn Hoddle has taken charge of the England side, Batty has been outstanding in his use of the ball, to the point where there are now few more valuable midfielders. Equally, it illustrates just how much the game has changed over the last forty years, the increasing emphasis on 'keeping the team's shape' meaning that few players can operate in isolation. Where once teams had specialists like Danny, who were free to play in an almost exclusively creative fashion from the midfield, even the greatest players are now expected to do their share of defending – wasn't it that that ruled Glenn Hoddle out of so many internationals? Someone like Batty is the archetypal modern-day footballer, having a toe in both camps, the constructive and destructive. Certainly his ability to find himself involved in off-the-ball incidents and the permanent Steptoe-like scowl that's etched on to his face are as far removed from Danny Blanchflower as one could get, but with the ball at his feet, the comparisons are valid and instructive. It also illustrates the fact that however much of a ballplayer he might have been, Danny was expected to make his fair share of tackles at Villa Park, since that was the character of the side – powerful, physical, aggressive. Later on, when he moved to Tottenham, no comparable physicality was required of him, and his colleagues there speak of him in terms of Cantona and Hoddle.

Villa were safe by mid-April, when a 3–3 draw was secured against Portsmouth. The *Mail* was clear on where the credit lay for this recovery: 'The tide turned in Villa's favour with the advent of young Danny Blanchflower. The signing of this brilliant young Irish international from Barnsley on the eve of transfer restriction day was indeed timely. His open play, combined with deceptive passes with which his colleagues are getting acquainted, has made all the difference to the team . . . he has soon settled down – off the field as well as on.' It was off the field and in the club's administration that the problems lay. When he came to the club to play right-half it was to displace Larry Canning who'd played there for much of the season. Canning recalls that they obviously thought Danny was 'the right man for the job. That was fair enough because Danny was a very good player, very good. The manager was so weak, that to soften the blow for me, he said, "They tell me you're a useful outside-left." Do me a favour! Suddenly I'm playing as a forward on the other side of the field! And I scored on the Saturday against Burnley, but I didn't care after that. Just as ridiculous, the assistant secretary at the club then got hold of me and said, "Larry, take the new lad around." This was the guy who'd taken my place in the team and they wanted me to look after him! So I showed him round the club and around Birmingham for a few days. I took him to the theatre, the cinema and we'd generally end up in a cafe. He was trying to get the atmosphere of the club from me, I suppose, asking me about the other players. We had wooden benches, like a continuous seat, all round the dressing room and Danny asked me, "Who's the guy who stands up in the corner on top of the seats shouting the odds?" It was Harry Parkes, he was the joker in the pack. Danny said, "I don't like people who shout in the dressing room." I thought that was fine, neither did I, but Parky was an exception because he was funny. Before a fortnight was out, Danny was up on the table outshouting Parky! He had to impose himself on every situation.'

He had the chance to do that during pre-season training prior to the 1951–52 kick-off, and it was at this point that Danny's disenchantment with the club started to grow. He wrote in his autobiography: 'Since the war, the club had done very little, except struggle to avoid relegation most seasons. Many thousands had been spent on buying players without much effect. No youngsters seemed to be finding their way into the team. It appeared that the older players ran the show to suit themselves and that organization, discipline and competition were big words that nobody cared much about. Mr Normansell obviously loved the club – everyone accepted that – but he was too soft in his dealings with the more influential players. George Martin, it was hoped, would change all that.' Martin's honeymoon period was swiftly at an end, however. Larry Canning notes, 'Martin was a nothing of a manager and Danny couldn't stand that. Martin was no good to football and anyone who was no good to football was no good to Danny. There were factions at Villa Park. Frank Moss was captain. His father had been captain and it never occurred to the club that anyone else could be captain or might do a better job as captain. Frank would come out training with a cigarette and a match in his hand, he'd go into the stand and have a smoke, shouting at us while we were trotting round, then he'd toddle over to Hubert Bourne, the trainer, and say, "I think we'll play handball." That was his training. Frank was a strong personality and a strong man – he was centre-half and he was admirable in that position. But that didn't make it right, certainly not in Danny's view! He was a push and run merchant, football was a beautiful game for him, he loved the way Spurs played. We talk about the passing game in this country but we don't pass the ball, we pass the buck, we do it for the sake of doing it. He didn't like to see people spoiling the game, being in a position to make it better but not doing so, and that's what Aston Villa was like.' That view is echoed by Tommy Thompson who remembers, 'Hubert Bourne was always in the dressing room at Villa Park and he could hear people coming up the passage, their shoes echoing down the corridor. By the time anybody got in, Hubert was always standing next to the skip with all the tackle in it. If it was one of the players, he'd just leave it, go and sit down again, but if it was one of the bosses, he'd stick his head in and start rooting amongst the kit. I think he used to stand there for hours!'

Danny pointed out that 'there was some truth in the claim that the older players had been too dominant at Villa Park. Older players are more important; their character shapes the character of the club . . . good management had been lacking at Villa Park. The older players had, probably not by evil intention or cussedness, but through sheer lack of desire and ambition, grown fat on their freedom and lacked real competitive urge.' Essentially, Danny felt that Villa needed the same sort of drastic surgery that Alex Ferguson undertook when he arrived at Old Trafford a decade ago. Danny felt that the older players needed to be moved on, the training staff overhauled and newer, hungrier individuals brought in to fill the key positions. Had Danny had his way, the likes of Frank Moss and Harry Parkes would have been shipped out to lower division clubs. Yet this was easy for him to say, harder for George Martin to do. He'd been at the club just a few months while these players were Villa legends and still useful footballers capable of doing a job in the First Division. Perhaps they had been given more latitude than was wise down the years, but each had the best interests of the club at heart – for Moss, playing for the club was a family tradition, something which meant a great deal. He and Parkes did represent the old guard and there was a desperate need for renewal but, with the right sort of management, that might have been achieved with them on board; indeed, they could have been crucial in steering the club in a new direction just as Bryan Robson was at Manchester United. Danny's problem was a blindness to the niceties of man-management as he focused purely on the need to tear down the traditions that bound the club. As Amos Moss explains: 'Football's not just about tactics, it's about people too. In that way, I don't know if Danny would have made a good manager, even if he'd gone straight into it after playing. He may have been a bit too dogmatic. You've got to be a bit of a psychologist. You can't just say, "My ideas are right." You have to listen too, and he wasn't quite so good at that! Football shouldn't be complex, but working out the management side, looking at the players you've got and the system to fit them, is a very difficult business. You can't always get the players you want, you can use those you have better, there's more to it than Danny would admit sometimes.'

With his usual tunnel vision, Danny tried to get over his ideas as quickly as possible, without necessarily realizing that he was upsetting people along the way. 'He ruffled feathers, and some people didn't like him for it,' says Larry Canning. 'Those who could have done something with the club just did enough to stay in the game, whereas Danny wanted to change things.' There was rarely any real animosity in the exchanges, for Danny was able to get on well with his team-mates, especially on the golf course. Villa managed a good start to the 1951–52 season with Tommy Thompson in a rich vein of form which saw him elevated to the England team for a game against Wales. According to Amos Moss, 'Tommy Thompson was interviewed for television and he was asked what he did in his spare time. He said, "I play a lot of golf, I'm in the big four at Villa,' which was Larry Canning, Tommy, myself and Con Martin. When he got in for training the next day, Danny was on to him about "the bloody big four, you're not the best golfers . . ." and all that type of thing! We happened to be going to Letchworth for special training, so we had to have a series of Ryder Cup matches with us against Danny, Harry Parkes, my brother and one of the other lads.' At this point Larry Canning noticed golf was an increasing passion of Danny's: 'He'd have loved to have been a really good golfer but he wouldn't take the time to do it right. He thought he could do it better than the pros, that he could teach himself. You can't dominate the game of golf, you have to let it tell you what to do, and Danny couldn't admit to that!'

Whatever he was doing, certainly where sport was concerned, Danny felt he was the master. That's not the same as thinking that he knew all there was to know, however, for he accepted that he had a lot to learn about football at the top. In that sense, Aston Villa was a good club for him. Although he might bridle at the fact that older players ignored the manager's authority, he had a lot to learn from them. Frank Moss was an excellent centre-half, and playing alongside him was an education. Harry Parkes, playing behind Danny at right-back, had been a fine right-half in earlier years until an injury forced him to move back; he too was able to teach by example. Ahead of him, Danny had Tommy Thompson to work with; his international class shone through and gave a new dimension to Danny's own game. The move to Villa, whatever its drawbacks, clearly did wonders for him. By March 1952, he was embarking on a long, uninterrupted run of games in the Northern Irish team under the inspired leadership of Peter Doherty, now installed as national team manager. On the home front too, he was adding a vital degree of consistency while still having flashes of rare brilliance to crown his play – in the 2–1 win at Anfield he was described by the *Birmingham Mail* as 'the guiding genius'. In that first full season at Villa Park, 1951–52, he was an ever-present, turning out in all forty-three competitive games – though once again he failed to get beyond the third round of the Cup, Newcastle ending Villa's interest at the first hurdle. He took this defeat particularly badly, as he had recently confided in the *Birmingham Mail* that his greatest ambition was to play in a Cup-winning side.

Five wins in the final eight games of the season saw Villa finish sixth in the League, but that was deceptive. The position was achieved when there was nothing left but pride to play for – had a couple of those games been lost, they'd have struggled to get into the top half. The local press remarked upon the number of games where points were let slip in the final few moments, a reflection that the side was not as professional as it could have been. Although Villa were physically strong, Tommy Thompson recalls that, 'You'd always find a couple of the lads in the toilets having a quick smoke before they went out.' And his colleague Stan Lynn adds: 'Some of the players would have a pint or two before they went to the ground for the game.' Danny, a virtual teetotaller throughout his life, was appalled by what he saw as this wanton disregard for trying to attain a peak of fitness, and wasn't slow to make the point. Little wonder that manager Martin noted that he was 'a good man to have on your team. He takes the game seriously as distinct from the slap-happy types'. Sadly, Martin seemed unable to weed out these unnamed villains that would not match the commitment of the others. Even so, as the season wound down, the local *Sports Argus* reporter, Citizen, recorded: 'Villa are now playing better football than at any time since the war. Win or lose, they play an attractive type of game that is more in keeping with the club's traditions. Throughout the season there has been evidence of planning.' A brief tour of Denmark and Sweden followed the season's end with the hopeful comments ringing in the players' ears.

It's ironic that Citizen should have filed such a report, for Danny was starting to lose patience. It was his time there that confirmed him in his view that victory at all costs is worth nothing; that good, cultured football can only evolve from a coherent plan which uses the inevitable reverses in fortune as a launching pad for future successes. He saw little evidence of that at Villa and it was becoming apparent to him that much of the trouble stemmed from the boardroom and the club offices – not for nothing did Villa historian Peter Morris entitle his chapter on the years 1945–59 'Decline and Fall'. Danny's greatest disappointment was that Villa didn't seem to learn from their mistakes and nor were they bringing through enough new talent for the future. For example, the surface at Villa Park was very poor, 'absolute murder' according to Dave Walsh, and deliberately so. As Peter Aldis explains: 'We were a fit side and if teams came to Villa Park when it was wet, they would struggle to compete with us. They'd put sand on it but it just made it heavier and deeper!' Danny saw this as wholly unacceptable. Had he had his way, he would have re-laid the pitch and turned it into a paradise for free-flowing football. The great Tottenham push and run side had just won the Championship by playing in such a style and Danny was absolutely enthralled by it. Having seen League football played in this delightful manner, he wanted all sides to play the game in the same vein. As Tommy Thompson says, 'He was just an enthusiast for football, such a good player, always talking and thinking about the game, trying to improve the side.' His whole distaste for the way the Villa was being run was expressed in one cameo at the end of the 1951–52 season. After a dismal performance at Middlesbrough and a poor showing at Chelsea, with four games to go, George Martin had discussed bringing in some new blood and leaving out Dorsett and Parkes. Yet when the next team sheet was pinned up both were playing. According to Danny, 'The story we heard was that, hearing of Mr Martin's intentions, they had gone to see the chairman and pleaded not to be dropped.' As Larry

Canning explains: 'Danny relished losing because you learn that way. If you lose, you know you shouldn't lose the next game because you've learned something new.' Those final few matches offered a perfect opportunity to experiment, games where defeat would not have mattered. This failure to alter the team was final proof that those who ran Aston Villa were incapable of learning anything. Whether the rumour was true or not, it fatally undermined Martin's credibility and left him a lame-duck manager. It was here that any progressive intentions foundered on the rocks of the club's stultifying obsession with its traditions. As a reaction, Danny decided that if Martin could not change the club, then he'd have to try to do it himself.

With Martin at the helm, there was always scope to make suggestions. One of Martin's few new signings, Peter McParland, an outside-left brought in from Dundalk, makes the point that 'George was a free and easy manager, he wanted us to express our opinions. You didn't have to encourage Danny!' Danny was typically blunt in his views for he had lost a lot of his respect for the institution of Aston Villa. It was clear that the directors ran the show, even more than had been the case at Barnsley. As far as Danny was concerned, most football directors were little more than jumped-up shopkeepers who went in search of the spurious charisma attached to an association with a major football club. If he had to share a room with a director who'd made his money in the grocery business, he might ask him whether apples or oranges provided the best value that week, but he certainly wouldn't ask him who should play at outside-left on Saturday because he would have absolutely no interest in their opinion. He would dismiss it as amateurish and ill-informed, the equivalent of asking a plumber his views on Picasso's blue period just because he'd got a tin of paint in his shed.

Against this background Danny became something of a footballing evangelist, preaching his gospel of how the game should be played. Maurice Tomlins recalls that 'I was working for Lucas, the electrical engineering firm, and Danny came and gave us a talk at the offices in the city. I remember him telling us how to take a penalty – he reckoned you should tap it to the side so that a colleague could just walk it into the net. What struck me most was his comment that fifty per cent of the game is the element of surprise, which was such an intelligent comment to make.' It was all the more intelligent at a time when English football was so stereotyped. At the club, Danny tried to make changes too. Cleverly, he realized that he needed to create a powerbase for himself if he was to achieve progress and that the only place to start was with the reserve team. He tried to instil his philosophy into them, very shrewdly anticipating that as outsiders they had little to lose from trying something fresh, while as youngsters they'd be more impressed by his reputation and be more adaptable.

Driven on by his vision of a team playing the kind of football that he wanted to play, Danny was altruistic and selfish in equal measure. He wanted to improve the game as a spectacle and give the long-suffering Villa fans something to savour, but equally he wanted to enjoy his football, play in a side that would further his international ambitions and let him get his hands on a medal or two. He was approaching his twenty-seventh birthday during the course of the 1952–53 campaign and recognized that time was passing. At that age he wanted the additional responsibility of captaincy too, since this would give him the greatest amount of control over the team's pattern of play. According to Stan Lynn, he was halfway to taking over that position anyway: 'He liked to do the talking in the dressing room before a game, he'd talk about us and the opposition and how we should play. He'd take over the team talks from the manager. Some of the more senior players weren't too keen on that because it wasn't what they were used to.'

Danny's determination to improve sometimes led him to be boorish. Larry Canning recalls that, 'He liked his own way very much. We played head tennis a lot and Danny wanted to play the way Manchester United played it because Jackie had told him all about it. So he called over to Billy Goffin, who was a lovely, unassuming guy, "C'mon, Billy, we'll play United's way." Billy didn't hear him properly, thought he'd said something else, and called out, "No." Danny just threw the ball down, walked off and got in the bath!' Such childish outbursts were rare though not unique. But if he caused any disquiet in the ranks it was because of his incessant conversation, his determination to shake Villa to its very foundations. Still naïve in the ways of English football and the machinations of internal club politics, he genuinely believed that he could make a difference to an institution as set in its ways as Aston Villa. Larry Canning, though sympathetic to Danny's ideals, was a wiser character and saw that Danny was doomed to failure: 'The older players respected him for his ability at first. They didn't like the other side of him, but they put up with it because Danny couldn't do anything about it. That wasn't enough for him, though, as it didn't change anything. Things began to grate. He was disappointed because we still didn't train much with the ball. It was too much bother. Danny came here thinking Aston Villa was this great club but pretty quickly he realized it was too ludicrous even to comment on. It was so backward that we met this guy who was the scout in the North-East and the man could hardly see! Nobody knew who he'd sent us in twenty-five years, but the trainer was delighted because "he keeps the bad players away"! But that was Aston Villa. We had some poor managers. It was just a disgraceful joke. If the supporters had known what went on, there'd have been uproar! We had one official who came in early to get the mail so he could see what was going on – then he'd write "Opened in error" on the envelope! He ran the Villa.'

The 1952–53 campaign saw all the promise of the previous season dissipate in double quick time. Although relegation was never likely, neither was a sustained bid for the title, and in those days before European competition it was the Championship or nothing. With just eighteen points from twenty-one games by the end of the year, Villa put all their eggs into the FA Cup basket. They duly dropped it in the sixth round when Everton won a close game at Villa Park. The season ended much as every season had for Danny during his spell in England – in mediocrity. On a personal level though, things looked brighter. He was now established as one of the finest performers at Villa Park. The local press were quick to laud his skilful play: in the 5–1 defeat at home to Blackpool the *Birmingham Mail* noted 'in the tackle Blanchflower was supreme and his passing was as near perfection as one could desire'. In a win over Derby, he was 'a stumbling block to many Derby raids and possessed the ability to turn defence into attack by means of an accurate pass', while at Old Trafford 'Blanchflower was outstanding for the visitors but he had to concentrate so much on defence that he could do little to help the attack'.

As the outstanding player, the lack of any direction or apparent ambition at the club was too much for him, and his frustration frequently boiled over as his desire to instigate and effect change quickly became increasingly problematical. 'He was always interested in new formations and things like that,' says Amos Moss. 'He had strong opinions. When he first arrived, it was a strict 2–3–5, and he was all for experimenting with that – any kind of formation just to give something different. The difficulty with that is that when you want to change formations, you need to have drill, lots of practice in it, but Danny was always trying to change things straight away. I always liked talking with him because I thought I knew as much about the game as he did – my old man had been an international and I'd been mixing with players of that standard since I was a kid on the ground staff. I was always in the company of great players, and you learn things, you formulate your own opinions. With Danny, what struck me most about him was his tremendous enthusiasm for the game. He could be a bit dogmatic in his ideas, but I admired him for that. Nowadays there are as many different formations as there are teams, so he was ahead of the game in that respect.'

It wasn't always the done thing to be ahead of the game though, and Danny continued to run into conflict. His frustration at Villa was exacerbated by the fact that things were looking up with Northern Ireland. With Peter Doherty now the national manager, Danny felt that things were moving in the right direction. He was now an established player for his country, operating within a progressive framework. Doherty brought 'an understanding, a vitality and a leadership to the players that had been so sadly lacking before'. The contrast between him and George Martin could not have been more marked. More important still, during a close season tour to Canada with Northern Ireland in 1953, Doherty appointed Danny captain of his country, a singular honour and a position which bestowed the authority to play the game as he saw it. It was a freedom he craved and on which he thrived.

Danny obviously wanted success at Villa Park and criticized those who stood in the way. That said, he was always ready to stand up for his own ambitions and put them before the club's if he thought it necessary. At the tail-end of the 1952–53 season, Larry Canning recalls, 'We played against Preston when we were in the doldrums and we won well, with Danny at inside-right and

I was behind him. He played a blinder, he was always in exactly the right place for me to give him the ball. So the management decided we should go on with the same team, and we had a decent run to the end of the season. But Danny kicked up a fuss because he thought it was jeopardizing his international career. They put him back to right-half for the next season!' Perhaps Danny thought that if others had got away with complaining to the chairman the year before, it was only right that he did so too, but it contrasts a little with the view that he was solely interested in the good of the team. He wanted to be in a good side, but on his terms.

With that in mind, there's every likelihood that he would have asked for a move early in 1953–54 had George Martin not been forced out of office. In his history of the club, Peter Morris wrote that 'it was apparent that everything was not well at Villa Park and there was rumour and counter-rumour among shareholders and supporters before manager George Martin found himself in a position where resignation was the only step left to him. Again, and distressingly, a Villa manager's departure was a matter of controversy . . . there were many attacks on the board condemning their attitude of *laissez-faire*.' Martin found the pressures exerted by the board to be too much for him, preventing him from doing the job as he would have liked. Although Danny professed a personal liking for Martin, he was not sorry to see him go from a footballing point of view, hoping that at last things might take a turn for the better at Villa Park. The omens weren't good. He now found himself in a side that was little better than that he joined two years previously, while the *Sports Argus* pointed out that the good form at the end of 1952–53 might prove elusive in the new campaign: 'Certainly Villa went into the final stages with great spirit and enthusiasm. They tackled with a zest and determination they had not shown earlier and dominated games by gaining possession in five out of every seven challenges . . . the switching of Blanchflower into the attack without a doubt improved the football standard. But while they admittedly showed greater football skill, much of Villa's success at the end sprang from the team's hard tackling, enthusiastic type of play and their spirited "we're going to win" approach to the game. I doubt whether any team can play through a whole season like that.' Villa's limited improvement had been built on determination and honest endeavour rather than the quality required to see them through to the glittering prizes.

A great deal depended on the identity of the new manager. When he was appointed, it seemed to confirm all the prejudices that Danny held. Eric Houghton joined Aston Villa as manager from Notts County. A former Villa player, he was a popular appointment with the supporters but had done little in Nottingham to excite. Notts County were, admittedly, a small club, having spent the past three seasons in the bottom half of the Second Division. To Danny, it looked as though an old boy had been appointed to appease the supporters and factions in the board and dressing rooms. He was equally upset by 'talk that Eric and Harry Parkes had been business partners for a while . . . that he had played and been friendly with some of the other players still in the team . . . and that it would be an embarrassment to have, as a manager, a man who had been so closely related to some of the players'. According to Larry Canning, Danny's reservations were well founded: 'Eric was a country boy and stayed that way. So naïve. Villa is a big club in a big city and you need a big man to run it properly. You know how you hear cliches bouncing round the game? Somebody comes up with a phrase like "early doors" or "tired legs" and then they echo round. That was Eric's speciality. He'd say, "If you come back the way you are now, you get a point!" and we'd just laugh on the way out.' Danny recalled him sending the team out to play at Highbury with the comment: 'And watch yourselves crossing the road!'

Whatever Houghton's failings, with the possible exception of Matt Busby, Arthur Rowe or Peter Doherty, there probably wasn't a manger in the country who would have satisfied Danny at this stage. That Northern Irish trip to Canada lit a fire under him that raged so strongly it consumed what was left of his diplomatic skills. The national side had played against a Swiss team in an exhibition match in Montreal. It was a game that caused Danny to go back to first principles and look at the English style afresh. 'I had not played very often against foreign opposition up to that time,' he later wrote, 'and was entirely steeped in the thoughts and habits of British play. They played a defensive system that was new to me. I found strange patterns of play during the game. I had always thought in terms of one goalkeeper, two full-backs, three half-backs and five forwards. It had never occurred to me that it might be better to play four full-backs, two half-backs and four forwards; or any combination that would suit the conditions, the players in hand and the circumstances of competition . . . the more I thought of it (at the time in relation to Aston Villa and the players they had) the more I was convinced it would suit us to adopt a 3–3–4 system.'

Although he was overly modest in suggesting he'd never considered different formations in the past, the Swiss had handed him an object lesson of which he took note. In a nutshell this was why Blanchflower was such an exceptional player for the times, for there is little evidence of many of our clubs learning from foreign competition and from defeats, certainly not in the 1950s. Perhaps it was because he had a naturally inquisitive spirit, but when Danny was confronted with something new, he was enraptured by it. At times he might fall for innovation for its own sake, but in the spirit of those times any kind of change was sensible, if only to confuse the opposition. Returning to Villa Park for pre-season training, he duly suggested that the team try a 3–3–4 formation in practice. Houghton half-heartedly agreed as long as Danny organized it himself. Con Martin, Peter McParland and Tommy Thompson were enthusiastic about the outcome, but Houghton was unwilling to take the responsibility for such a radical change that might end in failure. Newly installed as manager, his was a safety-first approach. Three months later, the Hungarians descended on Wembley and gave England an embarrassingly comprehensive lesson in international football with their deep lying centre-forward, incisive rather than unnecessary passing movements and their all-round flexibility. Yet still Houghton and 99 per cent of the managers in England clung to their rigid, redundant 2–3–5 formation. Little wonder that Danny wrote, 'I began to see the club in a different light. They were hanging their hats on old traditions, sitting on their asses and doing nothing to keep the club alive and vital. I told Eric I would not promote another idea for the club as I thought it a waste of time.'

However much Danny might have meant his last comment, his own enthusiasm often got the better of him and he continued to push his views. Early on in that 1953–54 season he masterminded a triumph over Manchester City and their Revie Plan. According to Tommy Thompson, 'Before the match, Danny said, "I think we should play the same way as them, drop someone back." City could play it but they couldn't defend against it. Danny said we should mark Revie as soon as we lost the ball – the inside-left was to go and pick him up. We snuffed him right out of it. Mind you, if we hadn't played that way, maybe Danny would've had to mark Revie that day and he wouldn't have relished running after him, so he got someone else to do that! We won with three goals, we walloped them, actually, and that was down to Danny. He wasn't bombastic about it, he didn't order you to play the way he thought, but he was very persuasive. He was popular with a lot of the players who could see the game needed to move on, and he had that quiet way of talking that made his ideas sound worthwhile. But really somebody had to take the team talks over because the managers in those days didn't do much.' Dave Walsh echoes that comment, adding, 'Danny took more on himself in the dressing room when Eric Houghton came because he thought he had to. Eric's team talks weren't too good. It was all for the good of the club in his eyes.'

Whether for the club's benefit or not, it didn't go down too well, the more so since Danny was busily transforming himself into football's renaissance man away from Villa Park. He appeared on a weekly local radio show with Stan Cullis, called *Talking Football*, and also contributed to a talk-in column in the *Birmingham Evening Mail* along with Ronnie Allen of the Albion and Birmingham's skipper Les Boyd. He used that space to launch the following attack on our game in general and, by implication, Villa in particular: 'Our training schedules should have been changed a long, long time ago ... two or three hours a day are enough if they are used properly. I want to see more use of the ball in training. When a team goes on to the field for a match, it doesn't do three or four laps round the track before kick-off. Everything should be done with the ball, even lapping and sprinting. It's teamwork that counts and I think this is often neglected ... one thing I am looking forward to is when we start to make films of our matches so that we can study our faults – we should be training to win matches.' This was revolutionary talk, but wherever you went in the West Midlands you could find Danny pontificating on the game in the most gently persuasive fashion, winning many converts among the general public. Had he not had those outlets, he would have surely gone mad. As it was, at the club, he still found himself banging his head against a wall. As Peter McParland explains: 'Some of the senior players were getting tired of him dictating in training or on the field, because Danny would be saying: "Leave it. I'll do that. I'll take the free-kicks. I'll run the show."' With so much ability at his disposal, it was natural for Danny to want to be in the thick of things for, as Larry Canning notes, 'Danny had a tremendous ego and you either liked him for it or you hated him for it. That was his life, in the middle, with the two sides around him.' Amos Moss agrees, adding, 'He ruffled a few feathers there, because in those days you had to be careful who you voiced your opinions to! He would start arguments because he loved to discuss things, it was a form of stimulation for him. He liked lively discussion, as a means of coming to a better conclusion.'

Danny was perpetually foiled by the reluctance of the Villa hierarchy to embrace the new world, but it's easy to attack the elder statesmen at Aston Villa for their head-in-the-sand approach to the game. The senior players weren't simply being curmudgeonly for the sake of it. Certainly there was an element of 'young players should be seen and not heard' about the place, but that had been the pre-war culture in which they had grown up. Equally, some may not have been convinced by Danny's arguments. What track record did he have? How many other clubs were adopting his ideas? If your side had switched to a 4–2–4 or 3–3–4 formation in 1952, you would have been on your own. Had results gone the wrong way, the manager and senior players would have been hounded mercilessly by a disgruntled crowd; that was a responsibility which Danny did not have to bear, giving him the freedom to be fearless. Finally, the fact that a player six or seven years your junior was suddenly dispensing instructions could be upsetting. If nothing else, it was a reminder to the older players of their own mortality and impending retirement. That fateful day of retirement might be accelerated still further if a new regime came into being, and so their suspicions were understandable – it might cost them their livelihood to follow Danny's ideas.

An intelligent man, surely Danny understood those fears? Perhaps not. As a younger man in a hurry he dwelt little on the feelings of older pros, who he felt had had their time and were holding Villa back in their alliance with the board. Villa's backward approach to the game first bewildered him, then frustrated him and finally, as the evidence backing change began to mount, angered him. But throughout, he remained on good terms with his colleagues – Tommy Thompson recalls that if they were out together, his rallying cry would be 'Never mind about getting the candle lit at both ends, let's get the bugger lit in the middle!' – but he did grow more impatient on the field. In turn this antagonized the management and his team-mates still further, creating a vicious circle. Away from the club, he remained as helpful to others as he'd ever been, seeking some solace in the company of ordinary football supporters. One fellow Northern Irishman, Billy Currie from Belfast, was on the receiving end of Danny's kindness: 'Myself and a friend, Joe Yeates, wanted to see the West Brom v Newcastle Cup tie while Danny was at Aston Villa. We worked with his father at the time and asked him if he could possibly get us tickets. Danny said that he would, but no way would he send them over. He said he'd meet us at New Street station in Birmingham and there he was with a car waiting for us at eight o'clock on the morning of the game. He took us to his home, gave us breakfast and lunch and then drove us to the Hawthorns. Danny was a big star at the time and we were amazed that he should take the trouble to make sure we had tickets and everything ran smoothly. After that, he still had to get back to Villa Park to play a match!' Danny played his part in a 2–2 draw that afternoon against Huddersfield.

As the 1953–54 season came to its close and England set off for the World Cup in Switzerland, Danny concluded that his days at Villa Park were numbered. The team had stumbled to thirteenth place in the First Division and once again gone out in the third round of the FA Cup. More damning, there was no obvious reason to expect that things would improve at all. According to Larry Canning, 'Danny wanted to get to the top, a bit too quickly in my view. He thought Villa was the rocket, and it wasn't. He was full of ideas and Aston Villa was archaic. Danny wanted to remodel the place and at the end he was dying of frustration. He discovered the damage the board were doing – they had no idea, they were a disgrace to football – and he wanted to go.' The final straw had come in January 1954 when the chairman had invited Danny into his office to ask his opinion on team selection. By going over the head of the team manager in this manner, Normansell had simply confirmed his culpability in the club's decline. As far as he and his board were concerned, First Division survival was all that mattered, with the added spice of the occasional decent Cup run thrown in for good measure. That wasn't enough for Danny, who craved success. It's possible to be a great player without getting a lot of medals – George Best didn't win the FA Cup or even appear in the World Cup Finals. On the other hand, a good, honest pro like Ray Houghton has a stack of gongs – fine footballer though he is, even his most ardent admirers would not compare him with Best. A player's worth is seen on the pitch, not necessarily a trophy cabinet, but Danny wanted it all ways, and why not? Certainly the lessons of the Swiss World Cup meant that he was yet more desperate to get away, to free himself of the shackles imposed on him. To be fair, he felt it to be as much a duty as a pleasure to escape. Gradually there was a groundswell of opinion that our game had to change. Naturally, Danny felt he should be in the vanguard of that process. In his new column for the *Evening Mail* he commented on the way in which that change would come: 'To reach that Hungarian standard will call for a gradual development with better policy and methods and more enthusiasm and hard work all round . . . let me leave you with this thought. Most of the teams which distinguished themselves in the World Cup employed the third back.'

Another consideration was surely that of sibling rivalry. His younger brother Jackie was at an exciting, progressive club, had played a couple of games in the side that had won the Championship in 1951–52, was working with the admirable Matt Busby and had a glittering career ahead, while Danny was rotting at Villa Park. Jackie recalls that, 'I think he felt Villa was just as bad as Barnsley. He told me that they got more money for not being relegated than they would have done if they'd won the League, from backhanders! Danny didn't like that sort of thing, he liked to do things properly. He thought Villa were stuck in the past. I think he was interested in going to London because the media was just starting then, the television and so on, but I think he really wanted to come to Manchester United. Unfortunately the club was broke at the time because they were rebuilding the ground, which is why the youth policy became essential.'

It's important to recognize that matters on the field weren't Danny's sole consideration at this point. Having dabbled in journalism with the *Birmingham Evening Mail*, his obvious gift was rewarded with his own column for the 1954–55 season. He began to view this as a more exciting post-football career opportunity than chartered accountancy and started to pursue it with typical assiduity, hence the interest in moving to clubs in either Manchester or London, the two great national newspaper cities. With a view to that future, it was just as important that Danny established himself as a major name in the game – he'd be a much better catch for any newspaper as a club captain renowned for lifting the game's great trophies. That wasn't going to happen at Villa Park. He noted in his autobiography that he finally got fed up there in September 1954, but that's being a little economical with the truth. According to Amos Moss, 'I knew he was going long before he went. I know that during the close season a deal was done with Spurs, because we ribbed him about it on the golf course. He wanted success, and you can't blame him for that.' Dave Walsh adds, 'He always had it in mind to go to London, to Spurs or Arsenal. He always said, "The place to get to is London." And that wasn't long after he'd got to Villa. He knew where he wanted to go.' Danny admitted as much in another article: 'I wanted to go to London but that was not the original reason for my request for a transfer. Once I had made up my mind that I wanted a change of club, however, I thought it might be best for me to aim at London.'

It's unclear whether the deal with Spurs was done between the clubs, or, more likely, between Danny and officials at Tottenham. Had it been an inter-club agreement, it would not have dragged on for such a time, for Danny did not leave until December 1954. Given that he and Arthur Rowe now knew one another quite well, it's probable that they had informal talks about such a move. It must have been clear too that he would be going to Spurs in order to become the captain of a rejuvenated team; the push and run side was at an end and Rowe wanted Danny to spearhead the new team. Of course, any such agreement would be unenforceable, for it was really up to the Villa where he went – if they didn't want to do a deal with Tottenham, he couldn't go. Still, Danny was cute enough to work the angles in his favour. Although it was suggested that he might be destined for Arsenal, it was unlikely, given his distaste for their defensive style. After all, would he have written this about his potential employers while on the transfer list?: 'Moscow Spartak came out of the recent game with Arsenal with a lot of credit – far more by my standards than the Arsenal. To their credit they played a hard, strong game all through but they did not play well and by that I mean they did not play good football. You might ask, "Who are you to have such standards?" Well, who do I have to be in order to be honest?' If anything was calculated to put Arsenal off his trail, it was comments like that.

Just as it had when he left Barnsley, Danny's transfer turned into something of a saga, beginning with a bizarre encounter between himself and Eric Houghton. Transfer requests had to be conveyed to the board in writing via the manager, but Houghton wouldn't take Danny's letter. Perhaps he thought that the chairman might follow ancient custom and shoot the messenger on receipt of bad news. When he finally got the letter, the chairman asked Danny to keep it quiet, but within days it was headline news, inevitable given his relationship with the city's major evening newspaper. The *Evening Mail*'s Tom Blunt asked the question: 'Has Danny Blanchflower asked for a transfer? His reluctance this week to commit himself on future plans for his popular series of articles moved me to ask him this point-blank question. Danny's answer was, "Sorry, no comment." . . . He is emphasizing his loyalty to the club he has served so ably . . . he has been a consistently outstanding player in some drab displays . . . This season it has been noticeable that his form for the Villa has been lacking in some of its old sparkle and penetration . . . he is always seeking to improve his game but it is hard for him to do just that in this present Villa side . . . there comes a time when even the most loyal player must think about his own future and nobody could blame Blanchflower for thinking that in present circumstances his career is coming to a standstill.' A couple of weeks later Danny's transfer was still officially under wraps. In an attempt to hasten the process along, he used his column to make a thinly veiled attack on the powers that be: 'It is my belief that a team cannot produce a consistent standard of play unless it is backed up by a consistent policy of approach behind the scenes . . . if the legislators of the team have a settled policy then reason suggests that eventually the team's performance will benefit . . . that in my opinion is the only chance for eventual improvement – to persevere with team and policy and attempt to overcome obstacles, not by-pass them.' Ostensibly, this was a discourse on the state of the English national side, but it didn't take too much imagination to realize that the criticism could equally apply to Aston Villa.

It was this outburst that pushed the chairman into granting his request. As Larry Canning notes, 'Directors were afraid of Danny because he'd ridicule them. Directors are in it for the reflected glory, they think it makes them big people and they hate to be made to look foolish, so Danny was never popular with them.' With the power of a newspaper column at his disposal, they must have feared the worst, that Danny would expose all the inadequacies of the club and turn the crowd against them. They were already restive, as one open letter to Danny via the *Evening Mail* illustrated: 'We have been privileged in witnessing your whole-hearted endeavours and football of the highest quality and as one who has been thrilled so regularly on the terraces, I deeply regret your recent transfer request. It is easy to perceive that your progress towards the peak of footballing ability is being retarded greatly at Villa Park ... but it is to you that people are looking to lead first the recovery and then the triumphal march towards the club's new greatness ... should you be transferred, all is lost for Aston Villa for many years to come ... if you go the supporters will not blame you but will admire you for seeking to attain the peak of your honourable profession.'

So ludicrous was the set-up at Aston Villa, they even made a hash of granting him his transfer. Several board meetings went by without their being able to make a decision until one bright spark decided they'd do better to actually discuss it with the player concerned. He was summoned to attend and waited outside while other business was discussed, where he was joined by a *Daily Mirror* reporter, Tom Lyons, looking for the story of his move. Danny left him for a few moments while he went to the dressing rooms, and when he returned he found that the Villa secretary, Billy Smith, had ushered Lyons into the boardroom thinking he was Danny Blanchflower. When Danny finally got in there, he sat through various attempts to persuade him to stay, one director claiming credit for making him 'the player he was now'. That was just a red rag to the Irish bull, making him all the more determined to leave. Eventually he was dismissed from the august gathering and, the following day, he was informed via the newspapers that Villa would put him up for transfer at a fee of £40,000, a new record (the existing mark was £34,000 for Jackie Sewell). For the first time in several years, Danny seemed unsure of his own worth and wrote, 'I find myself the centre of this week's sensation . . . the sum quoted as my transfer price is out of proportion to anybody's ability . . . desperate acts by certain clubs in the past have pushed the limit so high that negotiations are nowadays conducted by standards which are not logically sound . . . how can a player possibly attain a standard of performance in relation to the fee named rather than one which relates to his own standard and that of the players around him? If a record fee was paid for me they would expect a consistently outstanding performance in keeping with a fee which is more an illusion than anything else.'

Inevitably, Danny thought he had a solution to the whole transfer market mess, one which he expounded in the *Evening Mail*. It was a typical example of his provocative mind, but one which was based on sound logic. Most important, it challenged the supremacy of the clubs in all matters and suggested that the players should be allowed to profit from their skills as an incentive to raise their game: 'It is said that all men are born free and equal – but they soon grow up to earn graduated incomes. Therefore, each club should, by its own standards, value all the professional players on its books and register them at such values with the FA. Then, as this is the price they put on them, they should pay them accordingly – a £10,000 player would perhaps be paid £10 a week while a £20,000 player, being worth twice that amount to the club, should receive £20. The important thing is the incentive for the player to improve . . . if a £20,000 player was valued by another club at £25,000 then his own club would naturally want to receive a higher price for him than they themselves thought he was worth! Should the selling club be allowed to gain £5000 which they do not rightfully deserve because they have only been paying him on a £20,000 value basis? They can argue the player has improved with the aid of their facilities but if they believed that then they should have been paying him accordingly. The ideal solution seems to be that the £5000 be divided equally between the player and the club.'

High though the asking price was, there was no shortage of takers. Within the day, Tom Whittaker of Arsenal had flown back from a trip to Paris and was talking terms, while the following day Danny was locked in conversation with Arthur Rowe. There was renewed interest from Molineux too and Peter McParland recalls that, 'I thought he was going to go to the Wolves at the time because that was the talk in the club, but coming back from Glasgow in early November one night after an international, he turned to me and said, "I'm off to Tottenham." It dragged on for a few months because the Villa didn't want him to leave, but he was so determined to go he just wore them down. We had decent teams, but there wasn't really the ambition to bring in the extra couple of players to make the difference and Danny got fed up of it. Later on, when Danny had gone, Villa could have signed Dave Mackay for £25,000 but they didn't follow up on it. That was typical.'

When news of Danny's impending move was finally confirmed, there was an outcry from the supporters. Their feelings were summed up by Peter Morris: 'Villa had no basic style on which to endure. They appeared to play their games as the indifferent card player plays each hand – on instinct – and blindly rode their luck when the breaks came. To me, the greatest tragedies were the departures of Danny Blanchflower and Tommy Thompson, two of the three most talented players the club had possessed since the war. Both went for much the same reason – "the Villa, while a fine club who treated their players well, lived too much in the past and the team lacked inspiration and hope for better football" ... Blanchflower made no bones about his determination to leave at a time when supporters had come to regard the Irishman as an established player. Blanchflower had ambitions, ideas and ideals of his own. He wanted better football – at least of a better class than the Villa could offer him ... one thing stuck in the craw. Footballers of the calibre of Blanchflower and Thompson had *asked* to leave the Villa. Fifty years before, the leading players of the day were honoured to be asked to join Aston Villa. Such was the measure of the Villa's great decline.'

There were few who argued with such a conclusion. That Danny was moving for the sake of his game was underlined by his own comment: 'I have not had any violent disagreements with any of my colleagues at Villa Park. My intentions in seeking a move are not aimed at immediate gain, financially or otherwise, although I feel that eventually I would be able to better myself.' Later on, he revealed that, 'I would have been better off financially if I remained at Villa. There was a man in Birmingham who would give me £500 to stay. But I wanted to play some football and win something.' Having been kept at the Villa for longer than he felt just by the board's initial refusal to grant him a transfer, the matter was further prolonged when he picked up a nasty ligament injury at Hampden Park when Northern Ireland played the Scots there. Danny was out for several weeks as the frantic negotiations continued behind the scenes. Finally even Villa seemed to tire of it all and slashed the asking price once it became obvious that neither Spurs nor Arsenal would pay £40,000 for Danny's services. Arsenal refused to pay more than £28,500, causing him to worry that Arsenal might be going the same penny-pinching way as Aston Villa. He need not have worried that he might be forced to go to Highbury against his will, for Arthur Rowe seized his opportunity. Tottenham upped their offer to £30,000. In the final surreal moment of his Aston Villa career, the club tried to transfer his brother Jackie to Tottenham. Danny was away with Northern Ireland when 'Mr Blanchflower' was paged at the team hotel. Jackie recalls: 'I answered the call and the voice said, "It's Eric here. You've been transferred to Spurs." I told him he'd got the wrong one, meaning the wrong Blanchflower, but he said, "No, it's Tottenham all right, you're not going to Arsenal, they won't meet the price." Eventually I put him right and told Danny about the move. He was delighted, of course.'

In the end even his critics at the club were swayed by the sincerity of his footballing convictions, and when he did leave he was sent a telegram of good wishes before his debut for Tottenham. That generosity did not extend to the boardroom, for around the country, word was spreading that Danny Blanchflower was a first-class troublemaker, a reputation that even dogged him at Tottenham. Of course, if you succeed beyond anyone's wildest dreams, your critics are too frightened to speak out. Their views were unimportant and always remained so, for Danny Blanchflower had finally made it to the place he would call home.

4 Wonderland?

By Christmas 1954, Danny felt like he'd finally reached the promised land, White Hart Lane, a stadium where good football was treated with the proper respect. He had learned a great deal at Villa Park – had he not gone there, he surely wouldn't have been equipped for the challenges that Tottenham posed – but he was now able to dismiss it with a passage from his perennial favourite, *Through the Looking Glass*: 'Now, *here*, you see it takes all the running *you* can do, to keep in the same place. If you want to get somewhere else, you must run at least twice as fast as that!' Under Arthur Rowe's tutelage, he hoped that the same amount of running might get him twice as far. Danny was a fully rounded footballer having played alongside many seasoned players both with Villa and in the Northern Irish team. His natural ability was now harnessed and driven by an experienced football brain. As an individual he had matured too, and recognized that this move was crucial to his career. If he was to fulfil his dreams of lifting trophies and becoming a top-class international footballer he had to go to the right team, one which was in with a real chance, rather than an outside hope, of taking the prizes.

Marooned, as he saw it, at Villa Park, he became disenchanted with the cynicism he sensed in the game at all its levels. Prior to his move south he argued that, 'Too many complain about our play, that it was better "in my day". The game, I consider, has changed for the better. Looking at some of the old team photographs, I fail to see how, in those strange football kits, those players could possibly have produced anything to compare with the streamline style of the Spurs. There are too many bad losers in sport today. More clubs should adopt a style of play rather than merely produce a series of teams. Arsenal have been successful with a defensive style, Spurs and Manchester United even more so of recent years with an attacking style, no matter what happens. The team which changes its style weekly just doesn't have one . . . let's be constructive in our efforts to help improve the game and stop to reflect that although we all grumble about it, we shall all be sorry to have to give it up eventually.' Although he still had his enthusiasm for the game, it was apparent that he was tired of tales of Villa's past and needed the fresh impetus that a change of scene would provide.

At Villa, Danny was supposed to be the symbol of a change blowing through Villa Park. As soon as he'd had time to look at the operation which surrounded him on and off the field he realized that he was only the agent of change from one mediocre team to the next one. There was no plan, no sense of a seamless transition of personnel who would play in a similar fashion to those that had gone before. At Tottenham it was all going to be different. Here was a club of similar stature, but one which was still in touch with its glory days of a few years earlier. Admittedly the personnel was changing but the team had an established method, that of push and run, of good football for its own sake. With Arthur Rowe at the helm, Danny's arrival was the symbol of not simply change, but of renewal. There was real promise that he would be the bridge that would take Spurs from one great team to another, constructed in its own image. The chances of success were far rosier – Spurs were redecorating a thoroughly modern, solid structure, whereas Villa should have been renovating an entire house that had fallen into disrepair over forty years of comparative neglect.

The chance to work with Arthur Rowe had been a crucial component in Danny's decision to go to Tottenham. As a player Rowe had made a reputation as a centre-half who could create as well as destroy. He was an inspiring captain too. Just prior to the outbreak of the war, he had gone to work as a coach for the Hungarian government in Budapest. Although his stay was a comparatively brief one, he had the opportunity to absorb many of the ideas and disciplines which were to help make the Hungarians *the* international team in the immediate post-war years. It was vital intelligence which he brought back to England – and as an avowed admirer of Puskas and company this was important to Danny, who had already written that, 'I should like to see some of our teams go over to Eastern Europe so that we might find out something about them -- their style, tactics, playing and training conditions. I think the Hungarians proved to us that we are far too stereotyped in our game – they had several different plans they could have adopted whereas we always seem to play the same game.'

Taking over as Spurs manager in May 1949, Rowe led the team to the Second Division title in his first season with 9 points to spare, and then the First Division Championship in their first season back in the top flight. His trademark style was to push the ball to a colleague then run into space for the return. Done at pace with intent, it tore defences asunder: Newcastle were hammered 5–0, reigning Champions Portsmouth humbled 5–1, Stoke 6–1, as Spurs rattled in 82 goals to claim 60 points, the highest tally in twenty years. That team was built on diverse talents – the dour Bill Nicholson at right-half covering for the adventurous raids of Alf Ramsey, nominally his full-back; Ted Ditchburn keeping the goals out and Len Duquemin knocking them in; Eddie Baily providing the crosses for Sonny Walters to finish off. Much more than talented individuals, Spurs were a fine team. That was the essence of their triumph, for they did not possess great individuals such as Finney or Matthews. Rowe created a thoroughly modern side, one of industrial efficiency where each man knew his job and could do it without fuss. Any man could slot into the team in the event of injury and do a good job; no one man was relied upon to win games alone. Yet as much as they were efficient, they were unpredictable. They were thrilling to watch, players were encouraged to improvise, the ball moved along the ground at remarkable speed and with devastating accuracy.

In 1951–52 Spurs came within an ace of repeating their League triumph, but Manchester United proved to be too strong for them. The London side was an ageing one; at the end of the 1952 campaign Nicholson was thirty-three, Ramsey and Les Medley both thirty-two, Les Bennett thirty-four and Ron Burgess thirty-five. While push and run called for clear heads and clever footballers, it also required stamina and good general fitness, such was the tempo at which it was played. The years began to catch up with them and the next two seasons were ones of grim anti-climax as they slumped to tenth (losing in the FA Cup semi-final to Matthews' Blackpool) and then sixteenth. By Christmas of 1954–55 Tottenham's team was in terminal decline, as Rowe knew only too well. He'd refreshed things with the introduction of new faces such as George Robb, Johnny Brooks, Mel Hopkins, Tony Marchi and Ron Reynolds, but the team lacked its customary authority. With a mere 15 points from 20 games, Spurs were hovering near the foot of the table and relegation was a distinct possibility. Emotionally attached to players who had achieved so much at the start of his reign, Rowe found it hard to say goodbye to the past, as his new goalkeeper Ron Reynolds realized: 'He had one weakness, which was that he was too loyal to his players. He ignored the fact that they were all getting old together, especially the half-back line of Burgess and Nicholson. Alf Ramsey relied on them, especially Bill, who gave him the freedom to get forward by slotting back. Eventually changes had to be made.'

Rowe knew he had to act and act decisively, which was why he tracked Danny Blanchflower so assiduously for many months. With Bill Nicholson a spent force and with Alf Ramsey also coming to the end, the right flank needed to be reshaped. Danny was a crucial part of that process, but he was more than a simple replacement. He was to be the central plank of a new departure for the club. Rowe noted, 'I knew we had to change the pattern. I had it in mind to team Danny and Tommy Harmer as the heart of a different team. It wasn't merely that the players were getting older, the system of push and run as we played it then was being caught out. Opponents would sit back against us, there might be some man-marking. The team had to be renewed, but so did the style we played.'

If a new team had to be assembled, Rowe realized he needed an analytical player at its heart, one who could read the play and guide the team through the inevitable teething problems that would follow, much as Burgess, Ramsey and Nicholson had done earlier in the decade. The belief that Danny was that leader had been on his mind for some time: 'I first met him after Northern Ireland lost 3–0 to Wales in Swansea in March 1952. I congratulated him on his performance, and he thanked me. It was not what that young man said but how he said it, so nicely and sincerely, that really impressed me. I shall never forget, as we stood sizing each other up, as people do when meeting for the first time, the way he looked at me out of those big, sparkling Irish eyes. I instinctively thought, Here is a good guy. He was brilliant that day. He made other people play. He protected the players behind and supported those in front. I wanted him as a captain.

I had become convinced that he was a natural leader. He had the kind of commanding personality which compelled respect. In nine matches out of ten he had the ball more than any other two players. It was an expression of his tremendous ego, which every great captain needs.' Word soon spread around the club as the protracted transfer negotiations were carried out in public. Tottenham's outside-left George Robb remembers that, 'We were interested to hear that Arthur wanted Danny. When we used to play against Aston Villa, Eddie Baily was inside-left to me and we always felt we had plenty of scope because Danny was always going forward!'

If Rowe wanted Danny, what was it that Blanchflower saw in his new mentor? Given his run-ins with Frank Grice with Glentoran, Angus Seed at Barnsley and George Martin and Eric Houghton at Villa, his general opinion of football managers was not high. In Rowe, he saw something different, an individual who cared about the game and who was not afraid of progress, one willing to take chances and experiment. More important he saw a manager willing to give him his head. As George Robb notes, 'Knowing Danny, he'd have assessed the situation at Villa and could see that they weren't likely to win anything. He could see the Spurs side was breaking up, that there was an opportunity for him to make his mark on the club, which didn't exist at Villa Park.' That he was looking towards White Hart Lane was evident from a coded column he wrote in the *Evening Mail* as he filed his transfer request. On reading it, as he surely did, Arthur Rowe must have purred with satisfaction: 'To judge and analyse true success is a more difficult job than it sometimes is to attain it . . . I recall the successful Tottenham Hotspur team of two seasons ago giving a wonderful performance at Villa Park. What were the reasons for their success and the influence which combined to produce that pleasing blend of football? I'll agree that Spurs had great players. I'll also agree that was a big factor. But to me it was not the deciding one . . . a well-drilled team can make ordinary players look good . . . I don't think it was a coincidence that Spurs' great progress in the football arts came at the same time as the appointment of Mr Arthur Rowe as team manager. I believe his influence, knowledge and encouragement were the guiding factors to a style of football that people admired, but I frankly believe it was ahead of its time and not properly understood by most. They hailed it during its winning ways but were quick to condemn it when it did not show effective results ... the team grew to success but the higher they went the more difficult gradual progress became. Eventually they reached a peak ... some players must naturally decline but do so gradually and when and how to replace them is a difficult task, others naturally ease up when they reach their destination. These factors start slowly, creep in gradually and are very difficult to detect until the damage has been done ... the important point I want to stress [is that] worthwhile methods are the outcome of knowledge, good organizing and planning, co-operation, enthusiasm, faith and a great deal of hard work ... if our national game is to improve we must all be more constructive and work harder. Most of us don't really object to a full day's work – we just don't do it.'

It was obvious from that article that Danny understood just how Tottenham functioned, sympathized with Rowe's plight and fully accepted that on joining the club he'd have to get down to some really hard work. Small wonder that when he turned out for his first game, a goalless draw at Manchester City, Rowe remarked that 'it was the first time for weeks that I was able to sit back with confidence and enjoy the match', recognition of the tremendous strain he'd been under as he searched for a new pattern. For a couple of months the team's fortunes improved as they lost just one of eleven competitive games, winning seven, including a 7–2 victory over Sheffield Wednesday. Danny relished the new surroundings. He wrote that the difference between Spurs and Villa was simple: 'At Tottenham, the players are encouraged to pass the ball to each other. I was amazed at the skill and great purpose in the football habits at Tottenham when I moved here. The influence of Arthur Rowe and the example of his great players had left a wonderful impression, and the boys following in their footsteps were anxiously striving to emulate the same pattern of play.' The early exuberance that he brought to the Spurs team had to fade, of course, but he had made an immediate impression, George Robb noting that, 'He fitted in very well, got on with the lads straight away. He was always dressed well, very smart, and the lads didn't earn much in those days, so he stood out a little because of that. And he was always a bit apart because he had his own interests. But we all got on well. As a footballer, he was in front of Alf Ramsey and both were very constructive players, which helped Danny settle in quickly. If you come to a new club and can settle in on the field, feel happy with your game and what you're trying to do, it makes everything off the field so much easier.' Ron Reynolds agrees that he was fortunate that he could 'slot into a side that was suddenly doing reasonably well, which is always a help. His enthusiasm right from the start was tremendous and everybody took to him, apart from a few officials.' Some Tottenham directors weren't entirely enamoured of Rowe's latest capture. As the word from their Villa counterparts had been negative, they were no doubt worried that he might be a disruptive element in a hitherto serene environment, and as such were always wary of him, the more so when he exercised his right to write a column for the *London Evening News*, following the same format that he used so successfully in Birmingham. Given some of his outbursts there, the board at Spurs knew that Danny did not conform to the ideal archetype of a thick, docile footballer who would be no trouble. He would always pose a threat to them and their cosy position – that mistrust existed throughout his career at Spurs.

However, in marked contrast to his previous experiences, he and all the other players shared the same basic outlook. Ron Reynolds noted, 'Our beliefs about the game were similar, we loved stylish football and he talked to me because I was a qualified coach. When he wrote his instruction book [*Soccer, My Way*] he would draft a section and would hand it to me to have a look through, asking for comments. We went on a tour to Hungary in 1955 and I spent all my time looking through his sheets of paper!' Danny was able to discuss football in minute detail with like spirits such as Reynolds or Tommy Harmer, both of whom took to him immediately. The same was true of the rest of the playing staff; immersed as they were in the enlightened atmosphere that Rowe fostered, Danny's was not some voice crying in the wilderness but that of a man who could see the next step in the club's evolution. He won converts with both the breadth of his knowledge and the personable way in which he put his ideas across. No longer having to shout to make himself heard by those who didn't want to listen anyway, he could enjoy normal conversation about the principles of the game and be more persuasive for it. His hopes that he was coming to a progressive club were justified from the outset, at least insofar as his team-mates were concerned. As a result, he became a more relaxed character overnight. No longer did he have to fret about getting the ball in practice, no more was he in a minority relishing the prospect of an educational defeat almost as much as a straightforward victory, no more was he an isolated figure who looked, almost alone, to the Continental style of play with interest and envy. He eagerly anticipated Tottenham's forthcoming summer tour to Hungary, where the team might both get to know one another better and absorb new influences that could improve their all-round game: 'All this competition is bound to widen our outlook on the game and lead to improvements all round ... the result is not always the most important factor. It is the rage to make excuses rather than admit mistakes and of course we never make excuses for the other fellow. Therefore in the end costly mistakes by ourselves and others teach us nothing and progress is retarded ... we have become too result-conscious and want a win regardless of method. There has never been a completely infallible method but the best ones have been the result of much hard thought and work, of patience, skill and sacrifice.'

The brief upturn in Tottenham's playing fortunes came to an abrupt halt in the FA Cup. With things gradually taking shape there were hopes that Tottenham might go all the way to their first-ever Wembley Cup Final. Gateshead and Port Vale had been disposed of in short order and Spurs were rewarded with a fifth-round tie at York City, then in the upper reaches of the Third Division (North). They approached the game in good form on the back of four consecutive wins where they'd scored seventeen goals. On a treacherous, snowbound pitch, Spurs fell 3–1. Danny noted later, 'The atmosphere was thick with remorse on the way back to London, the worst I had ever known in a football club.'

The York defeat was the catalyst for a run of poor form which saw them win two and lose six of the next ten League games. For a team in transition, the abrupt end to their Wembley dreams was a terrible reverse. It knocked a fragile new team out of their stride. The push and run masters that had won the League in 1951 would have shrugged off the disappointment, but this new team had neither their experience to learn from nor their medals from which to take solace. Instead, the confidence that was born of the ignorance of failure was dissipated and the team's short-comings exposed, notably those along the right flank where Ramsey and Blanchflower were too similar in style. For Rowe, the defeat at York was an appalling blow, one which took a heavy toll on his already poor health. In a process of rebuilding, the FA Cup can provide a healthy dose of excitement and optimism, glossing over inconsistent League performances, releasing the pressure on the management – in recent years, Howard Kendall's job was saved when Everton won the Cup in 1984, the team responding by then winning two titles in three years as well as a European trophy, while Alex Ferguson was within a game of dismissal as Manchester United embarked on their run to the 1990 Final. For Rowe, time was running out and as the season dissolved to a disappointing conclusion, he fell ill, his nerves worn down. The team faltered too and it was only a run of three straight wins at the end of term which lifted them five points clear of relegation. As the season closed it was obvious that an era had passed. Rowe simply could not contemplate taking back the reins at Spurs and reluctantly stepped down as team manager.

Given that Rowe had taken Tottenham from the middle of the Second Division to the First Division Championship, playing some of the most memorable football seen in England on the way, one might have expected his passing to have been mourned in some way by a board of directors who owed him a very great deal. Not only had Rowe taken Spurs to the summit, he'd done so at the cost of his own health. In the circumstances, surely Tottenham would keep him on the staff in some coaching capacity, or perhaps as a general manager? They did not. Rowe had a contract until January 1956 – pending its expiry, Tottenham relieved him of his duties as team manager. They would pay him until the deal expired and then he would become just another ex-employee. Rowe saved them any embarrassment that his continued presence might cause and made a more dignified exit than they deserved by resigning from the club in July. Danny was, predictably, disgusted at the treatment meted out to a man he considered one of the sport's true greats. Ron Reynolds notes that, 'Danny thought Arthur was wonderful, he genuinely appreciated what he'd done for the game.' Danny went further and wrote, 'When his team faltered and the whole unreasonable reaction set in, [Rowe] was appalled at the ignorance and violence around him. It drove him back to the depths of a quiet desperation.' Angry at Rowe's constructive dismissal (as it would be termed today), he was equally annoyed that he no longer had the chance of working with the man for whom he had signed. Was his stay at Tottenham going to see him go down the same road of disillusion that he'd travelled with Barnsley and Aston Villa?

The club's assistant manager, Jimmy Anderson, had deputized for Rowe for six months when he had had an earlier breakdown in 1954. As far as the board were concerned, he was the obvious candidate to take over the mantle, with the recently retired Bill Nicholson taking the position of first-team coach. Not only had he worked closely with Rowe, but Anderson was a Tottenham man through and through, having arrived at the club as a groundstaff boy in 1908. None could question his dedication to the cause, but sadly dedication is not always enough. Had Rowe had the chance to rebuild his team and give it a style then Anderson might have proved a better choice, but he was left with a team that was only just undergoing that painful rebirth. Ron Reynolds recalls, 'Arthur had been a fantastic manager, and under him there had been some brilliant football. It was difficult for anyone to come in and replace him, and Jimmy did not have the imposing personality that was required. Anderson took over and things went crazy.'

The beautiful football that Tottenham had espoused since the war was quickly under threat. When the names for the close-season tour of Hungary were announced, Alf Ramsey's was not on the list. Though Ramsey was now thirty-five, Danny for one felt that 'he was capable of playing at least one more season in the First Division'. His demotion was evidence that Anderson wanted to change things, George Robb's opinion being that it was Danny's arrival that hastened Ramsey's end: 'Danny wanted to be creative, to build up the moves, he was a ball player. It could let us in for defensive trouble, especially as Alf behind him was so constructive too. Jimmy wanted the ball upfield quicker, out of danger!' Where Rowe would see the attacking interplay between Danny and Ramsey as a positive virtue, increasing the team's attacking options, Anderson could only see that it might leave the team exposed on occasion. Ironically, having dropped Ramsey, Anderson then gave Danny, the high-priest of attacking, slick passing football, the captaincy, just as Rowe would have done, though not from the same conviction. Presumably Anderson was trying to win over a man who was already highly influential in the Spurs dressing room. With Ramsey ousted, it was immediately obvious that Spurs would be operating with a rather more robust style. For Danny, this was intolerable, a betrayal of the ideals that had drawn him to north London in the first place. From the outset, he and Jimmy Anderson were destined not to get on.

Danny conceded that in the opening weeks of the 1955–56 season, Tottenham were 'playing the same constructive football'. Yet it lacked conviction, rhythm and the swagger that the best sides had played with. Ramsey had left to manage Ipswich Town but neither Charlie Withers, something of a veteran himself, nor Peter Baker seemed an able replacement. In attack they lacked a cutting edge, as Anderson tried a number of striking combinations with no tangible success. By the first week in November, 15 games had gone by with just 6 points collected. Spurs were bottom of the table having scored a mere 17 goals and conceded 32. As skipper, Danny was unable to stem the tide and Spurs looked doomed. To Anderson's credit, he then took decisive action. He replaced Ted Ditchburn in goal with Ron Reynolds and bought in Maurice Norman from Norwich City to play at full-back; a few weeks later Bobby Smith arrived from Chelsea to transform the team's attacking options. The tide had turned and over the rest of the year their results weren't far short of Championship form. The performances on the other hand left more to be desired, especially as far as Danny was concerned. Ron Reynolds remembers, 'It was unfortunate for him because he believed he was coming to the push and run club, but when you're in trouble, style goes out of the window, at least under some managers. We had a method of playing that was no longer successful for whatever reason, whether because it had been rumbled, because we didn't play it as well any longer, or because Jimmy was in charge rather than Arthur. Some of the players that came in just didn't suit the style and our method changed. You'd had Eddie Baily who buzzed around and loved push and run, so did Alf Ramsey, Ronnie Burgess and Danny. All of these fitted in that side beautifully. Within a matter of months, that style had gone in order to avoid relegation. Danny was very upset about it. It was extremely frustrating for him.'

This was another early example of Danny's aversion to the realities of club management: the need to get good results in order to please the directors and keep your job. To Danny, such preoccupation with the bosses to the detriment of the football being played was anathema, but then he was not under the same pressure. He knew full well that if Spurs didn't want him, Arsenal would have him, or if not them, then Wolves or Chelsea or Manchester United. If he had to quit playing, he could get a job in journalism. Although Danny had no interest in amassing money for its own sake, he also knew that he wasn't likely to find himself out of work. His livelihood was not under threat but Anderson's was. He may not have had the flair or vision of Arthur Rowe, may not have had the same keen tactical awareness, but he had a feeling for the club and a determination to keep them at the top of the English game, as well as himself in work. It was his misfortune that he was promoted one level beyond his ability and too late in his career for him to grow into the position. Nevertheless he did get Tottenham out of trouble in that first season and made a couple of crucial signings in Bobby Smith and Maurice Norman.

The signing of Norman illustrates just how important a figure Danny had become in his few months in London. At Villa he'd always been stuck in the role of the young upstart, even after he'd been at the club a couple of years. At Tottenham Danny was a senior pro, respected by his peers, who could see what a good player he was, and adored by the youngsters coming through, who felt it was an honour to be on the same side as the great international. As Tottenham were rebuilding and older players left, the new players looked more and more to Danny for help and advice, both on and off the field. Maurice Norman admits: 'I was a country boy and I hadn't travelled a lot beyond where I lived. Going to London and to a club like Spurs was a bit frightening, having had just about fifty games for Norwich in the Third Division South. I wasn't really a full-back when I came, but I was fortunate to have Danny on my side of the field. Playing behind him taught me a lot about the game. I was very raw when I came to Tottenham but he made me the player I was, without him I don't think I'd have made it!' While Norman may be doing himself an injustice – he did collect international honours, after all – it's clear that Danny was a pivotal influence in Norman's career. This was no isolated example. If others didn't need the early guidance that Danny gave Maurice Norman, his leadership on the field helped later signings like Cliff Jones, John White, Les Allen and even Jimmy Greaves make the most of their ability.

Just as in the previous season, the serious nature of Tottenham's League position was mitigated by an excellent Cup run. Easing through their first three encounters with Boston United, Middlesbrough and Doncaster Rovers – where Danny was in opposition to their manager Peter Doherty for the first time – they were drawn at home to West Ham in the quarter-final. Local derbies are fraught affairs at the best of times and this was no exception, with West Ham eking out a 3–1 lead. Spurs got back into the game with a Len Duquemin goal, but time was running out. Danny later noted that, 'One of our tactics was to send our two big defenders, Harry Clarke and Maurice Norman, up the field for corner-kicks. Their presence near the West Ham goal seemed to frighten our opponents and, as captain of the team, I decided to send big Maurice Norman up into the forward line in the latter stages of the game ... we got the equalizer and Maurice had some part in the movement leading up to it. Of course, in the weekend papers I was a genius of a captain for having made the switch. I was the commanding general of a great revival, so the papers implied.'

Nothing in English football generates the same emotion as the FA Cup, so it was no surprise that the players and press should be thrilled by Tottenham's fighting comeback after the game had appeared lost. Danny's decisive tactical change seemed better still when Spurs went to Upton Park and, with him and Tommy Harmer, playing in a deep lying outside-right role, combining especially well, won 2–1 to go into the semi-finals to face Manchester City. Already respected by his team-mates, Danny was now revered as someone on whom they could depend in the heat of a match. His generosity was also highly regarded, as Ron Reynolds recalls: 'On the way to that replay at Upton Park, Danny said to me, "Would you like to do an article at the end of the game for one of the newspapers? I'm under contract to the *Evening News* so I can't do it. If you agree, at the end of the game we'll be taken by car to Fleet Street, and we'll do the article together." We won the match and went over to the newspaper offices. We produced the article, and I'd say it was 99 per cent Danny Blanchflower and 1 per cent Ron Reynolds! I got the cheque and I said to him, "There's no way I can take this. I'll have enough to cover my time in coming here and you can have the rest of it." But he wouldn't take a penny. In those days, he wasn't earning a lot of money, it was still maximum-wage days, so he didn't have to do that. All the time I knew him, he was magnificent, an idol as far as I was concerned, and that went for a lot of the players. He was such a genuine fellow.'

Managers in any industry like to have the best of both worlds, particularly if they're weak or are going through a bad spell. Jimmy Anderson was naturally delighted that Danny's actions in that first match with West Ham had got the team out of jail at a crucial stage in the season, and he also recognized what a steadying influence he'd had on the side in the midst of their early season problems. In that sense, Danny was an ideal lieutenant, a clever tactician who could read the game and switch the play or the tempo accordingly. He had been a central figure in turning their season around and as such had strengthened Anderson's position with the directors. Yet Anderson was still finding his way as a manager, trying to exert some authority over the team and establish himself as the boss, not merely Arthur Rowe's replacement. The very fact that Danny was so popular with the first-teamers meant that Anderson regarded him as a rival. He was threatened by his remarkable composure, worried that he might usurp his authority on the field and demonstrate his own lack of leadership to the watching directors. He knew full well that he needed Danny playing at his best to shore up a still slightly fragile team, one that was only beginning to find its way, yet he resented his easy authority over the players. This made the vital relationship between manager and captain an uneasy one.

Prior to that semi-final, Tottenham fought out a draw in the League against Portsmouth in which Tommy Harmer, so influential in the West Ham tie, had a poor match. A slight figure, he came in for some hard tackling. Just a week before the semi-final most of the Spurs players could be forgiven for having their thoughts elsewhere, but Anderson seemed especially troubled by Harmer's lack-lustre display, giving an idea of Anderson's workmanlike philosophy on the game. Harmer had been out of favour for much of the season and, with the big game looming, was dropped again as the manager initially selected the more robust Alfie Stokes to play in a conventional right-wing role. He informed his captain of the decision which Danny accepted as being beyond his province. Things looked no brighter to him when, before the game, Anderson decided to leave out Stokes too and play centre-forward Dave Dunmore instead. Danny was amazed at the decision given that he was the hub of the side's creative play and that he had linked so well with Harmer in the first place. To suddenly give him a new partner for such a vital game seemed an unnecessary gamble.

The semi-final was played at Villa Park giving Danny the chance to return to his former home on St Patrick's Day, exactly five years to the day since he'd made his debut for Aston Villa. Danny 'went on smothered in shamrock', a very theatrical expression, indicative of his approach to the game, that it was entertainment not war. Even so, he was just as determined to win as his colleagues, hence his disappointment as things went against Tottenham. George Robb remembers, 'We went one down and just didn't look like scoring,' so with just twenty minutes remaining, 'Danny switched Maurice Norman up front to create something and brought one of the forwards, Johnny Brooks, back. Then a few moments later he sent Johnny back into the forward line too.' With six forwards and just one full-back, Spurs surged forward in search of the equalizer. With moments to go Robb was free in the penalty area with City goalkeeper Bert Trautmann sprawled on the floor. 'Bert held me back when I was clear, but the linesman and referee missed the foul. That was our final chance.'

As the dejected players trooped back into the dressing room, Anderson burst in to tear a strip off Danny, livid that he had made changes to the formation. Sitting with the directors, he had had to put up with their questions as to just who was in control, and their natural disappointment at being denied their day in the limelight at Wembley. When Danny argued that all he'd done was throw caution to the wind in the hope of salvaging a do-or-die Cup game, asked 'What had we to lose but my scalp?' and reminded him that he'd been only too pleased when it had worked in the previous round, Anderson replied, 'I'm the manager here and I'll make the changes. It makes me look silly in front of my directors.' Once again, Danny was confronted with a manager who hadn't the nerve to stand up to his employers, nor one who would stand by a set of basic principles. He'd been happy to share in the glory when Danny's tactics had worked but, now they had failed, he was happy to lay the blame elsewhere.

That defeat led to a dip in Tottenham's fortunes, such that relegation was still a possibility when they entertained the equally troubled Huddersfield Town on the penultimate Saturday of the season. Defeat would pull them back into the thick of things at the bottom, while a draw or a win would assure them of safety. Tommy Harmer, restored to favour, gave them the lead as they cruised towards the points. Midway through the second period, a misunderstanding between Maurice Norman and Ron Reynolds led to Norman heading into his own goal. Moments later, an opportunistic shot on goal gave Huddersfield the lead. With a quarter of an hour to go Tony Marchi pleaded with Danny to let him go up into the forward line. Where a more cautious or less principled captain might have refused in order to protect his own position, Danny had 'always leaned in the direction of encouraging those who wanted to try something and, as captain, I agreed'. The game was lost 2–1 and once more Anderson went ballistic. Ron Reynolds 'tried to intervene because the goals we'd conceded were partly down to me, but Jimmy wouldn't listen. Danny asked me to leave it and Jimmy stalked out of the dressing room. Danny and I had a chat after the game and he told me that because we needed a point to stay up he wouldn't rock the boat, but that once we were safe he'd hand in the captaincy.'

Danny fell foul of the age-old rule that those who sit on the sidelines cannot lose while those who take action risk losing all. Danny never shirked taking responsibility for his actions, believing that his authority as captain stemmed from that. With Jimmy Anderson as manager, he was stymied. Where Rowe had been adventurous and experimental in outlook, Anderson was cautious, stereotyped and more concerned with his directors than his players. Perhaps Danny had been wrong to allow Marchi to go into the forward line against Huddersfield, but to attack him in front of the team was bound to diminish his own authority. If Danny was willing to take the consequences of success and failure, so too should Anderson. Evidence of a generation gap was clear too – where Anderson was very pre-war in his forelock-tugging acceptance of authority, Danny was an egalitarian, judging people on merit. He and many like him were winning the argument. Maurice Norman provides evidence of the divide: 'I think Danny spoke his mind too often for some and it could upset people. He was his own boss, but if you were prepared to listen to him, as the players were at Spurs, you got the benefit from it.' That was the crucial point – the players listened to him and grew in their appreciation of the game, while the officials had closed minds. Of course Danny wasn't always right, but under Jimmy Anderson's strict regime he was guilty until proven innocent. As Ron Reynolds points out, 'Things went well for a time but it was obvious that Danny wasn't going to be able to get away with it under Jimmy, because his ideas were so far ahead of the times. He had such vision. His ideas were advanced to certain individuals and even at a progressive club like Tottenham, initially he had his leg pulled unmercifully because he had different ideas, but there was no friction there among the players.'

The team were due to travel down to Cardiff on the Monday after the Huddersfield debacle, in search of the single point they required for salvation. According to George Robb, 'Jimmy decided to leave Danny out. He felt that would make us tighter at the back because Danny would always be looking to attack. We only needed a draw and Jimmy decided that was our best hope of not conceding goals.' He was correct in his analysis, for Tottenham managed a goalless draw. However, rather than confront Danny with the tactical reasons for his omission, Anderson did not inform him of the switch. Danny arrived at the club ready to travel to Wales to be greeted by Tommy Harmer, who told him he'd been dropped. Anderson was not at the club, having gone to Swansea in order to sign Terry Medwin, but even so, it was surprising that he had not telephoned his captain to let him know of his decision. Equally ill advised was his decision to tell the local press that Danny was out injured, without letting the player know that that was the official line. Presented with a day off, Danny called his editor at the *Evening News* to discuss forthcoming articles and was surprised to be asked whether the injury would clear up in time for the final game of the season. Danny's response was, 'What injury?' explaining that he'd been dropped from the side.

Perhaps this was simply Danny being honest or perhaps he saw the opportunity for a little mischief-making at Anderson's expense, retaliation for the indignity heaped upon him. The most likely rationale was that by stressing he'd been left out of the team, Danny created a good excuse for handing in the captaincy which was now worthless to him. Had he simply waited until the end of the season and then relinquished his hold on the job, the supporters might well have taken this as a rejection of their club and the highest honour it could bestow without realizing what had gone on behind the scenes. Danny had become very popular with the White Hart Lane crowd, who recognized a player in the best Spurs traditions. That respect and popularity was very important to him. As an outsider of sorts, he craved acceptance, albeit on his own terms, and the crowd offered him that. Following the press reports, Danny was clearly the injured party and quite within his rights to step down. He did so in a long conversation with Anderson, in which the manager insisted that he had not been dropped but left out because of injury, a faintly incredible position to take with a man who should know the state of his own health! To Danny, it was obvious that Anderson was making a petty point in the aftermath of the Huddersfield game, proving that he was in charge. Danny insisted that, as captain, he should have some authority on the field; Anderson refused to give it. The two agreed to differ and the captaincy passed to Harry Clarke, who admitted that he'd have preferred to serve under Danny. Anderson asked him to say nothing to the press and Danny agreed unless he was asked a direct question. A matter of hours later, he was approached by Bernard Joy of the *Evening Standard* who told him, 'The club have told me that you've been deprived of the captaincy because they didn't want changes made on the field.'

All who knew Danny well agree that he was a fiercely proud man. Having been summarily deprived of the job he wanted in the most humiliating of circumstances, a transfer request would surely have been the logical next step. Perhaps Jimmy Anderson was even trying to provoke him, hoping that with Danny gone he might be able to reassert his authority over the club. Yet if Danny was a proud man, he was an intelligent and rational one too. Surveying the scene around him, he knew that with Terry Medwin now on board, Tottenham had the nucleus of a good team. They'd been one game away from the Cup Final and had enjoyed a prolonged run of good form from November through to March. If he did not see eye to eye with Anderson he had to accept that Spurs still played some nice football at times and that there was rich promise around the club, the more so with Bill Nicholson as first-team coach. He must also have calculated that Anderson would not be around for too much longer given that he'd already completed forty-eight years of service. He was gaining fulfilment from his role in the Northern Irish team and was enjoying his football more than at any time since he'd come to England. Weighing all these factors he came to the conclusion that, 'Though I was at variance with the club about captaincy I had no desire to leave . . . there was something vital about the place that had been missing at Villa Park. I could sense the same feeling at Wolverhampton – particularly at floodlit games – at Old Trafford, and in a subdued sense at Highbury and Goodison; but nowhere else.' He'd come to England to play his game but also to succeed.' His decision to remain with Spurs was a triumph for his increasing personal maturity. When he failed to get his way at Oakwell or Villa Park, he had stalked off the training field. Now he kept his temper in check and took the long view, secure in the knowledge that the next few years would justify his faith in himself and in the glorious traditions of Tottenham Hotspur.

Biting his tongue was not easy. As George Robb recalls, 'He was a perfectionist and he didn't mind who that upset! He gave Cecil Poynton, the trainer, terrible trouble. Trainers had to pack the skip with the gear in those days and Cecil would moan about the number of pairs of boots Danny would want packing. All the rest of us took two pairs, one they usually played in, one with a shorter stud in case of a hard pitch. Not Danny! He'd have four pairs so that he'd have the right boots for the ground. In that way, Danny was a breath of fresh air at the club, a ray of light, because he liked to take a new look at things. There was a great deal of wit, of humour in him. He was a great captain. Team spirit was good under him, the players found him amusing because he'd come out with strange ideas and he'd express himself in a different way. He'd deliberately come out with thought-provoking ideas, sometimes plain stupid statements, that would start the players off. I remember that when the record "I'm Walking Backwards for Christmas" came out, Danny was very taken with it, it was exactly typical of his kind of humour. He would joke in the dressing room, pull people's legs. But mainly his wit came out as a response to things others said. He was very friendly and a good motivator, so players took note of what he had to say.'

Looking back to Ronald Murdock's comment that Danny didn't suffer fools gladly, and Robb's assertion that he remained a perfectionist, it's a reflection of how far he'd come as a man that he managed to keep his anger in check, though as Ron Reynolds admits, 'He'd still have a go at authority, but he wasn't so abrasive.

He was aware of just how far he could go and the tongue-in-cheek way he'd do it allowed him to get away with it – he was this lovely, soft-spoken Irishman, and he charmed everyone. To be honest, the board we had at the time wouldn't have known they were being insulted! We'd go on away trips and on the way back we'd openly insult them – I never once knew a director at an away game buy the lads a drink. We'd be pretty blunt about that but it was water off a duck's back, they'd never take offence.'

Danny's decision to stay at Spurs soon looked a good one. They started the 1956–57 season at breakneck speed, winning twelve of the first sixteen matches played. They continued to fight for the title alongside Manchester United, the reigning Champions, until they were beaten by Bournemouth in the Cup and their form slumped. They managed to hold on to the runners-up spot, giving the season a very respectable look, but Danny was not fooled by their lofty position. He continued to find himself in conflict with Jimmy Anderson, such that when Harry Clarke was left out of the team there was no question of the captaincy returning to Danny. It passed to Tony Marchi instead. Although Anderson's team achieved good results, George Robb states: 'He wasn't an Arthur Rowe. He had very set ideas, very basic, so he wasn't the tactician that Arthur was. He didn't mould a side, but bought players who he thought were good in their position. There's a great deal of difference between those two ideas. He carried on in the same vein as far as he could, but simply wasn't as good as Arthur. He had limitations as a man manager too. He saw Danny's capabilities, but they soon disagreed. Bill Nicholson didn't always agree with Danny but he was able to keep things on an even keel. Jimmy was very basic, always telling us to hit the long ball. Danny would ask, "What exactly do you mean by a long ball? How does a long ball roll?" The lads thought that was very funny.' Anderson was not amused.

At thirty-two, Danny was hitting his peak. A cerebral player, at the start of the 1957–58 season he had played 249 games in the First Division and had 25 caps for Northern Ireland, the majority as captain. In short, he knew the game inside out and was still young enough and fit enough to make his vast experience count. Also, as his brother Jackie avers, 'I think he was even keener to win because by that season I already had two Championship medals. Maybe he was a wee bit envious!' Yet he did not approach the new season with confidence. Tony Marchi had left the club to go to Italy and Anderson needed to find his third new captain in little over twelve months. He appealed to Danny to take the job, but he stuck to his principles and refused, arguing that the same tensions would resurface once more, and Johnny Ryden was appointed instead. Danny expanded on his thinking in the *Observer*: 'Good captains, like dinosaurs, are threatened with extinction. There was a time, so we are told, when the captain was a magnificent animal. He set his charges a fine example, led them with a rod of iron and solved every problem on the field with quick and imaginative decisions ... they must have played a bigger part in the scope of things than do the present pretenders to the throne; they prospered in times better suited to their individuality ... [Today] twin tribes have been fostered – the officials and the press. They have tasted the power and fascination of the great game and suffer its hallucinations. Together, with careless abandon, they have safaried into the game's mysterious and dangerous lands which were once the accepted province of the manager and his aide, the captain. They have civilized the manager and enslaved the captain in chains of fear. He is permitted no liberty of decision or action and yet is judged as if he were. After a game has been lost, the Solomon will criticize him for not making positional or tactical changes. Yet if he bravely does those things in vain endeavour to save a lost battle, these same second guessers demand his blood ... football needs captains of character who have the encouragement and authority to act according to their own judgement. It is down on the field that the game is lost and won.'

After a poor start to the season, Spurs were never in contention for honours, even going out of the Cup in the fourth round at home to Sheffield United. Nevertheless, as they roused from their early season slumbers, Danny was simply inspirational. Accepting that he could no longer call the play on the field, rather than sulking, he chose to lead the team by example. Week after week, he was the star of an improving Spurs show in the season that he really came of age as a footballer. Away from White Hart Lane, Northern Ireland were closing in on qualification for their first World Cup. Danny's captaincy was absolutely central to their progress, making his position among the ranks at Spurs look all the more ludicrous, heaping further pressure on Anderson. People began to take note of just how good a footballer Danny had become. Supporters had always admired his ability to pass the ball, his flair for feeding his forwards with the right ball at the right time, and the way in which he was always available to receive the ball from a colleague who might be in trouble. As he ran, stiff-legged, through the middle of the field, he retained a strange elegance in spite of his ungainly style, and he rarely wasted an opportunity to put the opponents in trouble. By this season of 1957–58, he had come to full maturity. Not just an impressive footballer, he was now a commanding presence on the field of play. A buzz would go round the ground whenever he was in possession. Colleagues in the Spurs side would look to him for reassurance if things were going awry, and would regularly find it. The gentle probing of his passes into space would gradually become more and more threatening. As a weakness emerged in the other team, the tempo would be raised at Danny's instigation, imperceptibly at first, then suddenly the whole team would be striking with ferocity at the behest of their skipper. Admittedly, there was more time to be had on the ball back in 1957 than there is in 1997, but time can be a limitation as well as a luxury. Danny's skill was in taking the right amount of time – hitting a through ball first time if necessary, trapping the ball and looking around him if there were no immediate attacking options. Just as shot selection is crucial to a top-class golfer, selecting the right pass at the right time is vital for any footballer – the passing game only succeeds if it is done with purpose rather than for aesthetic reasons. Danny was the master of that art.

At the centre of the stage, where he loved to be, he clinched the Footballer of the Year award, due recognition for a truly majestic season. It underlined the quality of his play, for in a season where Spurs came a distant third, there were many other candidates. Wolves supporters must have been surprised when Billy Wright, Ron Flowers, Bill Slater and Norman Deeley were overlooked, the great Tom Finney, who inspired Preston to the runners-up slot, must have come close to retaining the trophy, and Spurs' Bobby Smith rattled in thirty-six goals to put himself in with a chance. Aside from them, post-Munich, Bobby Charlton, Harry Gregg and Dennis Violett all had powerful claims, along with others who performed well week after week, such as Fulham's Johnny Haynes, Villa's Peter McParland and Albion's Derek

Kevan. Yet that year, Danny stood head and shoulders above them all. George Robb concedes, 'He was a very good player, not a Pele or a Best or a Puskas, but a fine player. Recently, I've seen Cantona come up with a through ball that other players can't see early enough, and Danny was rather similar. In possession, he'd make a shrewd defence-splitting pass. He was intelligent and he used that with his excellent ball control to create time and space that others couldn't.'

Established at the forefront of the game, readying himself for competition against the greatest players in the world in the 1958 World Cup, Danny could finally feel sure that events were moving inexorably in his direction, that his time was about to come. The players were on the march, freedom of contract and an end to the maximum wage was on the horizon. Jimmy Anderson's methods belonged to yesterday, and the directors to whom he had bowed in such meek supplication wanted to recapture the club's glory years. The future belonged to Danny Blanchflower.

5 Rhapsody in Green

For any professional footballer, the pinnacle of his career must be to represent his country at a World Cup Finals. To captain your nation there and lead them to a level of success beyond anyone's wildest expectations is the stuff of dreams. That was Danny Blanchflower's experience with the Northern Ireland side in the 1958 series in Sweden. Yet after the four internationals he'd played or, more accurately, endured, when he was with Barnsley, Danny was left wondering whether or not he had an international future. Plagued by that rarest of emotions, self-doubt, and stuck in a rootless, directionless side, Danny was simply unable to get a grip on international football. With no encouragement from the officials that surrounded the team, he was unsure as to whether he should play his natural game or be more defensive. Equally, though he was proud to represent his country, he had no such feelings regarding their Football Association. He felt that they had allowed the team simply to drift, since results did not impinge on the active social life that went on around the games. If the officials could have a good meal and plenty to drink along with the occasional foreign junket, why should the team's performance matter to them?

The first footsteps on the long road to Sweden were taken as far back as 1952. As Danny explained, 'Suddenly it changed. A new secretary, Billy Drennan, was a young man with clear thoughts. There was an intake of new officials. In the early 1950s it became the trend to appoint managers at international level in Great Britain. Peter Doherty was appointed as team manager but the committee still selected the team. Peter advised them and managed their selected players. He was the best thing that ever happened to us. Peter's appointment was the beginning of the fairy tale. We had all respected him as a great player. He gave the team an identity. Now, we did not play for inefficiency and hypocrisy. We did not represent all those old men masquerading as important sporting figures. Doherty represented Ireland. It was an honour to play for the things he represented, his enthusiasm and adventure. Such was Peter's stature that everyone else began to believe in the same policy. If there were those who doubted they were afraid to say so too openly – they were overwhelmed by the campaign.' With Doherty's return to the international scene, all the elements that Danny sought from football were in place – enthusiasm, reciprocal respect for players and management alike, progressive ideals, a determination to play attractive football, and an air of excited anticipation over the future. Almost at a stroke, Northern Irish football was revitalized.

The arrival of Doherty and Drennan alone was not enough to guarantee World Cup qualification. There were handicaps which they could not overcome – the decision by FIFA to prevent those born in the Republic of Ireland playing for the North was a body blow, greatly reducing the pool of players on which they could draw. Approaching things positively, this did at least give younger players a chance of an extended run in the national side, a luxury that young Englishmen, for example, did not enjoy. Danny was soon identified by Doherty as a man for the future and returned to the colours in March 1952, in a team defeated 3–0 by Wales at the Vetch Field – this was the occasion of his first meeting with Arthur Rowe. In spite of this disappointment, the Irish selectors under Doherty's direction made just two changes for the home fixture with England, seven months later. This time a more cohesive Irish side delivered a highly creditable 2–2 draw, causing Danny to comment, 'There is purpose and method in everything Peter Doherty does with the side. We couldn't have a better inspiration.' Those of Danny's own age, players like Billy Bingham, Jimmy McIlroy, Alf McMichael, Norman Uprichard and Eddie McMorran were spellbound by Doherty. As boys before the war, they had grown up with Doherty's brilliance – he had been Ireland's star performer at international level, while his exploits in England with Manchester City and Derby County thrilled those reading about him back home. To work alongside him was the icing on the international cake – his impact was the same as the starry-eyed effect Kevin Keegan induced at Newcastle, a nice irony since it was Doherty who recommended Keegan to Liverpool in 1971. Peter McParland simply felt that 'the players idolized Peter, which was a big thing in our favour'.

The policy of continuity continued to bear fruit. At Hampden Park in November, the Irish managed a 1–1 draw, with Danny outstanding, revelling in the freedom which was bestowed upon him. The newspaper reviews were encouraging, the *News Chronicle* terming him 'the most accomplished player afield', while the *Daily Graphic* recorded that 'here, thank goodness, was somebody who raised the game to the near level of a pukka international'. There were still many reverses for the team, but more importantly they were heading in a specific direction, all working to a plan. In Danny's first five games following his return from a two-match exile, the team managed just two draws, losing twice to Wales and once to France, but the signs were promising. They used just fifteen players in those five games, with eight ever-presents, evidence that a rebuilding process was gathering speed.

Following the 1952–53 season, Peter Doherty took his charges off to Canada for some exhibition games. The qualification series for the 1954 World Cup was about to get under way – the Home International tournament acted as the qualifying group – and the manager wanted to both experiment with new players and create an enthusiastic and co-operative spirit within the camp. The pivotal game of that tour came against a Swiss team in Montreal, when the Swiss took the field with a formation which completely confounded the Irishmen. This was a revelation for both Doherty and Blanchflower, neither of whom had so far given too much consideration to employing anything beyond the standard British WM formation in a match situation – their thoughts on the subject having been confined to theory. Throughout the course of this brief tour, the two were locked in conversation, in part because they enjoyed one another's company, but largely because they were experiencing a tactical epiphany. By the end of the tour, the new Northern Irish ethos had taken shape. Danny had been appointed team captain with absolute authority on the field of play – his first game as such came against Manitoba in Winnipeg. In training he and Doherty worked in tandem to the point where Danny was assistant manager in all but name. The success of that Swiss team, coming from a nation of similarly limited resources, was inspiring, offering the Irish a model on which they could build. They readily accepted the lessons of defeat and turned them quickly to their advantage – if they could do the unexpected, they might be able to embarrass more gifted nations. As Danny had noted of Doherty's first few games, 'We didn't just go out and slay the world; but we quickly lowered the boom on those mammoth defeats.' The challenge now was to turn defeat into draws and then into victories. That Canadian tour had pointed the way ahead.

Team spirit is always crucial to the 'minnow' nations, as Jack Charlton and Billy Bingham have proved in recent years. Doherty and Blanchflower were masters at bringing out the natural national pride of their colleagues, turning that into a relaxed enjoyment of the honour rather than a clenched fist attitude of war that has scarred other sides. The Northern Irish team became wonderful ambassadors for their country wherever they went, winning neutrals to their side. In Canada, for example, they were contacted by Bob Stevenson, a Belfast man working for Harland & Wolff at Vickers in Montreal. Recognizing that a temporary ex-pat would miss his football, Danny, in his new capacity as team captain, arranged for a party to take in a tour of the Vickers yard and then provided Stevenson and his wife Margaret with the best seats in the house for the game in Montreal. This was no isolated incident, but one which made it abundantly clear that the players on the field did not just represent the Irish FA, but the people of Northern Ireland too. Such gestures were warmly received and ensured that the team received passionate support, crucial if they were to beat the better sides. It was further evidence too that, to get the best out of him, Danny not only had to be in an appreciative environment, he had to be at the centre of it. Once he was on the same wavelength as his manager and had been picked out as a key player, he relaxed and his core character came to the fore – authoritative, intelligent, personable, charming. Without such reassurances, as at Barnsley and Aston Villa, he could be more withdrawn, mistrustful, antagonistic.

Playing against the other home nations, especially England, meant that qualification for the 1954 tournament was always unlikely. Narrow back-to-back defeats against Scotland and England dashed any fond hopes of a miracle, but were evidence that Northern Ireland could at last begin to compete with their bigger neighbours on equal terms. When the final match of the series was played, in Wrexham in March 1954, it gave Doherty the opportunity to dispense with the services of some older players and begin the drive towards qualification for the 1958 tournament, an achievement already spoken of with optimism. For that game, fresh faces were introduced – Harry Gregg came in as goalkeeper, Bertie Peacock at half-back, Jackie Blanchflower at inside-forward and Peter McParland on the left wing, scoring both goals in a 2–1 win. Bertie Peacock feels that 'it all started to come together that day in Wrexham in 1954', while Danny wrote that 'it did my heart good to play in that team, and such a young side too, with an average age of twenty-three'. Danny was now not only team captain, but almost an elder statesman, and he took his responsibilities seriously, as Peter McParland recalls: 'While we were at Villa together, whenever I was picked for an international, Danny would just say, "Leave everything to me." He got the tickets, arranged the travel and so on, so all I had to do was just meet up with him before we left! I was a bit green early on, of course, but he was a great captain, he looked after you, put you right, on and off the field. Peter [Doherty] let Danny organize things once a match started, and Danny had the respect of the players so they'd do what he said. He was a great player as well as a leader. A lot of captains now are good at firing a team up, but they might be ordinary players. Danny could do it all, a lot of times he was the outstanding player in the game. He could take tackles and he was a very good tackler himself – people would say he couldn't win the ball, but I saw him win a lot more tackles than he lost, he had a bit of bite too.'

Danny was saddened not to have made it to the 1954 World Cup, but then he had few expectations that he would. Since the Northern Irish team had humble horizons, apart from the privilege of playing for his country, he sought other stimuli from the international scene. Prior to the jet age of the 1960s, matches against foreign opposition were rare, certainly for such a financially strapped association as that in Northern Ireland. The home nations provided most of the opposition but, approached correctly, this too could be turned to advantage. Naturally England and, to a slightly lesser extent, Scotland provided a greater test of a player's mettle than any First Division opponent, since every position was filled by a quality player. By playing the same, somewhat stereotyped opposition on a regular basis, it was possible to measure just how much the Irish side had improved in any given period. When playing England, Scotland or Wales, the Irish knew precisely the kind of tactics they'd come up against and so these games acted as glorified practice matches. If the others were less willing to experiment, the Irish were not so reticent. In November 1954, some months after both England and Scotland had returned from a fruitless World Cup campaign, Danny wrote, 'The more I see of other British national sides the more it seems to me that Ireland is the only association making any progress towards improvement ... a decision was made to pick what was thought the best team and to give the players selected a consistent run which would give them a fair chance to settle and improve their ability ... we have not covered all the ground we can and have by no means reached our limitations [but] our manager expects us to have completely absorbed his ideas and plans in another two years, and that is when he expects us to be a really good side. Then we shall still have a few playing years left to continue at that standard.'

Northern Ireland's greatest weakness was up front. Although they were a highly creative unit capable of making chances in any company, there was no forward who was able to accept them with sufficient regularity – Eddie McMorran, Fay Coyle, Billy McAdams and Derek Dougan were among those who played centre-forward without becoming prolific marksmen. This was a great pity, for in many other positions they were finding men as good as their English or Scottish counterparts: Gregg and Uprichard were fine goalkeepers, Danny and Bertie Peacock at half-back were a good combination, Bingham, McIlroy and McParland a genuinely inventive forward line. That Doherty was shaping a team of promise was recognized in August 1955. To celebrate the seventy-fifth anniversary of the Irish FA, a friendly between Great Britain and a European XI was arranged at Windsor Park. The selection was a highly politicized one, the authorities finally picking three men from Northern Ireland, England and Scotland and two from Wales; but the Irishmen selected – Peacock, McIlroy and Blanchflower as captain – were certainly worthy of their position in the team.

There was much debate as to whether Danny should have been given that particular honour, but there was no doubt in the mind of the team manager, England's Walter Winterbottom: 'He was captain of the side, and rightly so. He always felt the captain on the field should have authority, which I agreed with. As a manager, if you didn't have a captain who understood what you wanted, and couldn't make his own judgement on situations as they evolved on the field, then he wasn't a captain in my view. A manager can't do things from the sidelines because in senior football you're too far away. This business of talking through things at half-time is nonsense. A team should know what it's about and what it can do and it's then faced with problems on the field. The adjustment must be made there and then, on the field.' Danny enjoyed training under Winterbottom, whom he recognized as 'a most intelligent, pleasant man who cares very deeply about soccer and always has the best intentions for it'. Indeed, he also recognized the difficulties that Winterbottom worked under in trying to drag English football out of the dark ages, despite the prevailing media opinion that English football was still the greatest in the world. For his part, Winterbottom was impressed by Danny's ability and his wider vision of the game, something that was still surprising amid our insular clubs. Winterbottom recalls that, 'He was excellent in training. He was very thoughtful and provocative in the right way. He'd always be interfering, he couldn't stop it, that was his personality; he wanted to make suggestions, try out ideas.'

After a few days in training, the team took the field to be beaten quite convincingly by a slick European side. In a precursor of his troubles at Tottenham, Danny found his side 2–1 down with twenty minutes remaining and sent John Charles into attack, moving to centre-half himself. This enterprising idea led to Charles hitting the bar but the Europeans soon regrouped and ran out 4–1 winners. Where others attacked Danny for meddling with the team's tactics, Winterbottom defended him: 'I thought that he was perfectly entitled to make the change, although the press made a big thing of it, as they always do – if it works, they're in praise of it, and if it doesn't they all criticize! But if you had Danny in the team and had him as captain, you had to give him the opportunity to play the game as he saw it; he had such vision and so many ideas that he demanded your confidence. There aren't too many captains in that mould – he captained the side by acting virtually as a coach as well, and in that way you can feel as though you're actually among the boys and actively influencing them, that they're playing for you. You have to have a special way about you to do that and Danny was a fine example. But good sides are full of leaders who are there to help one another, working for one another and intelligently thinking through the problems together. New ideas and patterns emerge from this and a manager must be strong enough to allow players to voice their opinions, but to have the final say himself. In his early days at Tottenham, Danny's frustration was that that didn't always happen, he couldn't do what he wanted because he wasn't the manager, and there's a real difference, however influential you might be on the field. A captain must represent a manager's ideas. If he disagrees with those, he shouldn't be captain.'

Step by step, Northern Ireland became an ever more formidable unit, gaining strength from the patronizing attitude which some displayed towards them: when they were finally deemed worthy of a Wembley international in 1955, some were amazed at the honour bestowed on the tiny country. Trainer Gerry Morgan, known to the side as 'Uncle', pointed out, 'Great honour be damned. Sure, the greyhounds have been running there for over twenty years!' That indomitable spirit was a great asset, and much of it sprang from Danny, as Walter Winterbottom concedes: 'Danny was so effervescent, so full of Irish mannerisms, cheerfully exaggerating everything, using "Irishisms" to explain defeats, always positive.' Peter McParland recalls that, 'He was generally a much happier man after he went to Spurs – he'd always been a happy go lucky sort of fella – but also when he was with Northern Ireland, because we were building something that was exciting, a good achievement for the country. With Ireland, we had the feeling we'd be able to shake a few people up.'

As Doherty had promised, by the onset of the crucial 1956–57 season, his players were beginning to master all his tactics.

On reflection, perhaps tactics is too grandiose a phrase to cover what was essentially good common sense. Doherty recognized that he was fortunate in managing a crop of gifted players, probably the best collection that the Irish had had to date, although even then, how many would have made the England side is a matter for debate – Danny and Harry Gregg perhaps, McIlroy maybe. Certainly they were never likely to be a match for the Hungarians or the Brazilians in terms of pure ability. Nevertheless, they were intelligent players who, if employed properly, would be able to cause plenty of difficulties for opponents. Doherty made it his business to identify a nucleus of players who could make the grade and then stand by them through thick and thin, building them into the international equivalent of a club side with all the attendant benefits in improved team spirit, an intuitive understanding of one another's game and so on. If a new player emerged, as Dick Keith did at full-back, for example, Doherty was happy to bring him into the camp, on the strict understanding that he fitted into the group and the disciplined team pattern. Having achieved a solid blend among the eleven players – and Northern Irish football was distinctly a team, rather than squad, since they had so few players from which to choose – they produced a workmanlike display on the field, their tactics carefully modulated by Danny, Doherty's field commander. Danny's part was especially important. Such was Doherty's faith in him, he gave him the freedom to make any changes he felt necessary and this Northern Irish play had a fluidity that many other European nations lacked. Always likely to do the unexpected, teams found it hard to formulate tactics to cope with them, and had they been able to call on a prolific centre-forward such as England's Nat Lofthouse or Wales's John Charles, their results might have been yet more prodigious.

By producing a settled side, Doherty soon eliminated the problems that unfamiliarity had caused in the past when selectors chopped and changed the team. With that new familiarity came a confidence that seven- and eight-goal defeats were a thing of the past, and on the rare occasions when they might resurface, Danny would be on hand to boost morale by explaining away a four-goal defeat as 'the result of four breakaways'. Silly mistakes were eliminated to the point where opponents now had to earn their goalscoring opportunities. That immediately meant that rather than expecting a hammering, the Irish might hope for a good result. With that solid defensive foundation in place, it was an atmosphere in which the individual talents of the Blanchflowers, McParland, Bingham and McIlroy might flourish. Indeed, such off-the-cuff invention was positively encouraged for, as Danny noted time and again, 'If we don't know what we're going to do, how can the other side?'

There were some tactical changes that made the Irish formidable. Danny was often the fulcrum of attacking moves, for instance, unusual for a right-half. When the Irish goalkeeper won the ball, rather than launching it speculatively into the other half, he'd look for Danny out on the right. Possession football was the trademark of the Irish game. As Danny pointed out: 'If we've got the ball, they can't score.' Inside Danny at centre-half was his brother Jackie, whom Doherty had converted from a wing-half. As constructive as his brother with the ball, his presence was vital, forming, with Danny and Bertie Peacock, an imposing half-back line, all of whom could create chances for their forwards. Recognizing that goalscoring would always be a problem with the limited resources he had available, Doherty accepted that the pragmatic solution was to create as many chances as possible in the hope that some would be taken. It was critical that the half-back line should be creative, and those three certainly were.

With World Cup qualification in the offing once again, the side was coming to maturity. England were held in an international in Belfast, Scotland given a searching examination in a 1−0 defeat at Hampden, and then the crucial games were upon them. More than ever before, there was a genuine belief that this would be Northern Ireland's breakthrough. As Peter McParland puts it: 'Nineteen fifty-eight was a big chance for us because before that we'd been on a loser when they used the Home Internationals as the qualifying tournament, which was always going to be difficult for us. Portugal and Italy weren't easy meat either, but it was a different kind of game.' A solid side had taken shape, much along the lines of that chosen in 1954 − Jackie Blanchflower had moved to centre-half, Wilbur Cush had come in as inside-forward, and the never-ending search for a goalscoring centre-forward meant that several hopefuls had been tried, but essentially it was the same structure, a team with Doherty's imprint on it. As Bertie Peacock explains: 'Peter worked so hard for us, he could talk intelligently but simply about the game. He enjoyed his job and our team and that wasn't easy because selectors had a say in it and he had to fight to get his way when results sometimes weren't as good as the FA would like. Like Danny, he was a man of principle. Danny was no pushover, if he had something to say, he said it. He and Peter were very close, they agreed on how to play the game and they'd spent a lot of time talking, organizing and so on. They were lucky to have one another. Danny was a born leader, he wanted to lead and he could. That helped the team maintain Peter's disciplines. Danny could talk about the game, could coach people in what he wanted them to do. He was a workaholic too, behind the scenes, working on set pieces and so on. Peter and Danny didn't have us running up and down sand hills, it was all about football. The two of them were before their time, everything they did was about method, about playing, passing the ball with intention rather than for its own sake. The main thing was that when they asked the players to do something, we could understand how and why we were going to do it.'

Portugal and Italy certainly were not going to be a pushover, but the different challenge that the two nations posed was a refreshing alternative. Having been fed a constant diet of Home Internationals since a friendly in Paris in 1952, it was exciting rather than nerve-racking to be faced with the Continentals. As usual, Northern Ireland had nothing to lose from this foray into the unknown. Italy might have a great historical reputation in the game, but the Irishmen weren't exposed to their players on a regular basis, whereas they knew precisely what men like Finney, Wright, Haynes or Charles might do. The other British teams were perhaps given too much respect because they had performed brilliantly in front of and against the Irish players in the past, while their mainland European counterparts were merely names. As Danny pointed out in an interview with the Portuguese press, 'We do not know how your team plays so we can't detail a plan for them. We want to keep an open mind.' The group began with a 1–1 draw in Lisbon, a superb achievement that merely underlined the possibilities. Three months later, in April 1957, the Northern Irish team found itself in Rome. They distinguished themselves once more, being unlucky to lose by a single goal, and this with a team shorn of Jackie Blanchflower and Peter McParland, who were playing in the FA Cup Final the following week and could not obtain release from their clubs. That goal was a controversial one too. Danny explained that, 'We tried to do things that nobody else had ever thought of. We had to because they were better sides. We put up the first wall at a free-kick. They seemed to be frightened by the tactic. It did have its teething problems though. The referee had never seen it either, so when the Italians picked up the ball and moved it five yards away from the wall and shot it into the net, he gave a goal!' Recovering from this disappointment a week later, the same eleven humiliated Portugal by three goals to nil in the white-hot atmosphere of Windsor Park to close the 1956–57 season with a flourish.

Peter Doherty had masterminded a revolution of expectation

for the men in green, bringing them to within touching distance of the World Cup Finals. Yet he'd done it not by grinding out results, as Billy Bingham did in 1982, but by playing expansive, exciting football. Walter Winterbottom was thoroughly impressed with his achievement, noting, 'Peter was just a player who moved into management. He had no knowledge of the sports sciences or coaching or motivation, except that he was looked up to because of his own ability. Like all players of that ability, he struck a chord, a rapport with those under him who wanted to play like he did, and he was willing to let his team play football. He was fortunate to have a player as good as Danny who could be his right-hand man on the field. Between the two of them, they generated a wonderful camaraderie that meant they weren't put off by anything. They were a jocular group, they'd play cards, which was often dangerous – before we stopped gambling, in the England camp we had examples of players losing too much money, exchanging £80, which in those days was a lot of money – but they seemed to keep it all in hand.'

In preparation for the vital return game with Italy, Northern Ireland travelled to Wembley in November 1957 for another Home International fixture. For many of the players, used to heavy defeats at the hands of the English, this game assumed as much importance as the coming game with Italy; England were unbeaten in sixteen matches and Northern Ireland had not beaten them since October 1927; not in England since February 1914. Danny wrote that, 'At our hotel before the game we were all confident that we would beat England; we thought that on the day, we could rise to the occasion and with a better spirit undermine them . . . a team can raise itself to a standard on the day that it might not be able to achieve regularly. This was something that I think we achieved.' Watched by Italian scouts, anxious to learn more of their mysterious methods, the Irish decided to commit themselves to attack early on, to force their pace on England. Danny and Peter Doherty also evolved a tactical plan to nullify Johnny Haynes, using their full-backs to tempt him to play passes inside for his wingers which the Irishmen could anticipate rather than giving him freedom to set the central forwards Kevan and Taylor into the clear. Initially this failed and the Irish were lucky not to find themselves behind as Haynes released his forwards time and again. Taking responsibility, Danny changed the play, moving to shadow Haynes, forcing him to make the passes they wanted him to make.

Gradually Northern Ireland took charge of the game and went in at half-time one up, but England soon equalized after the break. Deliberately ceding possession on Danny's instruction, Northern Ireland were pinned back in their own half but remained in control, with Peacock and Jackie Blanchflower helping out the full-backs in man-marking the English forwards. As England looked in vain for an opening, the Irish hit them on the break to go 2–1 ahead then extended their lead a few minutes later. With twenty minutes to go England's unbeaten run was in danger, and though Duncan Edwards pulled a goal back Danny marshalled his troops through to the final victory, sharing the plaudits with his brother, Harry Gregg and Bertie Peacock, as the dominant figures in the game. Victory over England in a meaningless game hardly seems a great achievement, but psychologically it was a massive breakthrough. Peter McParland feels, 'That was a really great day and it was a stepping stone towards the World Cup. The greatest thing was we had an Irish team, we were all from Belfast, Derry, Newry, lads who'd grown up and played their football in Northern Ireland, which was very satisfying. We were a close bunch by then and beating England made us feel we could take on anyone.' Danny and Peter Doherty had set great store in the outcome of the game, knowing that if they could lay the English hoodoo, the forthcoming game with the Italians would seem far less daunting. The importance of that result was demonstrated in its aftermath. Maurice Tomlins, a friend from Danny's time at Aston Villa, had travelled to see the game and found him in ebullient mood: 'Danny had played England almost on his own that day and after the game, a party of us went to a Joe Lyons house for dinner. Danny sat there all night long signing autographs and chatting to supporters. I was playing local league football at the time and one of the supporters who'd come for Danny's signature thought he recognized me too. Danny said, "Of course you should know him. He's centre-forward for Dudley Town!"'

A month later, the scene was set for the final match with Italy. Other results in the group meant that Italy would go through with a draw while the Irish had to win the tie, arranged for 4 December. The appointed referee for the game was a Hungarian,

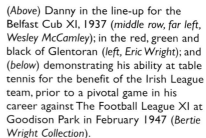

(*Above*) Danny in the line-up for the Belfast Cub XI, 1937 (*middle row, far left, Wesley McCamley*); in the red, green and black of Glentoran (*left, Eric Wright*); and (*below*) demonstrating his ability at table tennis for the benefit of the Irish League team, prior to a pivotal game in his career against The Football League XI at Goodison Park in February 1947 (*Bertie Wright Collection*).

(*Right*) Taking to the field at Villa Park, always with a ball at hand.

(*Below*) The Big Four? (*From left to right*) Tommy Thompson, Amos Moss, Larry Canning and Danny prepare for battle at Little Aston Golf Course (*Tommy Thompson Collection*).

The 1953 summer tour of Canada and the USA. Danny with Bob Stevenson (*left, Margaret Stevenson Collection*) and (*below*) in action in New York against a Liverpool XI. The original caption reads: '...note the "straight arm" J.B. Payne uses so effectively to thwart the Irish booter in this thrilling play. The Liverpool team whipped the Irishmen 4–0...' (*Corbis-Bettmann/UPI*).

Danny's one and only role model, the Northern Ireland international and manager, Peter Doherty (*above, Hulton Getty*); with brother Jackie, a fellow Irish international (*right, Hulton Getty*); and (*below*) Danny at the kick-off of the postponed 'friendly' with Italy (*Popperfoto*).

December 1954. The Great White Hart Lane Hope arrives in London (*above, Express Newspapers*), meets Spurs captain Alf Ramsey (*below left, Hulton Getty*), and warms up for his home debut, against Aston Villa (*Hulton Getty*).

In safe hands (*above*), sandwiched between Ron Reynolds and Ted Ditchburn, 1955 (*Hulton Getty*), and commanding the midfield (*left, Colorsport; right, Hulton Getty*).

Teetotal Danny keeps the cap on the bottle (*Express Newspapers*).

SOCCER EXPERTS SAY—

Extra energy makes the difference!

DANNY BLANCHFLOWER of the 'Spurs, Captain of Ireland, and one of the most brilliant half-backs in the game, says: *"Ninety minutes of top-speed soccer can be a pretty gruelling test! It needs extra energy and plenty of it. That's why I rely on 'Dextrosol' Glucose Tablets. They're the handiest way I know of renewing energy fast."*

Dextrosol
gives extra energy

To build up energy for that extra effort, to replace energy after exhaustion, eat delicious 'Dextrosol' Glucose Tablets. They are 99% pure glucose: the quick, *natural* source of energy. 'Dextrosol' requires no digesting but passes straight into your bloodstream carrying energy at once to the muscles. For extra energy anywhere, any time —carry a handy packet of 'Dextrosol' Glucose Tablets.

$1\frac{1}{2}$D & 6D

AT CHEMISTS
AND GROCERS
EVERYWHERE

DEXTROSOL glucose tablets

MADE BY THE PHARMACEUTICAL DIVISION OF BROWN & POLSON LTD

If only Maradona had stuck to Dextrosol (*Vintage Magazine Company*).

The team of the century? The Tottenham squad (*above*) on the brink of history, autumn 1960. Back row: John Hills, Bobby Smith, Johnny Ryden, Maurice Norman, Mel Hopkins, Peter Baker, Dave Mackay. Centre: Cliff Jones, Tony Marchi, Bill Brown, Johnny Hollowbread, Ron Henry, Les Allen. Front: Tommy Harmer, Cecil Poynton (trainer), Danny Blanchflower, Bill Nicholson (manager), Terry Dyson. (*Below*) Danny introduces the Duchess of Kent to the Spurs team prior to the 1961 FA Cup Final (*left to right:* Jones, Baker, Mackay, John White and Norman, *both Hulton Getty*).

(*Above*) Football League president and Barnsley chairman
Joe Richards hands Danny the Championship trophy. Manager
Bill Nicholson looks on, White Hart Lane, 29 April 1961.
(*Below*) The Double – Danny and the spoils of victory,
May 1961 (*both Hulton Getty*).

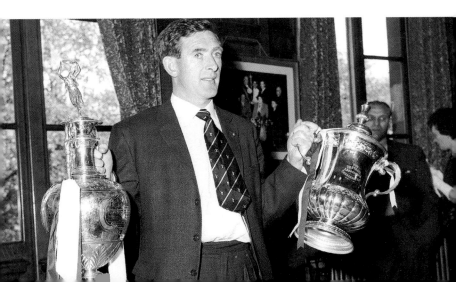

The show goes on: (*above*) signing autographs at a
pre-season open day, August 1961 (*Popperfoto*); warming up for
a League fixture (*left, Colorsport*); clinching the 1962 FA Cup
Final against Burnley (*below, Colorsport*).

(*Left*) Injured but informed, Danny lies in a hospital bed receiving the news that there will be no third consecutive trip to Wembley, as Spurs go down 3–0 at home to Burnley in the third round of the FA Cup, January 1963. He makes it back to ensure Spurs capture England's first European trophy (*below*), parading the Cup Winners Cup before the multitude, May 1963. (*both Hulton Getty*)

Managerial days: (*clockwise from top left*) always talking football in earnest, here with Northern Ireland's third-choice keeper, Alan Paterson (*Eric Wright*); with Johnny Giles, four years after Bill Nicholson hoped to combine their talents at White Hart Lane (*Football Archive*); chatting with groundsman Harry Canells on his first day at Stamford Bridge, 15 December 1978 (*Hulton Getty*); despair in the dug-out as Chelsea lose to Coventry, February 1979 (*Hulton Getty*).

In his prime at Spurs (*Colorsport*).

who arranged to fly into Belfast on the morning of the match, having stayed the previous night in London. The morning found London cloaked in a blanket of fog. His original flight was cancelled, but the Irish FA remained hopeful that a later plane might bring him into Belfast. Finally, at one o'clock, it became clear that he would not make the afternoon kick-off. Peter McParland remembers, 'Twenty minutes before kick-off we were up and ready for the game, raring to go, and Peter Doherty came in and said, "I've news for you. The referee hasn't turned up and the Italians won't accept the Irish referee." That was a good job, because he'd probably have gone out of his way to show how fair he was! So we had to play the game as a friendly instead. That was such a downer because we were really fired up for it. Anyway, they announced to the crowd that because the Italians wouldn't accept an Irish referee, the game would be a friendly. Now the crowd were very upset! All the shipbuilders, and whatever, had taken the day off. It was a full house, all worked up for a big World Cup game, and the next minute it's off, so they weren't too pleased. On the field it was tough, there were no prisoners, so the crowd got mixed up in the atmosphere of that too.'

The crowd began to boo as the teams took the field and continued throughout the Italian anthem, creating a very hostile atmosphere to which the visitors responded in kind. Bertie Peacock terms the game 'The Battle Of Belfast' and Danny obviously agreed with him. In his autobiography, he records his view of events: 'Very early I brushed past the opposing right-half and we had a bit of a struggle for the ball. I was completely surprised when he flashed a sharp uppercut to the point of my chin . . . Schiaffino flung himself brutally and deliberately into little Wilbur Cush. "Now forget all about it," I advised Wilbur, but shortly after he did the same to Schiaffino . . . right-half Chiapella jumped with both feet into the small of Billy McAdams's back.' Incidents such as this came thick and fast and the crowd grew more and more agitated. According to Bertie Peacock, it was only Danny's swift thinking that avoided a potentially nasty incident: 'Danny made a man of himself that day. Tommy Mitchell, the stand-in referee, gave us a penalty and their centre-half just picked the ball up and put it up his jersey, he wouldn't have it at all. I'm not sure the crowd knew what was happening, so Danny got to Tommy and said, "Don't worry, we'll take a free-kick." After all, it had turned into a friendly, there was no sense turning it into a fight! That was him, quick thinking because he knew the crowd were worked up.'

When the game came to an end, a few moments after a free-for-all fight on the edge of the Italian box, the crowd came on to the pitch, as was customary at Windsor Park. Peter McParland recalls that, 'Suddenly, the Italians were trying to be friendly, but the crowd were after their blood! We didn't want any bother and Danny got us to each escort an Italian off the pitch to help, he tried to handle it all that way. One of the Italians, big Ferrario from Juventus, who'd been kicking anything that moved, went to the crowd to be friendly, but it didn't work with the shipyard workers!' Ferrario found himself embroiled in a fight with a spectator and it was Danny who returned to the centre-circle to separate them and help the big centre-half from the field. FIFA ordered that the fixture be replayed in January, but no sanctions were taken against either team, given the special circumstances that had surrounded the game.

In those circumstances, the score was the last thing on most people's minds, yet it provided the most enduring legacy of the game. The Italians, strong and confident at the outset, had twice taken the lead but had been unable to assert their customary dominance, neither by dint of skill nor sheer physical presence. Whatever they tried, the Irish would not be quelled. Each time they went behind, they fought back with goals from Wilbur Cush. The final outcome was a 2–2 draw and, had Danny insisted on taking a penalty rather than a free-kick in that earlier incident, they would surely have won. The Irish acquitted themselves supremely well under extreme provocation and had won the psychological war. With a return to Belfast to play the critical qualifier in the forefront of their minds, the Italians knew that the Irish would not be the pushover they had assumed. Such was their fighting spirit, so intense had been the crowd's reactions, that several of their opponents clearly did not relish the idea of coming back to the province. Their superior skill had failed to rattle Doherty's side, his well-drilled players able to cope with anything thrown at them. Nor would tough players like Bingham, Peacock, Blanchflower and McParland be knocked off their stride by intimidation. As the Italians trooped disconsolately off, each with an Irishman at his side, it was clear that the home team were in the ascendancy. As Peter McParland reflects, 'That draw left us even more determined. We knew we had to get after them early on, because they could be rattled very easily. We knew we could win after the first game, and we set about it.'

As the qualifier got under way in January, the Hungarian referee, determined to stamp his authority on the game and prevent a repeat of the previous meeting, quickly sent off Ghiggia, the Italian forward, for a seemingly innocuous offence. Alf McMichael, the injured party, appealed to the referee to recall the Italian, but to no effect. Taking the new circumstances on board, Northern Ireland quickly made full use of the extra man, McIlroy and Cush putting them two goals clear at half-time. Italy, promised an astronomical bonus of £500 each if they won through, stirred briefly in the second half and an error by goalkeeper Norman Uprichard gave them hope by halving the deficit. On the brink of qualification for the World Cup Finals series, the Irishmen suddenly seemed aware of the enormity of their achievement. According to reporter John Calkin, in his book *World Cup 1958*, Northern Ireland's 'team-work fell completely away to nothing, the match was there for Italy's taking. Yet this team of stars failed utterly to rise to the challenge . . . [their] play was characterized by a marked lack of fighting spirit.' The Italians were simply demoralized by the Irish refusal to surrender in the game before Christmas. The brief respite of six weeks since that match was not long enough to heal the mental scars inflicted that day. Regaining their nerve, the result was rarely in any doubt and the team booked their passage for Sweden. There was an odd sense of anti-climax about it all, so confident had they been of victory, but nevertheless Peter McParland remembers that, 'We got a great ovation from the crowd but we didn't do a lap of honour clapping the supporters – we used to think it was their job to clap us!'

That game was played on 15 January. Between then and the first game in the World Cup, on 8 June, Northern Ireland managed just one competitive fixture, a 1–1 draw against Wales in Cardiff. Peter McParland 'had a bad game against Wales just before they picked the side for the World Cup, and I said, "I hope to God I get picked after that." Danny said, "You've a fair chance, we've only eighteen players anyway!"' That was fair comment. Peter Doherty didn't arrange any more friendly games because 'we daren't risk any injury because we just haven't any reserves'. Matters degenerated into farce when Northern Ireland could not furnish FIFA with the requisite preliminary squad of 40 players since the Irish FA pointed out that there weren't 'forty men remotely under consideration!' To compensate, Danny got in some useful work by joining the English side's preparation. Walter Winterbottom recalls that, 'He came to our sessions when we worked at some of the London clubs. Instead of just ball practice, we liked to get in an easy but thoughtful practice game, so we might go to West Ham, and they'd turn out and try to play against us as the French would or the Germans might do. Danny was keen as ever to show his skill.'

Irish resources had been further depleted by the tragic events at Munich on 6 February 1958. Not only did many great men lose their lives that day, others lost their careers. Jackie Blanchflower was one whose dreams were dashed, not only of participating in the World Cup, but of having a career in the game. An awful personal blow, it also robbed the game of a fine player. Ever since Doherty had converted him into a centre-half, his reading of the game and his distribution from the back had been a feature of Manchester United's play, as had his ability as a goalscorer – 26 goals in 105 games for his club. Just approaching his twenty-fifth birthday, there was a wonderful future ahead of him, which surely included succeeding his brother as captain of his country, perhaps even eclipsing his achievements; he might have won the Double with United before Danny did at Spurs. In his *Daily Mail* column seven months after the disaster, Danny wrote, 'So my kid brother Jackie has finally decided that he will never play football again. There comes a time when even an Irishman must give up fighting for lost causes. It has been a hard fight, a bitter fight and the price was a broken heart. There were times when he willed himself to believe that once again he would get out on that field. But somehow he always knew. He knew from that first moment as he lay in the snow beside the battered plane in which his great buddy Tommy Taylor, and so many of his other friends and colleagues, died ... Then came the real fight. He has pretended that he could not care less about football any more. He did not want to go and see the games. And all the time it was eating his heart out.' Jackie recalls that Danny came to visit him when his duties at Spurs allowed, but as George Robb, his Tottenham colleague points out, 'Danny was obviously very upset about his brother's accident, but at the club it didn't affect his game, he didn't fret about it.'

Danny was quite fatalistic in many ways, never wasting time or effort on things he couldn't change, be they professional or personal matters. He was deeply saddened by the Munich disaster, but no amount of wishing or worrying would change the situation. Moreover, he was a very self-absorbed character; he was extremely ambitious, wanted success and to make a great reputation for himself, and would not tolerate anything, even family sentiment, getting in the way. Ironically, the corollary to that was the fact that he could be selfless at one and the same time. His ability to work tirelessly for a cause and to give himself wholeheartedly to the team meant that he often made a greater contribution than some team-mates, helping lesser players through their problems while being happy to share the spoils of victory with them. Nevertheless, in this age, it's hard to grasp just how Danny could be so sanguine about his brother's injury. If such a tragedy happened now, there would be support groups springing up for the injured, the bereaved and those watching on television, charity records and concerts would be arranged, an entire industry springing up to help the victims. Back in 1958 there was no such assistance, perhaps in part because it was impossible to organize, but mostly because of the timing. This was just thirteen years after the end of the war. Tragic though Munich was, people were still conditioned to accept death and disaster as a way of life, still hardened by the relentless tide of loss that had carried on through six hard years. They were touched by Munich, desperately saddened by it, but such catastrophe was not quite the rarity that, thankfully, it is today. Having joined the RAF, albeit without seeing active service, Danny knew the risks he might himself run, had accepted the possibility of his own death, and consequently took Munich, if not in his stride, then relatively equably.

The Northern Irish team regrouped to cover the loss of Jackie Blanchflower, Willie Cunningham moving to centre-half, Dick Keith taking his place at full-back. They were ready to take on the world, but for a time it looked like they would not be allowed to compete. Because of the intensive schedule of matches at the Finals, some games took place on a Sunday. The Irish FA was the only association in world football which had a rule preventing its team playing on Sundays. It was a rule defended rigidly by the Church Leagues, who would not countenance such blasphemy, and Northern Ireland risked expulsion from not just the World Cup but the world game. As Danny wrote later, the problem was eventually resolved: 'A majority 75 per cent vote of the Irish FA decided we could not go to Sweden but, being Irish, we did.'

The Northern Irish team were fated to have to do things the hard way if they were to progress. Having overcome Italy and Portugal, they now found themselves up against the holders West Germany, Argentina and Czechoslovakia. With their first game scheduled for 8 June, the team did not assemble until the 2nd, though even then a number of players were still missing on club duty on post-season tours. Looking ahead to the tournament, Danny wrote an article for the *Observer*, commenting on the nation's prospects while simultaneously illustrating his growing confidence as a columnist: 'Northern Ireland is the Cinderella of the soccer world and that we are here competing with the elite of international soccer is an *Alice in Wonderland* tale . . . for little Cinderella to overcome the mighty Italians could, in terms of a "Wonderland" character, only make an unpredictable game "curiouser and curiouser" [but it is] a just reward for the all-round efforts we have made in recent years . . . one day along came our Prince Charming, Peter Doherty. We whittled down those defeats to the odd goal, drew many of our games and had the occasional win to gladden the heart. This year we have reached a great peak, with an unbeaten season of five games and qualification. What effects will the taste of this great competition have upon us? Will the partaking of it make us shrink as Alice did or grow as she did? Or will we, like Cinderella, get caught out after midnight?'

There was a lovely, relaxed attitude about the party, which certainly helped the team prepare for what were extremely demanding games. Revelling in their position as underdogs, the Irish went out of their way to enjoy themselves while in Sweden, adopting a young boy, Bengt Johansson, as a mascot, going to church with the locals, serving behind the counters in the village shops, all the while heaping pressure on their rivals by playing down their own ability. In the team talks prior to the first match, Danny helped ease any first-night nerves by pointing out the absurdity of Northern Ireland even being in Sweden. Peter

McParland remembers, 'Danny helped make the team feel like friends and family. He was always telling us that all we had to do was equalize before the other team scored, to make sure we got our retaliation in first and that then we'd be all right!'

The first game against the Czechs in Halmstad was a triumph of forward planning, even if training was delayed by a day when 'the officials went fishing in our tracksuits!' Danny and Peter Doherty had watched their opponents a few days earlier in a warm-up game and realized they needed to hustle the Czechs out of their easy rhythm. Peter McParland recalls: 'The Czechs were labelled as dark horses for the Cup, but after Danny and Peter went to watch them, we felt we had the edge. They didn't build them up, just said they looked quite decent, but that if we were on our toes we'd do OK. There were no peculiar theories or complicated ideas floating around, just the thought that if we did our best we would win. The Czechs came past in the coach before the game while we were waiting around, and all the curtains were drawn, the coach was in darkness, and I just thought what a daft way to go about life! They had to come out on the field so we saw them then! We got an early goal and beat them 1–0.' Danny recorded the game as 'one time when the artisan beat the artist', but Malcolm Brodie of the *Belfast Telegraph* was more expansive, calling it 'a triumph of tactics with victory gained as much off the field as on it. Manager Peter Doherty and Blanchflower evolved moves to exploit the weaknesses of the Czechs.' Nevertheless, victory wasn't won without a tremendous fight. Having controlled the game for the first hour or so, the Irish were still only one goal to the good when they began to run out of steam, such was the effort they'd put in. Their poor finishing gave the Czechs a glimmer of hope and the final twenty minutes saw Gregg's goal under siege. With Danny's form on the ball having deserted him, his distribution being uniformly awful, Northern Ireland were robbed of their main attacking outlet and were simply unable to wrest back the initiative when they most needed to. In normal circumstances, Danny would have been given the ball and would have relieved the pressure for a moment or two by releasing an attacker into space, but on this day in Halmstad he was incapable of doing so. As it was, it was left to Gregg and his defence to keep the Czechs at bay, much as they had done at Wembley a few months previously. Finally, a heroic victory was sealed.

By now, Danny's tactical acumen was being appreciated by the world at large. In spite of his own dismal display as a player, he had refused to disappear into the background. He had organized the attacking forays of the first hour and had continued to marshal the rearguard action in the final quarter of the game, eschewing his normal passing game for a purely defensive role. Such was their respect for him that despite the dip in his form, the players were utterly supportive and never questioned his commands. Equally, they were right behind Doherty, for, as Derek Dougan records, 'There was only one footballer in my lifetime who became a legend while he lived, and that was Peter Doherty. He, more than anyone, realized Danny's strong points, and he played to them. They made a great combination. Blanchflower, McIlroy and Bingham were a little trio who worked things out for themselves and the rest of us reacted to them and the way they played.' Bertie Peacock adds, 'With Peter in charge, Danny could do what he liked because Peter liked what Danny liked, and that's a good combination to have. Dictation is OK, but if you can get a fella like Danny on the field, who can lead by example, that's a better bet.' With the Czechs overcome, Doherty and Blanchflower had the sense to let their charges enjoy the moment, Danny reasoning that 'to save us from evening boredom we decided we could all keep an eye on one another and we went to the local nightclub together in a bus'. The squad staged a big party at which the locals were most welcome. Peter McParland remembers, 'We were free and easy in our ways, we sang our way to the grounds, "Irish Eyes are Smiling", or whatever. The people took to us in Sweden, especially Tysoland, a village just outside Halmstad, where we were staying, where we'd go and have a cup of coffee, or whatever. They were all behind us, they were nice to us and when we played, the Swedish public were on our side. We admired their way of life and we were grateful for what they did for us and their support. We only had about six or seven Irishmen with us – a couple had come over on an old Vespa – so the Swedish support was really nice.'

Following that Czech victory, there was no change in the routine, even though they were close to reaching the next stage. Even so, the dawning reality that Northern Ireland might actually go further in the competition started to have its effect. Thorough in their preparation, Doherty called in Jackie Milburn, then Linfield's player-coach, to give his verdict on the Argentines and the West Germans, whom he had seen play in their opening fixture, the European side winning comfortably, 3–1. With the Argentines, their second opponents, without a point, the Irish were underdogs no longer. 'Against them we were a bit tense,' admits Peter McParland. 'It was an important match but it was also the first game we'd played against the South Americans, and they had a great reputation. We scored first, but they didn't fold, they were an excellent side.' That goal came about through Irish invention, Danny and Billy Bingham working a short corner on the right – at the time, a highly innovative tactical ploy – giving McParland the chance to head his team into the lead. Oddly, the goal seemed only to increase the pressure on the side, and Danny recalled that, 'I had to call all the players together on the field and tell them to shut up as they were only causing confusion for one another.' With total authority to run the play, Danny made sure he used it. Bertie Peacock recalls, 'They got a free-kick twenty yards out and everybody was meddling, trying to line up the ball, and Danny just lifted it up and gave one or two a slating and said the line-up for the kick would be as prescribed in our training, then he threw the ball back down! But he could take it too. Gregg was in goal that day and Danny was bringing the ball away and he tried to turn and flick it through his legs but he slipped. They got the ball and Harry had to come out and dive at their player's feet. This was just after Harry had been involved in the Munich disaster, so his nerves were up a bit, and it was just coming to half-time. He gave Danny some stick from the goalmouth all the way to the dressing room. But Danny just smiled, he knew what he'd done but he seemed to get over his failures easily, he'd take it in his stride because he had powerful confidence.' In the end, as Danny admitted, the Argentines were simply a superior force, a team who could switch the play at breakneck speed, employing the 4–2–4 formation (which would eventually take Brazil to the crown) and bewildering the men in green. Even so, it took a dubious penalty to bring them level just before half-time; had the Irish held on to the interval, the game might have been very different afterwards. As it was, Argentina took heart and after Fay Coyle had missed a good chance in the opening minutes of the second half, the balance of power finally shifted. By the hour mark, they were 3–1 ahead and coasting to victory.

For some countries, the party would have been over, but not for the Irish. It had only just begun. Led by Danny, they returned to the local nightclub and once more regaled the locals with a selection of their songs and jokes. Despite having had another very poor game, his passing no better against Argentina than it had been against Czechoslovakia, Danny was still a leading light in both the side and the tournament, for his captaincy was remarkable at a time when coaches were starting to assert their authority. His ability to change the way the team played on the field, the emphasis between attack and defence, the pace at which they played, gave the Irish an incredible flexibility when compared with technically more accomplished sides who slavishly followed a pre-arranged plan. Less gifted in some areas perhaps, Northern Ireland had a settled side with an inspirational leader, a state of affairs which Walter Winterbottom looked on with a degree of envy: 'They were remarkable in Sweden, but that was the big joy of being a small country with so few players of truly international standard. You must stick with them, and that welds them together. If you have a wider choice, as we have in England, the committee always wanted to make changes. Playing for England became a reward for doing well for their club rather than trying to build a side to win matches or competitions. If you chop and change, you've problems. If you keep the team together, it builds up camaraderie and they get to know each other's style of play. The Irish lads gave of their all because they were so tightly knit.'

The final group game was against West Germany and was played in Malmo, seventy miles or so away from the Irish base. Such was their popularity, that many of the people from Halmstad followed their new idols across country to offer their backing as they tried to defeat the reviled West Germans; this was as well, since the Germans had 10,000 supporters of their own in attendance. Four years of work would reach their culmination in this game, but the tension of the Argentine game was replaced by a simple determination to succeed. Going into the final game, West Germany had three points, Northern Ireland and Argentina two each, the Czechs one. The assumption in the camp was that Argentina would win their last game, requiring Doherty's team to beat West Germany to book their passage to the quarter-finals, probably eliminating the holders in the process.

The Irish used their third centre-forward in as many games,

Derek Dougan and Fay Coyle having played there in the first two games without conspicuous success. This time Tommy Casey came into the side but played in a slightly more withdrawn position, as one would expect from someone who played as a wing-half for his club, Newcastle United. While it underlined the lack of fire-power in the Irish side, it was a move which was indicative of the way they would turn a weakness into a strength, for it was Casey who set up McParland to put the Irish ahead after eighteen minutes. Casey then limped off for treatment and in his brief absence, Rahn equalized. This time the Irish were undaunted and, with Danny having a rather more secure game than latterly, they more than held their own. With their captain back to better form their attacking threat could come from the right flank once more, and it was from a corner on that side that McParland scored again on the hour. Predictably the Germans fought back hard but by this point the Irish defence were absolute masters at soaking up pressure. That vital victory seemed assured when, with twelve minutes to go, Uwe Seeler hammered in a speculative shot past Gregg, who had been hobbling badly since being injured in the fifth minute, to bring the scores level. The Irish pressed forward in search of the goal they felt they needed, and a late effort from McParland grazed the bar, but the final score was 2–2. Remarkably, as the team trooped off the field, sure that they were out of the World Cup, news filtered through that the Czechs had beaten Argentina 6–1, so that they and Northern Ireland both finished on three points. Since goal difference or goal average was not employed to separate teams in those days, it meant a play-off two days later in Malmo to see who would go through to play France in the quarter-finals.

By now, the strain was telling on the limited Irish resources, with injuries mounting. Just as tiring was the journey back to Halmstad and then back again to Malmo for the play-off game, the Irish FA's organization being typically chaotic. In the only World Cup to feature all four UK sides, only the Scots had been ousted so far, with England and Wales also involved in play-off matches. National pride demanded that Northern Ireland should at least match their more fancied counterparts, and so talk of fatigue was banished.

With Danny back to his best, there was some optimism that the Czechs could be overcome a second time, even though Gregg was missing and was replaced by Norman Uprichard. Doherty and Danny were determined to come up with another trick to unbalance their opponents, though their minds were especially exercised by their shortcomings at centre-forward, the more so as Casey's injury sustained in the West German game ruled him out. Having seen McParland score three goals in two games, he looked the best bet. Casey was replaced in the number nine shirt by Grimsby's Jackie Scott, and that was how the team lined up. Within moments, Scott and McParland had switched places in a move that clearly confused the Czech defence. If nothing else, McParland's physical presence in a central role would cause consternation in their defence, and having him closer to the right flank, where so many Irish moves began, meant he could be used as a link-up player too. For once, it was the other side that made the breakthrough early on, Zirkan heading past Uprichard after nineteen minutes. Still, the Irish remained patient and continued with their measured football. That virtue was rewarded on the stroke of half-time when McParland scored once more, pouncing on a rebound after Cush had rained in three shots from close range. Once more, the injuries that cursed the Irishmen struck – Uprichard, having twisted an ankle early on, then broke a bone in his left hand after an hour, and Bertie Peacock became little more than a passenger in the latter stages. At the end of normal time, the game was locked at 1–1. So bad was Uprichard's injury that Doherty and Blanchflower discussed replacing him with an outfield player but decided against it. Nine minutes into the extra period, with the Irish flagging under the strain, they were awarded a free-kick out on the right, midway inside the Czech half. Recalling one of the set pieces they had worked on in training, Danny took the kick, floating the ball into the box, McParland rushed in from the left, met the ball on the full and volleyed the Irish ahead with his fifth goal in four games. With that, the spirit of the Czech side was finally broken, a fact emphasized four minutes later when one of their stars, Bubernik, was sent off for allegedly spitting at the referee. When the final whistle went, Northern Ireland had exceeded their fondest dreams, qualifying from a fierce group. Their collective joy could only have been increased by the news that England had gone out to the USSR, leaving themselves and Wales, long dismissed as the two poor relations, the only UK representatives in the tournament.

Just two days later, the quarter-final loomed in Norrkoping, a two-hundred-odd-mile journey by coach, lasting ten debilitating hours. Exhausted by their efforts, with virtually every man nursing an injury of some sort and of varying degrees of severity, this was the last thing they needed before a tough encounter with the rampant French side, for whom Just Fontaine had already scored six goals in three games. With Uprichard out, Harry Gregg had to play 'even if we have to carry him on' according to Doherty. Bertie Peacock also missed out, replaced by Wilbur Cush, moving to left-half from inside-right, with Tommy Casey coming into that position, even though he was far short of match fitness – his leg wound soon reopened during the course of the game. By the time they took the field, the Irishmen were dead on their feet. Rising to the occasion, they chose to fight a rearguard action, drawing the French on to them in order to marshal their reserves of energy. They battled gamely, but two minutes before the break, Wisnieski scored for the French. That opened the floodgates. Two goals from Fontaine – who ended the tournament with a record thirteen goals – and another from Piantoni put the French four up and clear by the sixty-eighth minute. Ruefully, Peter McParland recalls, 'I would have liked us to have a go at them on level terms. While we were playing the play-off matches and travelling here, there and everywhere, the French had got their feet up for four days just waiting for us. They were a very good team, but if we'd been as fresh as they were, we could have given them a game.' In spite of the heavy defeat, Doherty's team, with Danny in the vanguard, had given more fun and excitement to the 1958 World Cup than any side except the eventual winners, Brazil, who, incidentally, ended Welsh participation at the quarter-final stage. Danny was satisfied with their Herculean efforts, writing, 'If you needed an example of football people at their best this was it . . . the player carries on to the field responsibilities that would weaken the knees of any cabinet minister . . . I shall not forget the evidence of quiet despair as the Czechoslovakians retreated from the ground after we had defeated them. I felt sorry for them. And I will always remember the extreme exhilaration of the Argentinians as they defeated us.' But it was the lessons learned from competing in such a rarefied atmosphere that mattered most. Against the French, for example: 'They curled the ball round our defensive wall so we had to learn to line it up properly. We got round to the last man on the wall lining it up. It sounds simple, but it showed the planning that went into everything. That was the thinking we took back to the clubs.' So much had been learned that, on the flight out of Sweden, Danny turned to his travelling companions, Joe Mercer and Stan Cullis, and made a fascinating prediction: 'Tottenham are going to win the Double within the next few years.'

6 The Double . . .

Perhaps the only drawback of a World Cup or European Championship year is its elongation of the football season and consequent reduction of the summer break. On the few occasions where the home nations, particularly England, have enjoyed great success, as in 1966, 1990 or 1996, this is less of a problem, for that achievement heightens anticipation of the new season. If the tournament has ended in failure, the fans sometimes find it hard to rouse themselves afresh. Whatever, the outcome for the players who've had a long hard summer is that pre-season training becomes even more of a chore. Danny conceded that 'at the start of 1958–59 I lacked enthusiasm'. The physical effects aside, Danny did enjoy the fruits of his new-found fame off the field. In tandem with his agent, Bagenal Harvey – a prototype Eric Hall who also represented sports stars such as Denis Compton – he arranged a lucrative new press deal with the *Daily Mail*, writing a provocative column each Monday, entering a further contract to produce *Danny Blanchflower's Soccer Book* for publishers Muller.

It's a pattern commented on already, but with every progressive step that Danny made, he became a little more outgoing. Perhaps there was a degree of cynical self-interest in that too, promoting himself, but most of his good deeds gained no publicity. Maintaining his interest in encouraging youngsters in the game, especially those from Belfast, he was always on the lookout for visitors to the club. Peter O'Dell was leader of 'the Lower Shankill Boys' Club', and in the summer of 1958 he 'took about twenty or so of the more senior footballers to Chigwell for a week's holiday. I arranged a tour of White Hart Lane with the secretary and when we arrived we were welcomed by Danny, who had heard of the visit and had decided to act as our guide. He took us everywhere, gave us detailed information about the club, the ground and his ideas, and answered all the boys' questions. He even produced a pair of his boots explaining why he would wear a certain pair on certain days. After the boys had exhausted their questions – and Danny – he insisted on being photographed with each one in turn. He was such an impressive man and the boys remembered that day for a long, long time, boasting to the other club members night after night.' At a time when he'd just returned from being one of the most influential players in Sweden and could have been forgiven for wanting nothing more than to get home and put his feet up, this was a generous gesture. Clearly he hadn't forgotten the days when he worshipped Peter Doherty from afar, and realized just how much such a meeting would mean. It appealed to his vanity to hold court, but he also saw that looking after the youngsters was his chance to put something back into the game. In his *Soccer Book*, he wrote, 'These kids are wonderful young people who spend their leisure hours pursuing something they love . . . what better for a boy than hero-worship and something wonderful to believe in? What better for a boy than a romance with the great game? Its heroes are men of deed and action – real champions; not phoney images on some celluloid screen . . . they take football deeply into their hearts and it is a romance that nearly always lasts a lifetime. Those kids that do not become great players, those that do not make the grade, do not, often, jilt the game. They become the fans, the fanatics, the people upon whom the game really depends.' Later on he demonstrated his commitment to that ideal when John Parkinson, a Belfast schoolmaster, 'took forty boys from Dunlambert to London on an educational trip. Danny arranged for us to have a tour of White Hart Lane and then to meet the players at the end of a training session. He arranged for us to be guests at the game the following Saturday. His pride in having a group of Belfast folk there to see him was very evident.'

This concern for football's future was a genuine one. If Danny had been a romantic about the game before Sweden, he was now utterly besotted with its glorious possibilities. The pure joy of taking Northern Ireland, the country with the slimmest resources of the fifty-three nations who had initially entered the competition, to the quarter-finals of the World Cup, where they were finally beaten by fatigue as much as by the French, had left its mark on him. He wanted to play games with a flourish, with a heroic compulsion, producing the grand gesture at the appropriate moment to turn any triumph into a genuinely memorable occasion. Never a conformist, he was now intoxicated by the great adventure, of achieving the impossible. He was addicted to thinking the unthinkable, hence his concentration on the English game's Holy Grail, the League and Cup Double.

Returning to Tottenham under the leadership of Jimmy Anderson required a degree of adjustment, notably to the fact that he was no longer captain. That alone might have discouraged many, but that wasn't an emotion that Danny countenanced. He was rarely dismayed by any opposition, simply because he had the absolute conviction that he was right, that in the long run his ideas would be shown to be correct. If he was criticized for doing the unexpected, his answer would be along the lines of: 'If we don't know what we're going to do next, how will the other side?' If a manager complained that he spent too much time going forward, Danny would ask just how they proposed to win a match without scoring goals? He had an answer for everything, all delivered with a confidence that brooked no further argument. That could irritate those who didn't see the game the same way, but for the true believers, his views were liberating.

The omens for the new season weren't great, in spite of their third place the previous year. Danny had not been the only man at Spurs exhausted by the demands of Sweden. New signing Terry Medwin had played for Wales, as had Cliff Jones, although his need of a rest was soon catered for, in the most disappointing fashion. Ron Reynolds remembers that, 'We were training at Cheshunt and we finished up with a match, first-team forwards and reserve defence versus reserve forwards and first-team defence. We'd been playing a few moments when Cliff Jones was caught in a tackle and broke his leg. The same day, I was taking the car out of the garage. We had a steep drive and as I got out, the car started rolling so I jumped in to put the handbrake on and there was a helluva bang. I was still holding the car door and it had smashed into the pillar of the garage and guillotined the end of my finger off. So we lost two players in a matter of hours!'

If that was an inauspicious start to the new term, things got little better for Danny, once it was revealed that he'd be writing for a national rather than a local newspaper in future. George Robb points out that, 'There was no actual bar on writing an article – I did one for the *Evening Standard* – but Danny liked to put his views across. He expected the article to be his views, not those of the editor.' The fact that Danny would have a national audience caused alarm bells to ring in the corridors of power at White Hart Lane, as directors and management began to fret that he might use this new position to expose any problems that flared up at the club. He was summoned to a board meeting to explain his position, an indignity for which he never forgave the directors (Danny was a free man, not just number four). Little wonder that a few weeks later he mounted the following assault on directors in general, with regard to transfer policy: 'Usually some soccer-confused director, drunk with the power of his club's wealth, is determined to spend it somehow ... money can buy success, though it doesn't always do so. Newcastle have thrown a lot of money around and achieved certain successes in recent years but a lot of their buying has been unwise [no change there] ... Bristol Rovers have paid out about £100,000 in recent years on improving their ground facilities. They seem to know how to use their wealth.' Given that Bristol Rovers left Eastville some time ago, time has scarcely been kind to this comment, but in principle, Danny's view was sound. Prior to the Taylor Report and the wholesale sprucing up of our stadia that has ensued, how many grounds were in a state of terrible disrepair, club directors complaining of a lack of funds for improvements while simultaneously wasting fortunes on mediocre signings?

On the field, Tottenham began to struggle almost at once. Writing in the *Mail*, Danny tried to find humour in the situation, conducting an interview with himself about Spurs' decline: ' "You should worry," the troubled face in the mirror whined. "My football manager doesn't like the way I write and my sports editor isn't too satisfied with the way I'm playing football!" ' The loss of Cliff Jones was a terrible blow to their ambitions, and with eleven games gone they'd managed just three wins. The strain finally told on Jimmy Anderson and he left his job, ostensibly for health reasons, though as Ron Reynolds believes, it was more a case of jumping before the shove came: 'Jimmy never had any opportunity to last as a manager because everybody saw through him. Anderson never did anything with training, because he let Bill Nicholson take it, but he also brought in Jesse Carver, who'd been coaching in Italy for a few years, and it became farcical. He introduced a scheme whereby for several weeks he invited ordinary schoolboys from a local school to train with us, and we'd finish up with the youngsters in amongst us in five-a-sides, which was ludicrous. On one occasion I got a real kick on the shin from one of the kids – you couldn't blame them, they were just so enthusiastic – and I had this great egg come up on my shin right away. Basically, Bill was the coach and it was becoming more obvious that he'd have to take over and rectify a bad situation. Bill was a very good coach and he soon returned to the methods Arthur Rowe had used.'

Naturally there was some lingering sadness that Anderson's fifty-year association with Tottenham had come to a close, but Danny wasn't hypocritical enough to shed crocodile tears. He recognized that a new, and hopefully more invigorating and open-minded era was beginning. He accepted that 'Jimmy was a great scout, but there's a vast difference between spotting good players and being able to handle them. He was very unsure of the new tactics I brought back from Sweden. He even told the others to ignore them. I kept wanting to go up for corners and Jimmy kept ordering me back. In one match Tommy Harmer was taking a throw-in in front of the directors' box. I told him to throw it to me so I could volley it. I did. Straight into the box. Jimmy was furious. He screamed, "Why did you do that?" "It was safe," I replied.'

Having returned from the World Cup bursting with new ideas, new tactics, new thoughts on the game, to be hidebound by Anderson's trust in time-honoured conventions was too much for Danny to endure. Now, working under Bill Nicholson, a member of Arthur Rowe's push and run Championship side, Danny hoped that he might have a more receptive audience.

Initially, those hopes were to be dashed, in spite of an amazing 10–4 win over Everton in Nicholson's first game in charge (leaving the field, Danny told Nicholson, 'It's all downhill from here', while Tommy Harmer added, 'We don't do this every week, you know.'). But Nicholson wasn't fooled by that victory, nor a 4–3 win at Leicester, and he was right to be sceptical. Impressive going forward, Tottenham leaked goals with regularity and managed just one more win in the next eleven games, being beaten 2–1 and 4–1 on successive days by West Ham over Christmas to leave them in deep trouble at the bottom of the First Division. Danny had not been in vintage form, as a game for Northern Ireland at Hampden Park illustrated. Bertie Peacock, Danny's half-back partner, recalls, 'Danny was directly opposed to Denis Law. I don't know whether they told him to smother Danny or not but that's what he was doing that day – Denis was quick, hard, whiplash, he had that extra yard on Danny and Danny was kept dormant. We came in at half-time and Peter and Danny decided, "Right, we'll go down the left today and let Danny keep Denis busy." From 2–0 we got back to 2–2 and hit the bar with the last kick of the game.' Even with Danny in poor form, such was his reputation that opponents didn't dare leave him to his own devices, and he was still able to change the course of a game with his tactical appreciation. These were rare qualities in any player. How could any manager leave him out?

Bill Nicholson was still unsure where the team was going and needed them to turn the corner quickly. With another game with West Ham looming, this time in the Cup, he felt drastic action was required. Prior to Blackburn's visit to Tottenham on 3 January, Nicholson told Danny he would not be in the team. Coming at a time when rumours were rife that Danny was contemplating retirement at the end of the season, it added up to a dispiriting start to 1959. Nicholson noted that, 'Danny was a culprit in that bad run, taking too many liberties. He was an expensive luxury in a poor side.' Danny 'thought that was funny. It's the bad players in a bad team who are the luxury. It's fancy talk, a smart contradiction. The poorest of families needs some luxury, it gives them hope.' Bertie Peacock doesn't subscribe to the idea that he was a luxury either: 'He could defend – he was essentially an attacker with tremendous vision, but he wanted to be successful so he knew the value of a strong defence. He was essentially a flair player, but he could tackle too. I suppose he could give you a problem at the back sometimes – say the opposition had a corner kick, as the ball was coming over, Danny would read the situation, he'd say to himself, "That should be the goalkeeper's ball", and be on his way out to collect that ball thirty or forty yards out on the right.'

Nicholson was defiant in his determination to shore up the defence. With the younger Jim Iley now installed at left-half, Spurs had two wing-halves with attacking instincts, not the balance he was looking for, and so Danny was sacrificed. Trying not to close the door on Blanchflower, Nicholson suggested that he play at inside-right in the reserves with a view to coming back and filling that position in the first team, displacing Tommy Harmer. Danny's reaction was simple: 'I told him I had all that experience at wing-half and it was too late to change position. I suggested he might want to transfer me. He did not hesitate, he was definitely against that and would not agree to it if I put in a request.' With that, Danny knew that he still had a future at the club, though when Spurs won their next four game without him, he might have had his doubts. The transformation was a brief one, however, and they were thumped by Arsenal and Manchester United and held by Norwich in the Cup at home. By demoting Danny, Spurs had lost much of their ability to surprise opponents, had lost their mainspring on the field, and were little more secure at the back. Danny had to be restored to the side whatever the defensive implications, though Bill Nicholson argued, persuasively, that, 'After my prodding on the point, he became a better defensive player. When a move broke down, he had to be a defender along with the others.' To reinforce the point that Nicholson was the manager, Danny's first two games were at inside-forward, but that didn't last long. After a 4–4 draw with Portsmouth, he was returned to his rightful position at right-half.

That brief break from the first team rejuvenated Danny, restored his energetic enthusiasm. He'd admitted that that preseason had been tough after the thrills of Sweden, and that much of the season was anti-climactic in its wake. Not only had he found it hard to commit himself emotionally to the side, he must have been running out of steam physically. Although he was always supremely fit, at thirty-three, the effort of playing football at the top level almost non-stop for fifteen months would have taken its toll. Although he played for the reserves, these games were a virtual stroll for a man of his quality and he was able to regroup, restore his energy for the first-team fixtures ahead. Cliff Jones was delighted to see Danny back in the team, having only recently returned from injury himself: 'We were struggling and Danny always wanted to play football, and I think Bill Nicholson felt something more straightforward was needed to get us out of trouble. But if you've got Danny at the club, you've got to play him, and Bill soon recognized that. He was so good for us, always wanted the ball, wasn't afraid to make changes, wanted responsibility. He was such a good talker that he bridged the gap between the dressing room and the boardroom because he could talk to anyone at any level. Bill and Danny were a good partnership, he took Bill's ideas on to the field. We all had so much respect for Bill, he knew so much about the game, he worked harder than anyone else, though perhaps he did lack a bit of personality, which is what Danny had.'

Within a couple of games Nicholson fully appreciated what a gem he had in Blanchflower, that here was a man who could help drive his team. At the beginning of March Spurs travelled to Wolverhampton. Danny wrote that Bill 'hustled us into a private room in the hotel to announce the team and give us a talk. Then he said that he was making me the permanent club captain and that the players should all respect my position. The party started then.' It was a big admission for Nicholson to make, but it was an intelligent one which confirmed his credentials as a forward-looking coach-cum-manager, Bertie Peacock agreeing that 'Bill understood Danny and got the very best out of him'. Bill Nicholson was one of the first tracksuit managers, one who liked to get among his players on the training field and one who instilled his values and ideas into them by demonstration rather than by spouting incomprehensible theory at them. If Nicholson had a fault, it was that he was a typically dour, taciturn Yorkshireman, and needed the presence of someone like Danny as a right-hand man; Nicholson could instruct, teach and advise, whereas Danny could lead, inspire and improvise. The two provided an ideal foil for one another.

As Danny said, 'the party started' at Molineux with a 1–1 draw. Spurs picked up the pace and won three of the next four games to dispel the spectre of relegation. There was still much to be done, however, if Spurs were to progress. Nicholson had dropped Danny because he felt the half-back pairing of himself and Iley did not provide the requisite checks and balances. With Danny installed as the creative centre of the team, it was Iley who now had to lose out. A replacement was sought and when Wales's Mel Charles chose Arsenal ahead of Spurs, Nicholson looked towards Scotland. Hearts had surprisingly agreed to sell their star half-back, Dave Mackay, the man who had become the linchpin of the Scottish international side and, despite the fact that he was slightly hampered by a foot injury, Nicholson had no hesitation in taking him to London. He managed just four of the eight games left that season, but it was obvious from the outset that in

Mackay, Danny had the perfect partner, a player who would release him to go into attack whenever he chose, secure in the knowledge that behind him stood the footballing equivalent of a Sherman tank. George Robb feels that 'Danny didn't really fit into the Bill Nick mould as a right-half. Bill was a good player but he was hard, he went into the tackle, so there was a difference there. But finally Bill saw the value of Danny in a good side. I think that was the reason for bringing in Dave Mackay, because the two of them together were a great partnership. Mackay was exactly what you needed alongside Danny: dour, hard, a worker. Danny was the rapier as opposed to the bludgeon.' Interestingly, Dave Mackay was also the most blatant visual representation of the other side of Danny's own personality. Danny was always viewed as the great romantic, the lover of the beautiful game who wanted to see free-flowing, exciting football and, of course, that was all true. But he had just as much steel as Mackay, just as great a determination to win. Where Danny was so unusual was in his conviction that beautiful football could have its reward, a theory that was alien to most managers. Even so, he accepted that a team needed a man like Mackay who would liberate the 'artists', allowing them to play.

With 1958–59 over, Danny could look back on a season where he'd returned from the point of oblivion to grasp the position he'd always wanted, the club's captain, with the freedom to discharge that responsibility as he saw fit. Further recognition came when he acted as player-manager for Northern Ireland in April 1959 against Wales in a 4–1 win that Peter Doherty couldn't get away from his club for.

Telling the tale of any career, it's easy to over-dramatize certain moments as turning points, but in Danny's case it's hard to underestimate the importance of that chat he had had with Bill Nicholson when he initially asked for a transfer. Once Nicholson turned him down, Danny was confident that the changes that Nicholson was making were merely temporary, the experiments made by any new manager in search of a pattern. From the moment that he was told he must remain a Spurs footballer, Danny became convinced that his dream of taking Spurs to the Double was on once more. Nicholson treated Danny as an equal rather than a nuisance, listening intently to the ideas he had brought back from Sweden, implementing some, discarding others. Nicholson had plenty of ideas of his own too; he had worked with Walter Winter-bottom with the England squad and learned a great deal from him. Between the two of them, they turned the Spurs training ground into a melting pot for new tactics, new practice routines, new formations of play. For example, on the training ground, Cliff Jones was given licence to roam as he chose, sometimes appearing on the right, at others on the left. Free-kick routines were tried, polished and perfected. There was some experimenta-tion as to formations, the centre-half becoming more of a centre-back, or Danny trying some interplay so that he would finish ahead of his inside- and outside-right. No ideas were considered too outlandish to try, and if they didn't work they would move on to something else that might. More than anything else, they tried to employ the same patterns of possession football that the Brazilians and Hungarians had done. One football writer of the time, Ralph Finn, noted in his book *Spurs Go Marching On* that 'the ball goes from full-back to half-back to inside-forward, back to the full-back, out to the winger, back again to the full-back, inside to the half, forward to the inside-forward, it shuttles back and forth until the opening is made. The ball is always worked from one position to another. Players move around taking up places where it is safe to receive a pass. Patterns of incredible complication are drawn on the field of play by the moving ball and the darting players.' Such confident use of the ball came from long practice sessions where the basics of movement were mastered. Finn went on to say, 'It is foreign soccer that Spurs play. It owes a lot to the great Hungarians, not a little to the typical Scottish style of clever ball-players, something of its defens-ive strength to the Italians, much of its interplay and pattern-weaving to the South Americans.'

An integral part of Spurs' evolution was a close season tour to Russia. They played three games before huge crowds but the players were upset by having little to do in their free time and by the poor food and accommodation they encountered on the trip. They visited the circus, ballet, even the Mausoleum to see Lenin and Stalin lying in state, their immobility reminding the players of certain statuesque First Division defenders. Perhaps Nicholson had led them behind the Iron Curtain deliberately in the hope that such comparative adversity would bond the side; if that was the case, it was a stroke of genius, for Tottenham returned home with a team spirit which was second to none. Given the high level of skill and steel in every department of the game, this determination to work hard for one another on the field was the final ingredient which turned them from a decent side into one that could genuinely vie for the title. 'Looking back,' Cliff Jones believes, 'you could see that team starting to come together there, it was a really important time', while Bill Nicholson couldn't 'overstate the value of the trip in terms of getting things together'. In terms of the actual method of play, Nicholson made one crucial change – Maurice Norman moved to centre-half, giving further ballast to the half-back line alongside Danny and allowing Peter Baker to come in at full-back. Ron Reynolds believes that change, along with the acquisition of Mackay, 'permitted Danny to become a truly great player. Now he had the freedom to move around, look for space, support the forwards, prompt from the midfield, because Dave Mackay, the cruncher, wouldn't let anybody get past! Up to then, he still tried to express himself, but there wasn't the strength behind him – it was a transition period under a very weak manager. Although Bill was very dour, and for me, not a very good man manager, he and Danny formed a super team because Bill built everything around Danny.' It was important to flatter Danny in that manner, giving him the confidence to look ahead. His ego was a powerful motivating force in his life, illustrated by his driving around London in a Sunbeam Rapier with the personalized plate, 428BLF. He might have been a private man – as he proved when turning down *This Is Your Life* – but he still wanted people to know who he was.

Ron Reynolds was one of the only Spurs players to have any complaints about the outcome of that Russian tour: 'I'd not got back in the team after my finger injury in the close season, but Bill had told me in March 1959 that he was taking me to Russia in June as first-team goalkeeper, that I'd play two games of three, but not to say anything to anyone. We went there, Johnny Hollowbread played the first game against Torpedo, which we won, and then I played against Dynamo Kiev, where we won 2–1. Bill was pleased with me, then we played the national Olympic side at midnight in Leningrad, losing 3–1, and Bill again congratulated me on my performance. Danny was thrilled because we were good friends and it had gone so well in my first games for the first team in a year. We got back home and I went off on holiday, bought a newspaper and found we'd bought Bill Brown! I went to see Bill about it and he tried to put the onus on the board, saying they'd insisted, it wasn't his decision. I left at the first opportunity after that to go to Southampton, the following spring. I asked Danny for his advice on the move and he had no hesitation, he told me that I should go.'

The pre-season for 1959–60 promised to be a crucial one. This was the first full year where Nicholson was in charge with Danny beside him. From the off, things were very different from the way they'd been in the Anderson era. Nicholson insists, 'When I took over as manager, I introduced the best training schedules which any club had, the sort of organized training which all clubs brought in in the 1960s and 1970s. Danny once asked if I didn't think we were doing too much' – a question unheard at any of his other clubs. In that summer, the Spurs players worked for four or five hours a day, mixing cross-country runs with road walks, five-a-side games, practice matches and ball work. There were set pieces *ad infinitum* and endless repetition of a variety of moves, a discipline which Danny was to take with him to Chelsea in later years. Essentially, Nicholson was looking for the next stage of push and run, creating a team where there would always be a man looking for the ball, available in space to take a pass. Walter Winterbottom notes that, 'Tottenham were the best exponents of push and run which suited Danny's skills and his intelligence. He would always look for the ball, offering himself to whoever was in possession. I used to get cross with Jimmy Greaves because he'd sometimes hide if things weren't going well, which was wrong. No one could use the ball better than Jimmy when he had it and so I always wanted him to show himself to pick up possession. Danny never hid. However he was playing, he always wanted the ball, he was always looking to more than fulfil his potential.' Rightly, Nicholson concluded that the more people you had in space waiting for the ball, the more difficulties you could pose for an opposition unsure as to where it would be moved to next – this was the basic plan which Liverpool refined to give them their dominance of the 1970s and 1980s, going from push and run on to pass and move.

Dave Mackay noted in Ken Ferris's *The Double* that, 'Bill had us working overtime developing this kind of play. It was hard drill, but our manager kept it so interesting that no one lost concentration. And as we began to perfect this technique, interest developed into enthusiasm. We could hardly wait for the start of the season.' Fine coach though Nicholson was, his man-management problems were always in the background. Ron Reynolds recalls one bizarre confrontation with the manager during pre-season training: 'We'd done our leg work, had a break and were away to do ball work. Having bought Bill Brown to replace me, Bill Nicholson came to me and said, "Ron, in the practice games, Bill's flapping, he's not catching the crosses. For the next half-hour, take him with you, go to the far goal and coach him on how to catch crosses." I couldn't believe it! To compound that, a couple of days before the first match of the season, Bill Nicholson called me and Johnny Hollowbread, the other goal-keeper, into the office. He said, "You know the situation: Bill's the first-team goalkeeper and you two are in the reserves. I don't want to have to select which one plays, so you'll play alternately, and you can pick and choose between you. I don't care how you arrange it, you do what you like." That was diabolical because he lost our respect – if Bill Brown had got injured, one of us would have had to replace him. So Danny was crucial as captain because this wasn't the only example of that type of management. I think he initially helped to keep the peace, and then I think he was a good motivator on the field. The respect I had for him was head and shoulders above any other player.'

Danny's importance to the team grew as the season unfolded. Bill Nicholson put much of his effort into pre-season training, putting away the tactics board once they kicked off the first game. His reasoning was that they were sufficiently well drilled through-out July and early August in what they were expected to do that they didn't need to be told again. From the first game to the last, Spurs had their own plan of campaign and all that would alter that was the opposition. As Dave Mackay explained in Ferris's book, 'It's important that a team does not take the field with preconceived plans, for there is always the opposition to be borne in mind. This was a point we at Tottenham understood, so the moves we worked out were not part of a plan. The moves we developed became automatic, and fitted into the pattern of any game, and in no way did we allow ourselves to be mastered by tactical plans.' The most successful sides have long been those who have good technique but who can improvise, play off-the-cuff passes, do the unexpected. Danny Blanchflower was the instigator of much of Spurs' electrifying spontaneity, as well as being the key tactician through each match. Maurice Norman points out that 'Danny would talk the hind legs off a donkey, but you had to listen because he was such an outstanding personality. He knew what he wanted and he got it from us, everything we had to give. The tactics often came from Danny, he was full of it, and he'd keep us going in training, practising and practising to get things right. When we got on the field, Danny was the boss, we looked to him to run the game.'

Finally working with a responsive manager at club level, Danny's captaincy was phenomenal. The players clearly had the very greatest respect for Danny, and Bill Nicholson had the good sense to make the maximum use of that. It was a risky move because it takes a very brave, as well as intelligent, manager to delegate so much responsibility to a mere player. Jimmy Anderson and Eric Houghton had not had that courage in the past, but Nicholson believed in Danny every bit as much as Maurice Norman did and resolved to get the very best out of him. This was the watershed in Danny's career, but it was one that perhaps could not have come any sooner, being a function of his age and the prevailing climate at the time, one of great social and cultural change. When Danny was at Barnsley or Aston Villa, England was still in the grip of post-war austerity and the codes and values of the 1930s dictated every aspect of life. The old pros were men who'd come back from the war, some from actual combat, hard men who knew their own minds. To them, Danny was just some whipper-snapper, and a foreign one at that, trying to tell his elders and betters how to play the game they'd made a living from for many years. That sort of thing was just not done in 1952. Youngsters didn't offer opinions, they were told what to do and expected to do it without thought or question.

At Tottenham, the situation was completely reversed. In Bill Nicholson's rebuilt side, Danny was the elder statesman, the senior professional and club captain. Nicholson had given him virtual *carte blanche* to run the show on the field and had ordered the players – not that orders were necessary – to respect Danny's authority as their skipper. For comparatively inexperienced players making their way in the game, players like Maurice Norman and Cliff Jones, Danny was a fountain of wisdom. Not only did he demand respect by virtue of his seniority, he commanded it by personality, Cliff Jones explaining that, 'He was a lovely person to have around. He was a bit distanced from the players because he didn't smoke or drink, but we were all comfortable with that and it helped establish his authority. We all loved him, he was just a great personality, making the boys laugh. I used to throw small coins in the air, catch them on my foot, flick it on to my head and then head it into my pocket. I tried to get Danny to do it, but he just said, "When you can do it with a ball and a coin at the same time, then come and see me." As a youngster, I learnt my trade in Swansea as a ship's plumber, and he'd say, "You're a plumber, who's the God of water?" When I didn't know, he'd say "You call yourself a bloody plumber and you don't know that, and your trade's all about water! Tom Finney, he's the peerless plumber, but Jonesy, you're the bloody clueless plumber!" It was just lovely to be in the dressing room or a hotel with him.' Danny was fortunate to gain respect from his seniority and his personality, but alone, that would not necessarily have garnered interest in the new ideas he put forward. If the early 1950s were still a time of music hall, the late '50s was the age of Elvis. Danny was now playing alongside players from the rock 'n' roll generation, players who weren't restricted by convention but were willing to question everything that had gone before. In another age, Danny's iconoclastic approach would not have been acceptable. Post *Rebel Without A Cause*, rebellion was all the rage.

Danny *was* a rebel of sorts, perhaps the most effective sort, a smiling guerrilla fighter, insidiously working his ideas into the heart of the machine. So deftly did he make his changes, they'd often been put into operation before anyone could do anything about it, causing Bill Nicholson the occasional headache. Nicholson admitted later that, 'Danny always felt that making changes on the field was a captain's responsibility and it took two long meetings lasting more than an hour each before he would finally accept the job again after that first game at Wolverhampton. I told him we had probably the best players in the country in each position. That was a hell of a team, so why change them round? Danny saw this but I told him that if a switch needed to be made in a death-or-glory game I would leave it to him. He would do the sound, common-sense thing. He was very shrewd.' Danny's brief was not just to implement changes of that nature but to act as the pulse of the side, switching the rhythm according to the problems posed by the opposition, keeping each individual focused on their job, calming some, inspiring others.

Pretty soon, Danny was surpassing even the form he'd shown when named Footballer of the Year in 1957–58, yet it wasn't merely his precise distribution that garnered the plaudits. Opponents soon saw the difference in his game. Derek Dougan recalls: 'When I got into the Northern Ireland side and then went to Sweden, I was a very young man, and at that stage you don't really appreciate the intelligence of someone like Danny. I'd played against him at Spurs for Portsmouth when he was an inside-forward in the reserves and, as a youngster, I just felt, Oh well, Danny's too old now. Then Spurs bought Dave Mackay and Bill Brown and that transformed his career – they were the players he needed around him. Danny wasn't a quick player, even less so as he got older, but his mind was so fast. Virtually every ball that Bill got in goal, it'd be straight out to Danny, because in the time it had taken Bill to gather it, Danny would have created six or seven yards of space for himself by stepping away from the opposition. Immediately, Danny would be away to set up another move. He was what you'd now call their playmaker.'

It was obvious as soon as the season began that Tottenham were on the verge of greater things, losing just one of the first fifteen games. But, as Bill Nicholson realized, no team was perfect, there was always room for improvement. In October Danny played for Northern Ireland against the Scots. On his return Nicholson asked him for his opinion on one of their players, John White, Falkirk's inside-forward.

'First class. Good positional sense, and smooth ball control,' came the reply.

'I can get him for £20,000,' said Bill.

'Don't miss the first plane,' Danny told him.

That was typical of the relationship between the two, one based on solid mutual trust of each other's footballing instincts. 'We would talk over players,' admitted Nicholson. 'Danny would advise me about their mood. He might say that certain ideas of mine might not be well received. He was my listening post.' As Cliff Jones has pointed out, Danny was the bridge between the two factions of management and players, ensuring that no unhealthy 'us and them' situation could fester. He always tried to do the right thing for the players, whether he agreed with it or not, something which inevitably enhanced his popularity among them. On the subject of FA Cup Final tickets, for example, he wrote, 'I didn't feel it was right for players to be given a lot of tickets for the Cup Final, but although I didn't ask for them I had to remember that the players were not fairly paid in my time. All they received was £20 a week. As captain I had to put their views and mine to the manager. I felt that by asking for too many they would be encouraging greed and corruption. But I also had the responsibility to see that they were not worse off than any other team in the same circumstances.'

Prior to the season, Danny had started to discuss the prospect of the Double quite openly around the training ground, and such was Spurs' League form it looked a possibility. A firm believer in positive psychology, Danny noted, 'To do the Double we agreed that we all had to believe in it. We must create the right atmosphere. Bernard Joy of the *Evening Standard* quoted me on it so that it might seem a distinct possibility to everyone else.' Once Crewe were dispatched 13–2 in front of 64,365 spectators in the fourth round of the Cup, the talk began to intensify, but it was soon dashed by Blackburn Rovers, who won a tough fifth-round match in London 3–1. That was a grave disappointment, but there remained an excellent chance of taking the League title. Entering the final fortnight of the season, Burnley and Tottenham both had 49 points, Burnley a game in hand. Two points further back lay Wolves. At home to Manchester City, a win was essential. On the stroke of half-time Tottenham got a penalty. Cliff Jones struck it, Trautmann made a diving save but the rebound fell to Jones who knocked it into the net. 1–0, Spurs on the way to the title. Yet referee Gilbert Pullen disallowed the goal. He had extended the half to allow the penalty to be taken and time had therefore expired immediately it was saved. No goal. As the crowd bayed for the referee's summary execution, Danny waved away his players, put his hands on the referee's shoulders and demanded an explanation. Once the referee had satisfied him, Danny led the players from the field. Naturally deflated, Spurs couldn't put things together in the second period and went down by a goal to nil. Two days later, they went to Stamford Bridge and lost by the same score.

A season that had promised so much ended in failure, but

Danny was surprisingly upbeat about it all, accepting that Spurs had not been the dominant force they could have been, that they were still developing and noting that 'fate was testing us to prove we were good Champions rather than lucky ones'. Equally, it was no time to slide into despondency, for Tottenham still had to go to Molineux, to face the League leaders. 56,283 people were crammed into the ground for a match that could have crowned Wolves as Champions. An hour before kick-off Danny led the Spurs players on to the field, and for ten minutes, as the crowd booed, he lectured them about the game that faced them and his expectations of them, gesturing around the ground to empha-size his thoughts. Spurs tore into Wolves and dismissed them 3–1 to hand the initiative to Burnley, who took full advantage and clinched the title. Danny was delighted to beat a team that excelled in the typically English long ball, physical style and wrote, 'We made Wolves look old-fashioned that day and taught them that we were the new masters.' In view of all the great matches that were to come over the following few years, it seems odd to describe that game at Molineux as the most important that Tottenham Hotspur have ever played, but that was surely the case. Had Wolves won, the title would have been theirs, as would the Double – they took the FA Cup a few weeks later. Danny's great dream would have died. The absolute determination with which he approached that match, the calculating way in which he inspired Nicholson's flagging team at a time when others would have simply folded, was evidence that here was a visionary with the steel in his character to turn dreams into reality.

Not an especially superstitious character, Danny did enjoy the existence of good omens and used them as proof positive that Spurs were on the brink of their destiny. Like a Chinese New Year, any year that ends in '1' is supposed to be 'the year of the Spurs' – they had won the Cup in 1901 and 1921, and 1951 gave them their first League Championship. This, allied to their improving form of the previous season, seemed to indicate that 1960–61 would be a very good year indeed. Danny was so obsessed with the prospect that he told chairman Fred Bearman that this would be the year Tottenham would do the Double. The idea of the League and Cup Double was one that had preoccupied Eng-lish football for many years. Preston and Aston Villa had managed the feat in the nineteenth century, when the competition was far less intense, but so far as the twentieth century went, the Double seemed an unattainable goal. It had started to interest Danny as far back as 1954 when West Bromwich Albion were on the brink, Danny writing in the *Birmingham Evening Mail*, 'I hope the Albion can do the Double. It is a great thing to achieve and I think it's good for the game that it should be achieved.' Indeed, throughout the 1950s and on into the 1960s, the Double always seemed to be coming: Albion were denied the League by four points, having led much of the way in 1954; in 1957 Manchester United took the League but lost the Cup Final after goalkeeper Ray Wood was injured and were then denied further opportunities by the Munich disaster; and, of course, Wolves fell just a point short in 1960. Depending on your side of the 'half empty/half full' debate, this was either proof that the Double could not be done, or that it was simply a matter of time before it was. For Danny, the glass was always half full.

There was little change to Spurs' preparation for what became a momentous season. As Cliff Jones explains, 'Bill took training and that's where he was so great, in his organization. Plenty of ball work, always emphasizing that you play the way you train – if you use a method, put in the effort, that will carry on to the field. It was always good habits, very simple.' Even Bill Nicholson was infected with the idea of breaking new ground that season, though naturally he played the idea down. It was left to Danny to instil the idea that they were in search of history, Jones recalling, 'Danny was the first one to talk about the Double in that season, particularly after we'd had such a great start. He definitely thought it was on.' That great start covered eleven straight wins – a First Division record – sixteen matches without defeat, one loss in the first twenty-five games, which embraced twenty-two wins. By the end of 1960, Tottenham had forty-six points. Given that Burnley won the League the year before with a total of fifty-five points, it's little wonder that Cliff Jones felt, 'It was virtually over by Christmas, we'd have had to play badly to have lost it and with Danny, Bill and Dave Mackay at the club, that wasn't going to happen.' Ron Reynolds believes that much of the credit for that barnstorming start must go to Danny: 'He had a brilliant mind, there was no situation that could overwhelm him. He could assess things in a second that others hadn't seen until it was too late. He was playing backheels through his legs into the path of the forwards, switching the game, opening up the pitch in a way that very few others could. Recently, Eric Cantona was like him in that respect, more vision than a dozen other players put together (Cantona's influence on United's Double team in 1995–96 was similar to Danny's at Spurs, in a similar set-up. Cantona had Keane behind him where Danny had Dave Mackay, who was hard as nails – we used to say if Dave had played against his grandmother, he'd have kicked her to death!).'

Throughout those first twenty-five games, Tottenham had been virtually irresistible, a force of nature. Cliff Jones feels that, 'Dave, Danny and John White were the engine room, the rest of us sparked off them. Danny and Dave were totally different personalities but both loved Tottenham and both were winners. We were all good mates, and that helps you work for each other on the field. That comes down to good management and captaincy. Danny was good at dead-ball situations, corners, free-kicks, throw-ins – lots of variety, new ideas all the time, he used to work so hard at that. There was no getting a free-kick on the edge of the box and just whacking it and hoping it might go in, he'd want us to get behind their wall, changing the angles, bringing players into the game. He was instrumental in that. He'd say for dead balls: "The hardest thing in the game is to get the ball. Now we've got it. Let's keep it, let's use it." We had a lot of success from set pieces.'

With the League almost in the bag, the focus switched to the FA Cup. It's a myth to say that concentrating on one trophy must help a team succeed. In Spurs' case, six matches were all that stood between them and history, and as Maurice Norman concedes, 'There was terrible pressure on the Cup ties because we knew what it meant. In the League we were really going through the motions waiting for the Cup games to come round.' Charlton and Crewe were brushed aside in the early rounds, with Aston Villa drawn as their opponents in the fifth round. A League fixture meant that Spurs would be visiting Villa Park twice in a week. The League game provided Spurs with the key to the Cup game, Villa manager Joe Mercer revealing his tactical plans a week too early. To his credit, he had succeeded in shackling Spurs early on, marking Danny especially tightly. When the team came in at half-time, Danny noted that 'some of our players would not pass the ball to me. I took my shadow back into his own defence and advised John White to exploit the space I had left. I told them that Villa didn't want me to have the ball. "You're doing their job for them! The solution is push and run, isn't it? We're supposed to be good at that, aren't we? Give it to me and run forward, and I'll knock it straight to you and then you go on with it." We beat them 2–1.' A week later, Spurs played out a comfortable 2–0 win in the Cup to advance into the last eight.

Watching Spurs that year was to experience real footballing beauty. The team was dissected and subjected to lengthy analysis, but there seemed no way to counter them. The *Daily Mail* provided this anatomy of success, which was as good a basic explanation of how they operated as any:

1 – The build-up of pressure incorporates unorthodox moves.
2 – All-round ability of every player.
3 – Supreme confidence bordering on cockiness.
4 – Ability to vary game.
5 – Failure of teams to smother attack or overwhelm defence.
6 – Uncanny positional sense of Blanchflower, White & Mackay.

To that, Bill Nicholson added, 'The intense pressure must come in spells and they are intelligent enough to know when just such a spell is on. During it, or them, they should score enough goals to win.'

The only thing missing from that recipe was perhaps the most vital ingredient – Danny Blanchflower's captaincy. Without that, the Cup might have been elusive once more. Remember that Spurs had never been to Wembley and so they weren't only pursuing the Double, they were trying to lay a thirty-eight year hoodoo. Sunderland at Roker Park provided their sixth-round hurdle. The Roker Roar is now no more, but back in 1961 it was still a fearsome prospect, the more so when their incentive was to be the Second Division side that stopped the 'southern softies' winning the Double. Danny wrote in his autobiography, 'I have never seen such excitement, anywhere, as I did that day at Roker Park.' Spurs took control and were one ahead at the break. Then 'Sunderland forced a corner – and all hell broke loose behind our goalmouth. That great Roker crowd, starved of glory for so long, could not contain itself. A corner ... the possibility ... the equalizer ... you could feel the tension behind that goal. They shouted and whistled and screamed and fainted with expectancy. The noise was unbearable; I could not feel my senses or clear my thoughts or concentrate properly because of the shrieking din ... that great ear-splitting emotional roar was hammering at, and looked like cracking, the invisible links of our defence. It was chewing away at the bonds of confidence between us, and choking the words of encouragement and the shouts of understanding with which we rally one another. The ball flighted over and there was a wild scramble. Confusion and then the ball was scrambled behind for another corner. Over came the ball – another corner. The pandemonium increased. Over it came again and in the frothing panic, it was smashed into the net.'

The Sunderland crowd burst on to the field 'like mad Hindus waving their arms to the glory of Allah for the equalizer'. As the pitch was finally cleared of intruders, Danny called the team together. 'Now keep your heads and let's get going after a goal. We don't want that business down in our goalmouth again.' The game was drawn, Sunderland thrashed 5–1 in the replay. Cliff Jones asks, 'How many captains do you see nowadays? Danny could see things and change them. You need that on the field. Players are usually wrapped up in their own game – for myself, it was, "Give me the ball, I'll get on with it", which is the same with most players. Danny was concerned with the whole team, and that's a big difference. Bill Nick used to say the best and easiest thing was to play, the hardest thing was to manage, thinking about the players, directors, supporters, press, keeping them all happy. Danny played that role on the pitch on Bill's behalf and you don't get many players who're capable of that.' Maurice Norman agrees that Danny was 'one of the greatest captains you could wish for. He was intelligent and he had everything revolve around him, he was the hub, always in the thick of things, organizing everything.'

Tottenham were back at Villa Park for the semi-final against Burnley and after struggling in the early exchanges, Spurs gradually exerted their authority and clinched a place at Wembley with a 3–0 win. Having achieved that much, they returned to their League chores with renewed vigour and reeled off five straight victories to power to the title, going mathematically safe on 17 April when they defeated their closest rivals, Sheffield Wednesday. With three games to go, they had won their first Championship in ten years and had done so in the grand manner which Arthur Rowe had instituted a decade earlier. Danny had been the inspiration, pulling the strings, bringing everyone into the game. Cliff Jones remembers, 'That season I played at outside-right quite a lot. I used to love to have the ball and so did Danny, and I was playing in front of him. We'd been playing for half an hour in one game and he came up to me and said, "Do you realize that the ball's round?" I asked him what he meant and he said, "It's round so that it rolls so that you can pass the bloody thing!" It was a nice way of putting it, it was a nice way of getting players to do something a bit different.' For all that, Danny enjoyed working in tandem with Jones, as it allowed him to indulge in one of his party pieces: he'd bring the ball up the right, the ball at his left foot, then suddenly swing his right foot behind his left leg and knock the ball into the path of Jones. Danny explained that, 'It gives the fans a laugh. But who's noticed that switching the ball to my left foot brings the defender two yards off my winger? And hitting the ball in that daft way gives my winger an extra yard of space.'

All that was left was to win the FA Cup and the miracle would be completed. To be ninety minutes from immortality is a daunting prospect. The build-up for the big day was especially ferocious but Danny handled it with typical aplomb. Speaking to the press before the game, he made the following observations, which were so phlegmatic they'd now be regarded as Gullitisms: 'Where's the strain? We've won the League. Now there's only one game to play. It just happens to be the Cup Final. If we lose, it's only one game, after all, and the Double will be there as a challenge next year ... the Cup Final is all glitter and glamour – then the teams come out and spoil everything! There's a big crowd who've come to be entertained. Let's entertain them.' For all that glitter and glamour, there were still things which, quite rightly, grated: 'As captain of the team, I was given an official FA programme so that I could see how to lead my team out. There were a lot of pages of how arrangements had been made to entertain the various officials and a few lines, almost hidden away, as to how the teams would be received. One did not begrudge the officials their day out but one knew there were many injustices in their administration. The handling of Cup tickets, for instance. All those social climbers and gadabouts at Wembley on Cup Final day at the expense of the long-suffering supporters.'

To calm the side's nerves the team went off into the West End on the night before the match to see a late night screening of *The Guns Of Navarone*. Unusual preparation? Perhaps. But, as Danny said, 'I've never forgotten a story about Walter Hagen, the golfer. He was up late the night before an important play-off. Somebody said, "I suppose you know your opponent's in bed?" "Yes," said Hagen, "but do you think he's sleeping?"'

Waking the next morning, the side were refreshed and ready to take on Leicester City. This was a slightly worrying prospect since they were one of the few sides who had interrupted Tottenham's serene passage to the title, winning 3–2 at Filbert Street. Even so, a team who finished twenty-one points adrift of the all-conquering Spurs were generally considered mere sacrificial lambs. In the Tottenham camp, no such liberties were taken. The pre-match preparations were every bit as thorough as usual. Cliff Jones recalls, 'Bill took the team meeting and we listened – most footballers aren't great talkers, they just want to get on with the game, but when Bill finished he asked if anyone had anything to say and, as usual, Danny was there: "By the way, Bill . . ." and that was it for half an hour! He'd have been a natural on the after-dinner circuit now, the only trouble would have been getting him to stop!' Danny even made sure he got the better of the FA's guest, the Duchess of Kent. As she was presented to the teams 'she remarked to me that Leicester had their names on the tracksuits. I replied, "Yes, ma'am, but we all know one another."'

In spite of that relaxed attitude, Spurs played poorly. Paradoxically, they weren't helped by an early injury to Leicester's Chalmers, Cliff Jones noting that, 'Ten men always defend well. They don't usually win games but they make things much harder. They usually played an open game too, but at Wembley they shut the space down a lot more and made it hard for us to play. It wasn't a very good game, Danny and John White weren't really involved. Danny was thirty-five, which people forget. He was still at the top at a pretty advanced age, though I suppose Stan Matthews was still playing at about fifty, so perhaps people didn't notice Danny's age so much! But for older players, Wembley could be an exhausting pitch to play on.' Danny agreed that, 'I don't think we played particularly well but I think that was due to the conditions. Wembley is soft and luxurious and it slows up the ball sometimes. The trick is to know your own capabilities and to recognize a bad day when you see one, ride with it, take less chances.' As a result, the Wembley final was not the glorious spectacle that it might have been. Nonetheless, Spurs retained control and edged remorselessly towards their goal; with Bobby Smith and Terry Dyson on target, the fabled Double was theirs. Danny led his team to collect the Cup, but it was with a weary tread that he took them on their lap of honour, disappointed that Tottenham hadn't completed their wonderful year by playing with their customary verve and swagger. It wasn't until the following day, when Spurs took the spoils of their victories through the London streets past crowds that numbered hundreds of thousands, that he was finally satisfied: 'Here was the real glory . . . to me that was the day that summed the whole season up. A season of victory and crowds, a season for Tottenham Hotspur and football to remember.' Even so, there was still no real sense of euphoria. Reflecting on the season, Danny saw it more as just another job well done: 'I'm glad this has come in the twilight of my career. It's the right time for it. I feel sorry for the younger lads. The rest of their soccer lives must be an anti-climax. As for me, I haven't just got on a bus to get here. I think I deserve it. I've given the game all I had over the years.'

For all that the Double was a fantastic team achievement, that team including players, manager, club officials and fans alike, the embodiment of Tottenham's triumph was Danny Blanchflower, a fact recognized when, of all the great players on show at Spurs, Danny was the one selected as Footballer of the Year once more. The visionary who had chased the Double now had the chance to take his philosophy to the Continent once more, for there was yet more new ground to be broken. No English club had won a European trophy.

7 ... And Beyond

Achieving success is one thing but, as most clubs have found over the years, remaining at the pinnacle is another. Once you are proclaimed as the best team in the land, every other side takes a special pride in beating you, knocking you off the perch. If you've just landed the Double, then everybody's even more determined to wipe the smile off your face. To a degree, Spurs found themselves in that position at the beginning of the 1961–62 season. There can be little question that they were still the finest side in England, but having quenched the fires of their ambition so dramatically the previous year, what appetite remained for battle? And what of the strain on players now asked to compete on three fronts – the First Division, FA Cup and European Cup? Back in 1961, pan-European travel was not as easy nor as comfortable as it is today, particularly when travelling into the heart of Eastern Europe. That alone could take a massive toll on the players.

Surprisingly, given the workload that lay ahead, Danny chose not to take advantage of the summer break. Instead, he spent a couple of months in Canada, playing for Toronto City along with other great names such as Johnny Haynes and Stanley Matthews, who recalls that, 'At that time, you just needed the permission of your club to go out there and play in the close season – a couple of years later, you'd have had to have a proper transfer. So we took advantage of that while we could. The club was owned by Steve Stavro, he was the president of a supermarket chain out there and he wanted to field a good team in his city. It was all very exciting because it was such a dramatic change from what we'd been used to.' Given Canada's strong ties with England and their sizeable post-war influx of Italian immigrants, there seemed a ready-made market for football. The idea was to launch a professional league on the back of a four-team competition; there were to be three locally based teams, from Montreal, Hamilton and Toronto, plus a special guest team, Toronto City. Danny noted that, 'Our team was to be British at heart because it hoped to attract the ex-patriots.'

'There was no England trip that year,' Johnny Haynes recalls, 'so I agreed to go, and it was a lot of fun. The general standard of play was relaxed but very good, and it looked like catching on. The kids were very interested but after a couple of years it died out, as has happened quite often over there. It was exhausting because it meant we played right through the year and, of course, we had to do a lot of promotional things for the club, some coaching and so on. It was extremely tiring – Canada gets very hot in the summer – but it was very enjoyable, the football especially so because Danny was the captain of our side, and it was very interesting to work with him. He was a real thinker about the game, he always had plenty of ideas of his own and, in Canada, he didn't have to answer to a manager as much as he did in England. He had the freedom to experiment because we could please ourselves, really. Danny loved that!' Although the team was together for only ten weeks, Stanley Matthews, certainly the most experienced and perhaps the greatest of all English footballers, has no hesitation in saying, 'Danny was far and away the best captain I ever played with, a great leader and a great football mind.'

Danny returned home from his Canadian odyssey to a very different footballing culture. Following the strenuous efforts of the PFA, the maximum wage had finally fallen in early 1961 and the players were now in a position to negotiate their own contracts. Of course, when the clubs giveth, they also taketh, so although the players could now earn as much as their clubs were willing to pay them, the clubs demanded their pound of flesh in return, inserting a clause into player contracts that restricted their right to freedom of speech: 'Spurs offered me a wage of £3000 a year instead of the £20 a week I had received the season before,' wrote Danny. 'It was a fair rise but it was not such a big deal considering we had just won both the League and the FA Cup in one season and Johnny Haynes had been offered £5000 a year . . . I did not disagree the money terms but refused to sign the contract because of the restriction of speech clause. "It's not my idea," Bill Nicholson pleaded. "It is not mine either," I argued. "Why should I sign an agreement with you to please someone else?" Bill and I were on very good terms. We trusted and respected one another. Perhaps he sought legal advice on the matter because some days later I was given written permission [to speak freely]. That was not the end of the matter. Pressures were brought to bear on me. "What would you think if I fined you £5?" Bill said to me one day. "Not much. I don't know what it is I've done but if you're going to fine me then let's make it worthwhile – how about £500?" He had learned to be patient with my direct approach to delicate matters. "Forget it," he said. "It's just that we're having a bit of pressure from the League."'

After having curtailed his journalistic activities while Spurs were in pursuit of the Double, Danny was now back to his pungent, acerbic best, often writing for the *New Statesman* – a considerable departure for a professional footballer. Was it what Danny said or the way that he said it which caused such alarm? After many years where footballers had been portrayed as lacking any intellectual credentials, men like Blanchflower, Jimmy Hill and Derek Dougan were proving that that caricature was now redundant. Those in power at the FA and the Football League were clearly worried that giving intelligent, articulate men the opportunity to speak freely about the absurdities and iniquities of the professional game was asking for trouble. It was time to clamp down on it before it got out of hand. In clubs all over the country, the more voluble players were being summoned to the boardroom. At Spurs, Danny was informed that he'd been known as a troublemaker when he was at Villa. Danny's answer was characteristic: 'Still am, it's just that the results look better now.'

According to Danny, the discomfited chairman continued his gentle probing:

'"Well, I want to talk about some of the articles you are writing," he said. I pulled out a notebook from my pocket. "What's that for?" he asked.

'"If anything interesting is said I'm going to quote it."

'"But this is a private meeting."

'"Not if it is about my rights regarding freedom of speech . . ."' there were no bad feelings between the Tottenham board and myself. The restriction of speech clause in the contract had not been their idea. No doubt one of them had been at the League general meeting and voted for it. Whether they knew the implications of it all or not I do not know. But I was not going to give up my rights without a battle. And I was not going to lose that battle to my friends just to please my enemies.' Journalist Patrick Collins recalls that, talking of that meeting, Danny told him that one director said, ' "The trouble with you is you think you know all the answers." Danny beamed. "Ah, God love you," he said. "You don't even know the questions."'

By this stage Danny was in an insuperable position. He was captain and personification of the Double side and as such was almost fireproof – if Spurs had tried to dispense with his services on the flimsy excuse that he spoke his mind, there'd have been uproar. In the words of Lyndon Johnson, it was probably still safer to have him 'inside the tent pissing out, than outside pissing in'. Equally, although he wanted to continue playing as he entered his late thirties, premature retirement would not be quite the blow it would have been when he'd had his run-ins with Angus Seed a decade earlier. From Bill Nicholson's point of view, with Spurs heading off into the European Cup, he just could not do without Danny's international experience out on the field. Danny understood that everything was running in his favour and chose to exploit that to the full. Perhaps this was his most enduring gift to the game, greater than any of the dazzlingly intelligent displays he gave on the field. Most important of all, Danny Blanchflower showed the world that footballers had brains like everyone else and that they should not be underestimated. In so doing, he helped attract new people to football, those who became enraptured by the tactical side of the game rather than the simple physicality of it.

Ironically, it was tactically that Tottenham were found wanting in their first European Cup tie, away in Poland. The team had had a mixed start to the season with both White and Mackay missing a number of games through injury. The visit to Gornik Zabrze in mid-September was viewed as just the tonic the team needed to kick-start things, the impetus of a new challenge hopefully reinvigorating a side that had overcome every obstacle the domestic game had to offer. The preparation for the game was poor; Gornik were watched just once by Spurs officials because of the difficulties in reaching their ground – to get there, Spurs had to fly into Warsaw and then take a train on a four-hour journey to Katowice. Danny wrote, 'They didn't look a very good team to me when I first saw them run on to the field in Poland. But they were much better than we were that day.' That was something of an understatement. Playing their typically expansive game, Spurs were comprehensively defeated by a Polish side roared on by 90,000 fans. Bill Nicholson admitted later that 'We had practised normally and had decided that we would adopt the same sort of philosophies and principles that had helped us to win the Double. What we did not know was how to play in Europe. We did not know how to play games over two legs.' Within 47 minutes, Spurs were trailing 4–0. They were lucky to see their opponents' left-half limp off following a challenge with Dave Mackay and, regrouping, they pulled the game back to 4–2, giving them a semblance of a chance in the return.

That game was set up for Spurs to simply do what they did best – attack. Danny described the evening as 'virtually a religious feeling' and Cliff Jones doesn't disagree. 'That Gornik game really stands out in my mind. We'd not played well there, they were a good team and we had a bad press after that, rightly so. We were really up for it at home and so were the crowd. As we walked out, I've never experienced anything like it. There were 65,000 people all wanting us to really take this team. At their ground, there was the pitch, the running track, a moat, then the crowd, ten or fifteen yards away from the pitch, whereas at Tottenham the crowd are right on top of you. We walked out and you could see the Polish team thinking, What the hell is this? Right away we broke away, hit the bar and the crowd went mad. For ninety minutes it was a continuous roar, and that night, I think, was the best performance by any English club in Europe. We'd have taken anybody apart that night.' Certainly Spurs were too good for Gornik, winning 8–1.

Spurs were nothing if not adaptable. By the next round, against Feyenoord in November, changes were made. Cliff Jones admits, 'We'd gone to Gornik and had an education. From that we learned that away from home in Europe, we always had to have an extra defender.' In Rotterdam, Spurs made good use of that tactic, killing the tie with a 3–1 win. But the European Cup was already having an impact on their League form – in the four League games that immediately followed these first four European games, they won one, drew one and lost two. Injuries were starting to cause problems too, as were international calls – Danny became the first man to win 50 caps for Northern Ireland, at Wembley in November 1961. When he played against Leicester the following Saturday, it was his twenty-sixth competitive game of the season in just 105 days. To refresh the side, Bill Nicholson secured the signature of Jimmy Greaves, bringing him back from his Italian exile, able to pay him his due now that the maximum wage had been abolished. With a hat-trick on his debut, his genius revitalized a flagging team – he scored 21 goals in 22 League matches to put Spurs back in with a shout of the title, even another Double, or the Treble. Certainly, post Greaves's arrival, Danny led them with greater conviction than at any time that season. Time and again, he would set Greaves free on goal, the two forming a mutual appreciation society – Cliff Jones states: 'Jimmy absolutely idolized Danny, he thought he was wonderful. He even named his son after him.'

That fruitful partnership saw Spurs powering towards Wembley in the FA Cup – having been held to a draw by Birmingham City in the third round, they had no further truck with replays in an already congested season. Instead, they steamrollered the opposition. By 21 March, Spurs were in the semi-finals of both the FA Cup and the European Cup, Dukla Prague having been defeated 5–3 on aggregate in February, but six points adrift in the League, their early season lapses giving them too much to do, which was a regret for both Danny and Bill Nicholson, who felt that back-to-back Doubles would be an unrepeatable feat. That being so, yet more emotion was invested in the European Cup, in becoming the first English side to lift the trophy, something which couldn't be matched. The semi-finals paired them with Benfica. Away in the first leg, they entered the most hostile atmosphere they'd yet encountered – in Lisbon's Stadium of Light – which alone would have been enough to account for most teams, but as Danny wrote in the *New Statesman*, the pre-match hype was almost exclusively slanted towards Benfica: 'The newspapers, our main source of information, completely lost sight of reality. I read that Benfica were a multi-million pound team, that Germano, the greatest living centre-half, had a beard, that Eusebio, their young inside-right, had been dragged out of the swamps of Mozambique in tattered trousers just a few years before, and that they played in a fabulous stadium with ice-blue walls. I found that the stadium was a fine one, but I saw no sight of the ice-blue walls – they were plain dull concrete grey. Germano is a world-class centre-half but he has no beard. Eusebio is a skilful young player, much embarrassed by the wild pen pictures of him that were painted in the British newspapers.'

Spurs had lost the mind games that went on around the contest but on the field they were far from disgraced. Although they lost 3–1, they were very unfortunate to have two goals disallowed, Bobby Smith being penalized for offside despite squeezing the ball past two defenders who stood on the goalline! In spite of the defeat, Cliff Jones remembers that, 'We all felt we could pull two goals back at home, no danger at all. All the European keepers were upset by Bobby Smith's presence, but the Benfica goalkeeper wouldn't be intimidated by him. We won 2–1, Jimmy Greaves had another goal disallowed, Dave Mackay hit the bar, and we were unlucky to go out.' Despite the dejection in the dressing room Danny put their season into perspective: 'Spurs were not as unlucky as Manchester United in the European Cup. Spurs lost a semi-final but United had already lost a team.' Out of the competition, he had time to reflect on the European season as a whole, its greater glories: 'It would be difficult to conceive a more potent or popular soccer competition. Though the conflict is at club level, the club stands for its country and this allows national fervour to fall in and march behind the parochial banner of the club. Because it is at club level, the feelings of the player are more intimate, more intense than in international soccer, the family feeling is uppermost . . . a club crowd is more prejudiced, more personal and more passionate. This I do know – playing in the European Cup has been the greatest emotional experience of my soccer career.'

If Benfica had disappointed them, it was a valuable arc on their learning curve and they did still have the consolation of an FA Cup Final to come, having dispatched Manchester United in the semi-final. Falling short in the League – third to Ipswich Town – it was vital that they take the Cup so that they could qualify for European competition once more and build on the lessons learned. After the poor display in 1961, they were equally determined to put on a show for the watching millions around the country, to prove that Spurs were still a great footballing side, not the rough, tough footballers that Benfica had complained of – they had never encountered anything like Dave Mackay or Bobby Smith before! On the day, it was an emphatic victory, but one which illustrated that Danny was approaching the end of the line as a footballer. Cliff Jones believes Danny 'was obviously not quite the influence he'd been. John White was starting to beat him in road runs and Danny had been unbeatable in those. He was one-paced but he could keep going and nobody could get near him until the end, when his knees started to be a problem.' Age and the assorted ailments collected during a lifetime in the English game were restricting his mobility and, on this day of all days, he was required to play an almost entirely defensive game, shadowing Burnley's strikers. In a sense, he was playing an early sweeper role, using his agile mind to snuff out danger before it had flared to life, using the extra space he found at the back to thread telling passes through to the wingers or inside-forwards. His final job on the field, fittingly for this most glorious of players, was to secure the game, coolly slotting home a penalty to make the score 3–1 with ten minutes remaining. Tottenham had retained the Cup in the grand manner.

As the season wound up and the likes of Greaves and Norman set off for the World Cup in Chile, Danny was left to reflect that his own career, both at club but especially at international level, was in its own final stages. Northern Ireland had peaked in 1958, as Peter McParland admits: 'A few of the team were getting old even then, and they weren't going to get to the 1962 World Cup, especially when we drew the West Germans. It was asking a lot to get back to that peak again because Danny was in his late thirties by then, as were a few of the other lads. It was time to rebuild.' Danny was fatalistic, knowing he could not turn back the clock, but he was also annoyed with the way in which that team had been allowed to slide and how the behind-the-scenes feuding had restricted the opportunities for a revival to take place: 'Peter Doherty gave us encouragement and confidence and constantly picked us up when we were down. We seldom realized it when he was down but when I became captain I occasionally realized that he was in conflict with the committee. He fought battles for us we never knew about and was frustrated by the ignorance of some committee men ... Sweden was the pinnacle and deep down we all knew that afterwards it was a downhill tread. We had worked the greatest three-card trick of all time. Doherty had roused us to believe in things that were quite impossible. We had mortgaged our energies and talents up to the hilt, limited as they were, for one great crusade. Gradually the scene changed. People lost faith, some in themselves, some in Peter as their own abilities faltered, and some of the players simply grew older and disappeared. Peter left too. He knew the full story. There was nothing more he could do. I did not believe with any great conviction that I could help a lot. Our resources were too small and the giants were getting bigger. We had to save up for a good sling and stone for another tilt with them.' His final game, his fifty-sixth in the green of Northern Ireland, came in Belfast on 28 November 1962 when Poland were beaten 2–0. Injury denied him further caps. Danny's thoughts on the passing of a vital part of his career? Relentlessly logical: 'I had captained Northern Ireland for almost ten years and I had been a player longer than that . . . if the selectors are intent, as they ought to be, on building a team for the future, then the sooner the better for replacing me.'

The injury that finished Danny's Northern Irish career almost did the same at club level. It came against Rangers at Ibrox in December 1962, in the first round of the Cup Winners Cup. Danny remembered, 'I was nearing my thirty-seventh birthday and feeling I could play until I was forty. I liked the big games, they bought the best out of me. I was playing well until I was struck from behind. My knee felt like the twisted strings of a harp.' Age had robbed him of his previously rapid powers of recovery and the next three months were a race against time to regain fitness for the big games at the end of the season. That game against Rangers saw Spurs secure their passage into the quarter-finals of the competition, where they were pitted against Slovan Bratislava. Without their eminent captain, Tottenham were beaten 2–0 in the first leg in Czechoslovakia, causing Bill Nicholson to lash his side in the press, accusing them of losing sight of the basics of team play. Even so, just as Gornik had been brushed aside a year earlier, Slovan were demolished 6–0 by a highly motivated Spurs side determined to prove that the away game had been a momentary aberration.

As Danny toiled on the sidelines, desperately searching for the fitness that would see him back in the team for the climax to the European competition, in order to share out the burden of responsibility, Bill Nicholson appointed him as an 'assistant to the manager'. It was an interesting, if temporary move, and one which the players seemed to enjoy. Taking yet more responsibility on the training ground, Danny's 'attitude didn't change', according to Maurice Norman. 'Danny was always on his own in a way, never really one of the boys playing cards, he'd sit there with a book, and that gave him more authority, I suppose. I don't really know how well liked he was in the game because he'd always point out if something was daft, and so he upset people because there were so many daft things in the game! But we really knew him, and all the players thought he was marvellous.' Cliff Jones agrees that this sudden elevation 'didn't bring any problems, and it was an interesting change. He'd get us dribbling with two balls when some of us couldn't dribble with one! But it was all about making you think, about control, your awareness, not taking anything for granted. He'd talk over your head at times, which was a failing for a coach, especially with young players, but for the older lads it was very enjoyable.'

Desperate to get back into the side Danny went under the surgeon's knife. A cartilage was removed unnecessarily, costing recovery time, but four weeks later he turned out for the third team at outside-right, from then on using regular physiotherapy to get him through games. As he remarked, 'I was determined to get back on the field again as quickly as possible. I was too old to sit around waiting for recovery. I had to keep in motion to have a chance at all.' He played in a 4–1 win over Bolton on 27 April, just four days before the Cup Winners Cup semi-final second-leg tie with OFK Belgrade. On the morning of that game he was caught in a tackle in training, but with Spurs already 2–1 ahead, he chose to play, knowing that if he did not, his place in the Final would be in jeopardy. 'I was lucky. Two excellent passes in the early stages led to two goals. That deceived the critics, but really I was a passenger who had not been challenged. I just kept out of the way.' Those critics were fulsome in their praise, the *Daily Express* terming the game 'BLANCHFLOWER'S TRIUMPH', as Tottenham won 3–1.

Labouring under a great deal of pain, Danny kept his place in the two League games that followed: 'Each time my knee was stretched, the torn ligament was bleeding,' he recalled in *And the Spurs Go Marching On* . . . 'If I stopped soldiering on to nurse it, it would sleep and the muscles in my leg would get out of condition. So I limped through the rest of the season, learning new tricks. How could I make it more difficult for opponents without tackling? By quicker anticipation. When you move slower, you must think quicker.' Two days before the biggest game of the season, the European Cup Winners Cup Final in Rotterdam, against Atletico Madrid, Danny was still doubtful. Just before the team flew out, he had some old fluid removed from the knee and some physiotherapy, then boarded the plane to see what would happen, in hope as much as expectation.

By now, the mood in the camp had turned from optimistic to trepidatious. Danny was hobbling and his great partner, Dave Mackay, was definitely out. Cliff Jones admits: 'We were getting worried before the Final. I know I was very apprehensive, simply because Dave wasn't playing. He was the main man at that stage. And to be fair, Bill could be a little bit defensive as regards the opposition, he could build them up because he never liked us to get complacent.' Nicholson had already told his men how good their opposition would be and, in a repeat of events before Spurs flew out to play Benfica a year earlier, the press insisted that Atletico were a team of supermen. Danny, the captain through the glory years, knew the moods of his team better than anyone. He read their doubts: 'There was a strange lack of faith in us when we flew off to Holland for the final days of preparation. It was like one of those absurd royal moments when a royal figure is taken ill and lots of eminent medical advisers crowd around the body to diagnose and predict. They whisper suspiciously among themselves, pronounce grave little statements of warning that say nothing dependable or definite but somehow bode ill. They do not really help anybody. They do not usually commit themselves and give an honest appraisal. They play the banker in a sort of weird roulette game with the fears and doubts that might be gambled on in the situation. That's what I felt when I read the British press. They had lost confidence in us. I felt they were overawed by the occasion in some strange way. I read in one paper that Griffa, the Argentinian centre-half, could be brutal. There was a story of how he had been arrested in the bath after one match.'

Using all his intelligence, Danny reminded his colleagues of their adventures against Eusebio – he had been a fine player, but not the irresistible force that the press had painted him in advance. It would be the same with Madrid: 'We read about six foot three inch black wizards who were second in the table to

Real Madrid. Perhaps we thought of Real Madrid as they were on that magic night at Hampden, and not as they are now, a less formidable and more human team. "Let's respect these Atletico fellows," I said, "but let's not get carried away with all we say and read about them. They are probably having a team meeting at this very moment and somebody is saying, 'They've got this big six foot three inch white fellow . . .' They've got quick players? Cliff Jones can catch pigeons. They've got hard men? When Maurice Norman takes his teeth out, he frightens me. Jimmy Greaves invents ways of scoring goals."' The pep talk was worth its weight in gold. Cliff Jones recalls, 'We needed him to remind us that we were a good side and we went out thinking they weren't in our class.' Maurice Norman agrees, adding, 'They were a very good side but we just blew them off the park, we slaughtered them.'

From the very outset, Spurs took control of the game, Greaves turning in a cross from Jones. Further chances followed with Danny and Terry Dyson coming close before John White doubled the lead. With Spurs apparently home and dry, there was still a severe test of their character to come. A minute into the second half, Madrid pulled a goal back from the penalty spot and Spurs were suddenly thrown into crisis. For fifteen minutes, Madrid surged forward, winning corner upon corner as Spurs struggled to get out of their own half. Having settled on a 4–2–4 formation with a flat-back four, their typical away line-up in European ties, the defence of Baker, Henry, Norman and Marchi were under intense pressure as Blanchflower and White tried to stem the flow in the middle. Finally, the Madrid storm blew itself out and Spurs began to emerge as an attacking force once more. With just over twenty minutes to play, Terry Dyson put in a tentative cross from the left, the Madrid goalkeeper flapped at it and turned it into his own net. From here, Spurs exerted their dominance once more and further goals from Greaves and from Dyson, following a twenty-five-yard run, clinched the trophy. A side that had been good enough to win the trophy the previous year and who had been tough enough to fight back from two goals down were comprehensively beaten. Tottenham's triumph was all the more impressive for that.

This was the crowning moment that Danny had sought, a thrilling 5–1 win over one of Europe's finest clubs. Always a little reserved in victory in the past, this time he admitted, 'That win was all the greater for us because we finished the thing off properly. I carried that Cup high because I felt we had truly earned it. We had wandered through foreign fields and we faced our moments of trial and tribulation, our moments of doubt and frustration, but in the end it was deservedly ours. For myself, I had had to play matches and took a chance in doing so before I was properly prepared. In some ways that had been a little unfair to the other players. I added something in the games in which I played but I had to add their effort to my experience to get through. But it was a calculated risk done with the best intentions. I wanted to be ready in case I was needed in Rotterdam. If Dave had been fit and I had not played I would have been a little disappointed but somehow satisfied that I had done my best to get there . . . the team played well but our wingers did most to win us the match. Terry Dyson has never had a better game. It's a myth about Blanchflower winning the match without playing. It was the last really good match I did play. I never felt the knee that night. I feel it was an emotional thing. I was roused for the big occasion – a fresh and bigger injection of inspiration dulled all doubts and feelings of injury.' If Terry Dyson had caught the eye, for all Danny's modesty, he had been the key to victory, in the dressing room if not out on the grass itself, inspiring his men to victory like a great general.

As Danny conceded, that wonderful glory, glory night in Rotterdam was the end of the road. He hoped that the knee would heal, would carry him through a further season or two, maybe another Cup Final at home or in Europe. He was well aware that he'd be a long time retired and did not want to go too early. As he pointed out early on in the 1963–64 season, 'Some were telling me to quit at the end of the season we won the Double. I would have missed another FA Cup medal and a European Cup Winners Cup medal. I have no doubt their advice at the start of the present season was better – two years better . . . after the first match at Stoke one reporter pointed out that I had a shocking match and that I had fingered my left knee continually during the game. I have not the heart to tell him that the cartilage was taken from the right knee!' However Danny tried to bluff his way through, he knew the end was in sight. He had a poor game at Manchester United as Spurs went down 4–1, just a couple of weeks before

Tottenham set out to defend their European title in a tie against Busby's men. Danny's name was missing from the teamsheet for the Burnley game seven days later. The name of Blanchflower would never grace it again. He had come to Tottenham as the symbol of Arthur Rowe's desire to build a second great team. His passing was the symbol of Bill Nicholson's determination to succeed where Rowe had not. Danny knew as much, writing, 'When he dropped me from the team he didn't say much. But I knew he intended it to be the end for me. He could not really say that because his caution advised him that he might have some slight need of me again . . . it was part of his duty to take the club forward. It would be better if I were out of the way. I did not want to hang around in the wings like some pathetic old actor waiting for a chance to get back into the act.'

Danny refused to become sentimental or emotional about his impending retirement, accepting that no man can hold back time indefinitely. The closest he got to any sadness came in quoting F. Scott Fitzgerald. From *The Crack-Up*, he likened his retirement to the 'blow that comes from within – that you don't feel until it's too late to do anything about it, until you realize that in some regard you will never be as good a man again'. He might equally have quoted another line from the same story – 'show me a hero and I'll write you a tragedy', a tragedy that such a glorious footballer should have his career terminated one day sooner than was necessary. Typically phlegmatic, he simply noted, 'I feel no sadness. I have no regrets. I have had as good a career as anyone else and I have never had false illusions about immortality.'

Leaving the stage for the final time, it was obvious that Danny Blanchflower was a footballing immortal, a name that would be remembered and echoed down the ages. What made Danny an icon of the game? Cliff Jones has a host of reasons: 'He was a one-off, I've never known anyone like him. He always did things his way – he wasn't nasty about it, he was always charming – but he was very determined about getting his own way. He was so far ahead of his team that when people let him get on with things that might seem a bit odd, they generally worked out. When he refused to go on *This Is Your Life* in 1961, that was typical Danny. We were all at the TV studio, there were loads of people there: family, people from South Africa had come over. This bloke came in and said, "We've been doing this show for so many years now and this is the first time our subject has said no." Bill Nick turned to me and said, "Jesus Christ. Trust him to do it. Trust him. I've wasted a day's work coming up here," which was what really upset Bill, because he always wanted to get on with the job. But it took guts to do what Danny did, knowing what had gone into the programme and that it would make all the papers. But he didn't want his private life made public, which was fair enough.'

Danny's captaincy is an integral part of his story. Cliff Jones remembers, 'He was always good company, telling little jokes. He'd say, "How do we bring crowds back to football? Easy. Let them in for nothing and charge 'em to get out!" Daft little things, but they released the tension.' 'Danny was an original piece of art work,' Hunter Davies wrote in Danny's testimonial brochure. 'He was certainly too early for his own good . . . Danny had boundless footballing skills but did his leading from his head. He played in effect player-manager, the conductor of the orchestra, able to see patterns emerging, strengths fading, spaces opening up, and made changes accordingly while the game was in progress. I can't imagine Spurs ever having a better captain. Or being allowed to.' That final sentence is the crux. Only under Peter Doherty and then Bill Nicholson did Danny have the freedom that allowed his genius to flower. He wrote, 'There have been times when I have caused the Tottenham directors some concern by standing up for the things which I have believed. But the trouble has included me being a part of the team that won the Double, the FA Cup for a second year and then the European Cup Winners Cup.' It was Danny's footballing principles that played a major part in making Spurs great. Surgically remove those principles and he wouldn't have been half the player. As a captain who questioned everything, he could be hard work, but it was that same enquiring mind that helped unlock defences all over Europe. Tell him not to think – an impossibility anyway – and he'd have been a mundane right-half, ponderous and uninspired. Bill Nicholson knew how to use his gifts to the full, springing them on opponents when they least expected it.

Walter Winterbottom believes Danny was 'a natural footballer in every way. He loved to play, and the Tottenham style suited him because it meant he could influence things. He had a quick brain on the field. The balance of play is so important between those who win the ball and those who use it, and they had that at Spurs. Danny could use the ball as well as anyone in the game.' Cliff Jones agrees with that sentiment and compares him with Glenn Hoddle. 'He was a terrific passer of the ball, with great vision. He'd split defences. When he was on his game, he'd do the tricks, looking one way and playing it the other. Because he had such great control, his lack of pace didn't matter – he'd make time for himself by bringing the ball down immediately. It showed in his play, he had a beautiful balance, it showed how deeply he thought about the game. He was always on his feet, he was never on his backside, unless somebody put him there. We played Manchester United and Danny came up against Nobby Stiles. Little Nobby was snarling away and eventually he caught Danny. Danny went down and Nobby stood over him and said, "Blanchflower, you're finished!" Danny looked up at him and said, "Excuse me, son, I haven't read the programme yet. What's your name, by the way?" That was a lovely put down. None of that jumping up and having a go back – Dave would have picked him up by the scruff of the neck! – Danny handled him and that was the end of Nobby that day! Nowadays, he'd be priceless. Mind, he was then!'

With all those different pairs of boots hung up for the last time, Danny Blanchflower had to decide what to do with the rest of his life. He wrote in the *Sunday Express*, 'I doubt I will become a football manager. In my time as a player I have been continually at odds with officialdom. I have fought for my rights as a player. If I became a manager I think I would have a bigger fight on. But it wouldn't be a fair one. I would be too much the victim of officialdom. I believe in a Super League and a lot of other things. If I decided to take up that battle then journalism or television might be a better launching pad. We shall see . . .'

8 Writes and Wrongs

As one who had been described as a player-manager on the field, when the time came for Danny Blanchflower to quit playing the game he loved, most observers expected him to make a move into football management, perhaps becoming assistant to Bill Nicholson. Those who knew him better were much less confident of that. Cliff Jones 'never thought Danny would stay at Spurs. I always thought his future was in the media, the press and television. I remember him doing one thing on *Sportsview*, where he was basically the team manager and captain of Northern Ireland, because Peter Doherty was stuck in Bristol. Danny took the part of presenter too, and said, "I'm now going to interview the manager", and he interviewed himself, before saying, "And now I'm going to talk to the captain of Northern Ireland." It was all really well done. He had a flair for that type of thing.' George Robb believes that Danny was just too cute to be trapped by the lure of management, adding, 'I think he realized that there were other spheres that were easier and less fraught. He was intelligent and he had other things he could do, his writing and so on. He didn't suffer fools gladly, he'd made it clear that he didn't think there was too much intelligence on the average board of directors, very much in line with Len Shackleton's thinking. He'd tolerate them rather than enjoy their company.'

If any one thing kept Danny away from day-to-day involvement with the game for so long, it was the fact that he would forever be beholden to directors. Writing in the *Daily Mail*, he'd already noted that, 'As I see it, most directors have no real knowledge of the game. If they had they would know how to pick the right manager. Maybe they should let the manager choose the directors.' Holding that view, it was obvious that Danny was just not cut out for the challenge that football management offered. In the past he'd always been ready for a fight if it was on equal terms; his early up and down relationship with Bill Nicholson was a case in point. If it was a mismatch, he'd simply beat a tactical retreat – as at Barnsley and Aston Villa – going on to win the war with Tottenham. At managerial level, he just felt the odds were too heavily stacked against him. In that regard, he makes an interesting contrast with Bill Shankly. Shankly was as great a romantic about football as Danny, every bit as bloody-minded, just as determined to get his own way, but far less constricted by the boardroom. He was just as aware of their influence, but he didn't go through the same agonies of intellectualization that Danny did. Thinking about management, Blanchflower would look at all the obstacles, rationalize them, realize that the directors held the chequebook, had the power to hire and fire and would always get their way. As manager, he would not be able to express his opinion as freely or forcibly. In short, he understood their power. Shankly, on the other hand, rarely thought about the directors because he had no interest in the business side of the game. When he did think of them, he simply regarded them as footballing midgets, tiny people, simply because they weren't football people, they were greengrocers with a bit of spare cash. Their job was to provide him with the money to build a club and then keep out of his way. Danny empathized with that view but had the wider vision to see that they were big men in terms of the club's destiny. He saw no way round that whereas a man like Shankly, or for that matter, Brian Clough, was so sure of his own genius, so confident that he could mobilize the community behind him, that he would make himself indispensable and directors redundant, a courageous ploy but one which didn't always work.

With management apparently out of the question, Danny turned to the obvious alternative – writing about the game. By 1964, he was already a veteran journalist of ten years' standing. It was the *Birmingham Evening Mail* which gave him his first real break, initially inviting him to contribute to the crosstalk column with Albion's Ronnie Allen and Les Boyd of Birmingham in 1953, and then allowing him to pen his own piece the year after, an agreement cut short when he left Birmingham for London. His first article appeared on 21 August 1954 and it opened in what became a very recognizable style:

'I intend to be honest and often contradictory and argumentative . . . sometimes you may completely disagree with what I say.

Often I shall leave you wondering what I'm going to write about next. Sometimes, no doubt, I shall be wondering myself. However, my main aim is that you may find it interesting . . . I reserve the right to change my mind whenever I want to as I don't mind admitting I have much to learn. But let me assure you that I'm awful hard to convince.' That was the source of both his strength and weakness: fiercely opinionated at all times, generally entertainingly so, there were occasions when he became just as rooted in his ideas as his enemies were attached to their conventional wisdom.

From the outset he was something of a populist, writing that 'football is run for the public'. That was no mere sloganeering. He genuinely believed that to be the case. As the momentum for the 1966 World Cup was gathering pace, he penned this excoriating attack on the Football Association, one which still has relevance today: 'The England team has been sold down the river. Somewhere in the past, its soul was cut out and hired to Wembley for nothing better than money, money it did not always need, money that added up to a profit that would make the officials of Lancaster Gate wealthy and pompous-looking. It had become the habit of the England team to play most of its games at Wembley. It did very little touring of the provinces, it was too toffee-nosed to visit those loving relatives in Merseyside or Manchester or up in the North-East. It was too much trouble for those officials to get up off their asses and take the attractive foreign teams to Goodison Park or Old Trafford, Maine Road or Villa Park. They could not strut about up there the way they could at Wembley.' Today, of course, the debate as to whether to have two national stadiums, a revamped Wembley and another in the North, is still raging. If Wembley's resurrection is being largely funded by lottery cash, why can't the FA build another stadium? Clubs like Middlesbrough, Sunderland, Derby and Bolton have managed to build new stadia. After all, the FA sold the soul of the Premier League to Rupert Murdoch and the 125 years of history that was the FA Cup to Littlewoods. If they didn't get enough from that to fund such a project they should be locked up.

Danny's stock in trade was to be provocative. Larry Canning, a colleague at Aston Villa and a distinguished radio journalist in his own right, comments: 'Danny loved to throw a pebble in the pond and see how it was received. Then he'd throw a bigger one, to push things as far as he could, to get a reaction.' As such, he could be rather more honest than some employers would like. His problems with American television have already been documented, but he endured similar difficulties in England. At the BBC's Pebble Mill studios in Birmingham prior to the 1964 FA Cup Final between West Ham and Preston, he was asked who he thought would take the trophy. 'I don't know who is going to win. That's why they're playing the match.' Cue collapse of interviewer and producer with a further five minutes of air time to fill. 'He was a natural for television,' says Cliff Jones, 'but he upset various people within the BBC, and that finished that. Which was a shame, but it was like being at a club: those in charge didn't always like people who thought for themselves.' Derek Dougan was 'very disappointed that he didn't go on to do greater things in television and radio because he had strong views that would have benefited the game and the way it was reported. But he always fell out with the executives who had fixed ideas on how the game should be represented – he wanted to give it to the audience very truthfully, which didn't go down well if a game was dull.' To be fair to the television moguls, compromise was not an idea that held any appeal for Blanchflower. It would not have been impossible for him to tone down his language, to avoid some needless confrontations, without fawning to authority. Had he done so, he was one of the figures that could have transformed the way in which football was broadcast. Instead, he was content to snipe at those who followed him on TV, particularly contemptuous of the panels who talked for hours without saying anything.

The written word quickly proved to be Danny's forte, Bertie Peacock pointing out that, 'He wrote the way he played, he liked flair, he was always stylish. Certainly he was more suited to that than he was management.' By the time of his retirement, he'd already created a niche for himself with the *Sunday Express*, a haven where he felt perfectly at home. There were other possible distractions, but he turned them down in favour of his career in journalism. In October 1964, for example, there was a possibility that he might end up as manager at Manchester City. At that stage businessman Peter Donoghue was trying to win control of the club and announced that if he did so, he would 'appoint Danny Blanchflower as manager, offer him a job in which he could earn up to £10,000 a year'. It was an attractive opportunity for, as Danny said, ' As a small boy, I cherished the name of Manchester City . . . my dreams each night were full of the sky-blue shirts. I waved the flag for no better reason than that Peter Doherty played for them.' The prospect was flattering and Danny gave it a few moments' consideration. Eventually, he came to a conclusion: 'The wonder of young men is that they think nothing is impossible; the disease of the old is that nothing is possible – it's just too much trouble. For one mad moment in the company of Peter Donoghue and the young men he says will be his board, I imagined I was their manager. "Now there's the rub," I told myself. "You are older than all of them. You have always thought of directors restraining you – but you would surely have to restrain them. Either that or get an older team." It was a moment not to be taken seriously.'

Pretty quickly in his post-Tottenham days, Danny evolved a very pleasant lifestyle, keeping in touch with the game, but also indulging his passion for golf. He had a small but devoted social circle, including the Compton brothers and Walter Winter-bottom, who remembers, 'You couldn't keep Danny down, no matter what the company. We used to have a regular get-together, six or seven of us, at the home of Bernard Joy and his wife – he was a journalist too, having played for Arsenal. We'd have a meal and a chit-chat and Danny would turn up full of life and before long he'd taken it over! Some people might object to that, thinking he was full of himself. He had a lot of whims, he'd read a lot and he'd take ideas from books and philosophize on them and give us a round lecture on the pattern of life. Some thought he was odd for doing it! For that reason he had a few very close friends rather than a host of acquaintances.' Frank Keating testifies to Danny's voluble nature: 'I was with him on a chat show on Granada. I was nervous. For a full hour, bless him, every question Brian Trueman asked me was answered by Danny. "You were very good," he told me afterwards.' Talking, writing and playing golf offered an enjoyable way of life, not something to be given up lightly. Having been out of the game a matter of months, it was quickly apparent that it would take a lot to draw him back into it.

For the better part of a quarter of a century, Danny's column appeared week in, week out on a Sunday, with just the occasional break, allowing him to touch on many, many subjects, not solely footballing ones. All were addressed in a fresh and provocative manner, his calling card being a rigorous logic and a perpetually questioning attitude, one that refused to accept the received wisdom on anything. How many other writers, for example, have suggested that the Matthews Cup Final of 1953 was anything but a fantastic spectacle? Danny did on seeing a re-run of the game a decade later: 'I had that occasion fixed somewhere in my memory as one of the greatest Cup Finals of all time. Seeing it again, divorced from the emotions of the time, I had to remuster my values. If I had said back in 1953 that the Final was mostly bad football and that Stan's last twenty minutes were far from his best play I would have been considered a nut for saying it. Well, that's what I'm saying now. It was from a hopeful rather than a good cross from Stan, which the Bolton keeper caught easily enough but did not hold, that led to Mortensen scoring Blackpool's second goal ... [for the fourth goal] I would have sworn Stan slipped as he played the ball and that he fortunately pulled it back to Perry *because* he slipped.'

His articles were regularly unorthodox in tone, though many now lack their original impact because of the passing of time. Even so, it's obvious that Danny was no run-of-the-mill writer. He admitted as much when taking some colleagues to task in one piece: 'They are seduced by their own medium. It is one of black and white and it does not lend itself to subtler shades of opinion.' Just as he had trodden on toes when he was a footballer, he did so again as a writer. Larry Canning recalls that 'among journalists, they felt Danny would lead you down a lovely path with his column but that it wouldn't take you anywhere, there was no punchline. A professional journalist wouldn't like it; romantics about the game would.' Therein lay the reason for Danny's popularity: he tapped into a seam of similarly disaffected football supporters who felt that the game could be so much better than coaches and directors allowed it to be. Danny retained a childlike love of the game. He was cynical about much of life – that cynicism kept him out of football management, unlike real innocents such as Shankly – but that never tainted his view of the game. Indeed, he felt it was sacrosanct, that it should not be contaminated by greed or stupidity. It was this belief that forced him to satirize the upper echelons of the game, burst their pomposity by likening their discussions to those held in Alice's Wonderland. His favourite ploy was to discuss the latest decree from the FA through the medium of the Mad Hatter and the March Hare.

Equally, where a professional journalist would need to round out a story with an opinion or some form of revelation, Danny never operated under quite those restrictions. At the *Express*, his editor was John Junor, who idolized both Danny and his cricketing equivalent, Denis Compton. While Junor was editor, both had enormous freedom to indulge their flights of fancy and as such were often able to ask questions that their more conventionally trained peers could not. It's a matter of opinion as to which school of thought was the better, but the fact that Danny was different made his column all the more readable, although he could be a little too self-indulgent at times. He did write as he played in some respects, notably in reserving his judgement until all the facts were in. On the field he was bright, alert, but did not commit himself to making a tackle or placing a through ball until the right moment. He did not lunge thoughtlessly in the white of Spurs and nor did he in the black and white of the *Express*. Thus at times he was annoyingly vague and open ended; but better that than commit rashly to an opinion that time would prove ludicrous. The only exception to that rule came in respect of directors and authority figures in general. These were guilty until proven innocent, at all times. Like all rebels, his condemnation could be simplistic, and his blanket distaste for them as a breed earned him enemies where there was no need. Not all directors were malign, in spite of his own personal experience, and his attacks on them were simply storing up trouble. It was also a reflection on a weaker part of his nature, a thoughtless, almost casual intolerance for those who disagreed with him, drawn from his overwhelming self-belief.

Perhaps his writing deserves to be anthologized, for even though some pieces have dated, certain important themes crop up time and again; and when at his best, he was simply superb. He had forthright opinions on racism in sport, for example, as illustrated by his perceptive article for the *New Statesman* on the first Muhammad Ali/Joe Frazier fight: 'This is Joe Frazier's big chance. Like Joe Louis, he has become the white man's hope – the black with a good punch who knows his place outside the ring. Imagination would never choose Frazier as an obvious threat to the greatest looking athlete of all time. Liston looked more

like it – but he withered unbelievably in the confrontation ...
Cassius Clay, grandson of a slave, has wholesome roots. Muhammad Ali, stepson of the Black Prophet, has heavenly ideals. There
has never been a performer like him before. He has out-talked
the journalists, out-promoted the promoters and out-boxed the
contenders. We have come to scrutinize Superman, to see if he
has feet of Clay ... Frazier catches Clay in the last round and
sends him to the floor. Cassius gets up quickly but it is all over.
It is a terrible blow for the optimists. What they have lost is a
beautiful illusion, that a man can be so good that he can leave
the pack and all its pedestrian little ways behind. The boxers and
administrators have claimed back their game.' The impact of the
outside world on sport was something else that he understood.
Back in 1963, Denis Law received a lengthy ban for violent con-
duct, but Danny came to his defence, arguing that the punishment exceeded the crime and had been arrived at to placate
outsiders who demanded that 'something must be done'. Danny
pointed out that '1963 has been a severe year, a year when violence roused itself to strange and bloody deeds. It began with a
harsh winter. It shocked us with the Profumo affair. It stood and
watched religious figures burn themselves to death in Saigon. It
saw the political end of Harold Macmillan and the assassination
of President Kennedy. Doesn't violence beget violence? And
doesn't the mood of the day reach out and touch our every act
– awake or sleeping? Why was Denis Law not suspended [for
similar behaviour] in 1962 instead of 1963? And if he had been,
would his punishment not have been less? Instinct and feeling
take over our judgement.'

Those two pieces are absolutely typical of his approach to his
second career. Nothing exists in isolation, sport cannot be
divorced from politics or the rest of the world. Equally, football
could not simply be kept afloat by its traditions. Failure to adapt
would sound its death knell, as he noted in 1965: 'I hope the
powers that will pursue the future of professional soccer are keeping an eye on the cricket scene. They will see how a great institution dies. They will learn how a business that does not keep up
with the times will slowly perish and fade away.' And, of course,
Danny was not short of new ideas, the footballing equivalents of
the one-day game which revitalized cricket and brought it into
the post-war world, all of which he was only too happy to share.

In particular he felt that the punters were being short-changed, that clubs preferred to fritter away their incomes on transfer fees rather than on improving the facilities for supporters. He wasn't always right, for anyone putting forward innovations is there to be shot at. In the 1980s, for example, he was vociferous in his support for Luton and their chairman David Evans as they introduced the plastic pitch and a total ban on away supporters: 'Some people thought Luton were wrong to switch to a synthetic pitch. Well, they have been renting it out successfully to a lot of sporting teams and companies – profitably. They charge £200 for its use and the customers are rolling in . . . things are looking great for this progressive football club. If any football club deserves to prosper, it's Luton Town.' As an Irishman, Danny was never so tied to convention as an Englishman might be. He felt that given the climate of hooliganism, it was better to ban all away fans on a better safe than sorry basis. Yet to prevent away supporters attending games was totally alien to popular football culture of the last thirty years, and, more, something he singularly failed to address. To play on a plastic pitch completely changed the game – those who saw these experiments with AstroTurf will recall a very different game to that played elsewhere in the country, the initial expectations of a faster and more cultured passing game, which would obviously appeal to Danny's instincts, quickly dashed by the more prosaic reality. Change was tremendously appealing to him since he enjoyed confrontation and chaos, believing that such an environment could bring forth better solutions. In so doing, he often ignored the danger that tearing something down for the sake of it might also pull up the roots. In that vein he wanted to see a British League or Cup competition, arguing as far back as 1965 that, 'Gates are getting smaller, alarmingly so. Football needs higher standards if it is to survive. That's what the distant trumpets warn. We need a British League now before it's too late.' Once more, the fact that he was Belfast born and bred meant he did not have the same sentimental attachment to the League set-ups in England or Scotland as a native of those countries might; as such he failed to appreciate the huge emotional upheaval such a move would entail, failed to understand why such an idea was out of the question.

One of his biggest dreams was to see the introduction of a United Kingdom team, an idea still being aired and shouted down with monotonous regularity. That preoccupation led him into one of his more controversial periods, one which illustrated that he was less reliable as a tipster than as a defender of the best traditions of the game as it should be played. Having retired from the game, over the next two years he indulged in firing regular broadsides at the England manager Alf Ramsey: 'When he took over the England manager's job I was full of new hope. But he has done very little to reassure me as the days have passed by. Perhaps the thing that bothered me most was a picture I saw of him sitting with a selection committee, practically announcing to the public he was just one of a committee. I lost heart in him after that. The Indians had captured our lone scout, he was sitting around the camp fire smoking the pipe of peace with them and our dream of a new empire was going up in smoke.' A year before the 1966 World Cup Finals were due to start, he added: 'A man who chooses thirty-eight players in a couple of seasons to find one good international team might very well know what he's looking for, but it seems to me he certainly doesn't know how to find it.'

Once it was all over and England were crowned Champions, Danny's view on Ramsey's inadequacies had barely changed: 'In intention England were as defensive as any team in the tournament. At times they looked less so because they were urged on by the crowd. The defence was given too much credit and talked of as the best in the world. In fact, the forwards, written off in the early stages, were selected more as initial defenders than attackers. In the end it was Ball and Hurst who did most to win the Final. Persistence and stamina were the qualities that carried the team through. England endured.' Some might accuse Danny of sour grapes and of voicing the anti-English prejudice that permeates the other three home nations, but it was less England's victory that affronted him than the way in which they achieved success, the wingless wonders robbing the game of the beauty and excitement that he demanded. Given the dismal legacy of 1966, the game's vocabulary cheapened by the pre-eminence of workrate over ability, it's hard to disagree with his views. As Derek Dougan explains, 'Danny encouraged people to play like he played. He was a purist, a cultured player, probably the thinking man's footballer. At that time, we weren't supposed to think, we were supposed to have other people around who did the thinking, and this still prevails.' Even so, the orgy of English self-congratulation that surrounded that day at Wembley must have coloured his views.

Even if it was impossible to agree with everything that Danny said, objective readers would surely admit that he was at his best when he was crusading. Although the war over players' contracts was largely over before Danny hung up his boots, his journalistic reaction to it all was fascinating. Equally, it played its part in reinforcing his distaste for directors. As soon as he became a national newspaperman with the *Daily Mail* in September 1958, he began the job of exposing the football authorities. He'd had indignities heaped upon him for nine years by this stage, notably the shameful way in which he was treated when he moved from Barnsley to Aston Villa. He saw it as his moral obligation to set the record straight, but he must also have allowed himself a smile as he wreaked revenge on those who would subjugate him and his colleagues: 'Professional football has flourished. The men in authority should have realized this and changed the laws to match the progressive realism of modern times ... it's not that the maximum wage of £20 a week isn't fair for the average player, it's just that it is no incentive for the best. The present system imposes limitations and consequently produces them. Everybody is coached the same way. Everybody is paid the same. Nobody may talk out of turn. Rewards are for long service rather than better ability. The whole system breeds uniformity. A uniform system leads to a uniform product and mediocrity ... I am in favour of bonuses ... it is my profession and I think I am entitled to take out as much as I put in ... authority should respect us, not dominate us. I believe our authority is a bad one. How can footballers respect a contract which the FA and Football League have publicly confessed is invalid in law?'

Given Danny's strong opposition to the status quo, it was a little odd that he didn't become more involved with the players' union. Ron Reynolds remembers, 'He could be a rebel and so could I. The only difference between us was that he was very much more diplomatic! He'd tell me, "Simmer down, take it easy, you'll get there in the end." But I'd batter my head against the wall. It was a volatile period, one where Jimmy Anderson told me to just look after myself or I'd get myself in trouble. But I was the union rep! Anderson kow-towed to the directors and had always been that sort of man, which was up to him. Danny agreed with what I was doing and he believed in fighting for your rights, but he was more tactful about it! Danny tried to smooth things over, advised me not to stick my neck out while I was the rep and so on.' Derek Dougan, a long-time PFA activist, had 'long talks with Danny about the PFA. Danny never really played the active role he should have, perhaps because he realized he could look after himself. It happened to me later in life, but Danny was one of those guys who earned more from outside the game than as a player.'

As an older player and one with outside interests, there was no real reason for Danny to get involved in the PFA for, in purely selfish terms, he wasn't going to reap the benefits. Even so, he did make a principled stand, ultimately to his own cost. Johnny Haynes, who became the symbol of the changing times by becoming the first £100 a week player – though he never got another increase afterwards! – felt 'The support of someone like Danny, with a voice in the press, was important. He helped point out that we were very strong as a body and that the authorities had no choice but to give in eventually.' It's probable that Danny felt it better to play the long game – he'd have been a very able politician. Rather than trying to change the game from within, his view was that it was better to educate the supporters and get public opinion on their side, creating an irresistible movement for change. Although his role in this struggle pales into insignificance in comparison with the work done by the likes of Jimmy Hill and Cliff Lloyd, it was still an important one. He understood that the supporters could be their biggest ally or their greatest, most implacable enemy if the maximum wage and potential strike action wasn't handled carefully. With that in mind, in 1959 he went on the BBC's *Panorama*, along with Jimmy Hill, chairman of the PFA, to discuss the players' contracts with the Arsenal manager George Swindin and the president of the Football League, Joe Richards. This was the selfsame Joe Richards who had left Danny to eat in the hotel kitchens while he sold him to Aston Villa. Writing of this programme, Danny produced one of his most affecting pieces and one which was important in helping change the climate: 'Before slavery was abolished in America every negro was not a slave. But it *could* happen to them. Most footballers are rarely treated like slaves but . . .' Having established the principle of his argument, he continued, 'The maximum wage should be scrapped – it's a prop for weak administrators who haven't the judgement or the courage to value a player and pay him accordingly. I have nothing to gain by being critical of the footballer's conditions – they won't change in my time. On the contrary, I may rouse the "High Priests" to seek a spiteful vengeance. And I shall be called a nutcase, a Red, a troublemaker and a discredit to the game.'

That was very much the case. Previously mistrusted by directors, he was now reviled by them. He did not mind that for their opinion of him could scarcely be lower than his of them. The sad thing was that ten years after his retirement from football, those views towards him had not changed. That was to cost him the job that he wanted above all others.

9 The Thing With Feathers

Everyone, even the most opinionated of journalists, is allowed to change their mind from time to time. Where, in 1964, Danny Blanchflower would not have countenanced the idea of becoming a football manager, distance from the game added enchantment. Equally, perhaps, he'd forgotten quite how sizeable were some of the obstacles. Whatever the case, as the 1974–75 season began to pick up pace, there were rumours that Danny was about to be lured back into the heart of game. That campaign had opened very poorly for Tottenham with four straight defeats. By the end of August, Bill Nicholson decided that it was time for him to resign as manager. In spite of great opposition from the club and players, he was adamant that his decision was irrevocable, though he did finally agree to mind the shop until a replacement was found.

After sixteen years as manager, having led Tottenham to the Double, a further two FA Cups, two League Cups, the European Cup Winners Cup and the UEFA Cup, Nicholson had proved himself to be a modern manager *par excellence*, fit to rank with the likes of Busby, Shankly, Clough and Paisley. As such, it was widely expected that Nicholson would have the opportunity to anoint his successor; at the very least, surely the board would take careful note of any recommendations he might care to make. It was this that got tongues wagging about Danny's prospects. Certainly Bill Nicholson was never in any doubt that Danny was the man to fill his shoes, in spite of the length of time he'd spent on the fringes of the game. Speaking to Harry Harris, Nicholson remarked: 'It was my opinion that [Danny] would have made an exceptional manager for the club, the outstanding candidate. He had similar ideas to mine about how the game should be played. He knew the set-up and the tradition.'

It was that tradition that attracted Danny. Having spent the best years of his footballing life at White Hart Lane, he had formed a powerful emotional attachment to the club. That alone wasn't unusual – how many former players have been seduced by their former stamping grounds? Just as Venables and Ardiles would be drawn back to manage Tottenham in later years, so Danny was seemingly being offered a challenge he could not refuse. Within days of handing in his resignation, Nicholson was in contact with Danny, calling him into his office for a chat. 'I interviewed him for the job of manager. Typically he wanted to know all the details and, after a long talk, he decided he'd like the job. He said he wanted me to stay on in the background and I was prepared to do that. It would have been the ideal working relationship.' With typical foresight, Bill Nicholson also envisaged attracting Johnny Giles to the club, a prospect that thrilled Danny, who had long been an admirer, seeing a great deal of himself in his play. Nearing the end of his playing days at Leeds, Nicholson saw Giles performing the role of player-coach, pulling the strings on the field on Danny's behalf in much the way that Danny had done for Nicholson a decade and more earlier. It was a tantalizing prospect that caused much comment. Certainly the Spurs players were excited by the possibilities, the more so since Bill Nicholson would still be on board. Pat Jennings remembers, 'We were looking forward to Danny taking over as manager, and at Tottenham he would have had so much respect that it would have stood a good chance of working. Whether he and Johnny could have worked together is another thing, but it sounded a good combination.'

Danny himself was enthusiastic and let word slip about Bill Nicholson's approach, which he assumed had been made on behalf of the club. He knew that a board meeting was scheduled, one which he believed was ready to rubber stamp his appointment. He spent the day with journalist friends on the golf course at Wentworth. He mused on whether a Jaguar would be a suitable car for a Spurs manager, displaying his love for both style and affectation at the same time, before discussing with the *Daily Mail*'s Brian James his beliefs and intentions for the future: 'If I threw a football at you, you'd trap it, juggle it, have a hell of a time trying to do tricks. And I'd enjoy watching, ready to cheer if you perform, or laugh if you fall on your backside. We'd both be having fun. What you would not do is round up a couple of mates and then rush off to find someone to mark. Because that is not, instinctively, what the game is for . . . if I play two men up, they'll have three to cover them. So if I play four, they must defend with five. That suits me. I'll make defenders start earning their living, doing their own job. Life's become too easy for them . . . could I fail? Of course I can. But what does that matter? I'll gamble on making enough noise and disturbance in the game for someone else to come along behind me and carry on. I want a club that's an academy for the kids, a club where the fans could have their moan about things in the programme. And where they'd know that any player who stuck two fingers up to them would be an ex-player at the end of the game. Maybe it can't be done. But the point is, do you want me to try?'

After his round of golf, Danny went home in good time to receive the call from White Hart Lane, like a putative Prime Minister waiting to head off to Buckingham Palace. The call never came. They didn't want him to try to build this footballing Utopia. Bill Nicholson recalled: 'During my second week as temporary manager, a board meeting was called to discuss the new manager. To my great surprise I was not called to the meeting. I was shocked by the response from the board, Sidney Wale in particular. He was upset that I had interviewed [Blanchflower and Giles] without his knowledge or approval. The other directors appeared to share his indignation. I told them in no uncertain terms that what I had done was for the benefit of Tottenham, using the experience of my lifetime in the game to find a man capable of taking over a great club. My recommendations were ignored. Perhaps they felt threatened.' In hindsight, there's no doubt that the directors felt put out that a mere employee, even a Double-winning one, should take it on himself to try to appoint his own successor without reference to the all-powerful board. However, to refuse to give the right man the job simply because they didn't choose him is ridiculously childish. Surely there must have been some other motivation in rejecting Blanchflower's claims?

His clarion call to attacking football might well have sent a few shivers down the collective spine of a board whose club lay rooted to the bottom of the First Division, in serious danger of relegation. In such circumstances, footballing lore dictated that you required a team that could kick rather than play its way out of trouble. Although Danny had steel in his character, a hugely competitive nature and a great desire to win, no one was under any illusion that he would betray his footballing principles purely for the sake of results. Talk of playing with four forwards in the ultra-defensive 1970s was deemed suicidal and must have counted against him. Was it the deciding factor? That's unlikely. Throughout his playing career, he'd won few friends at board level. He was viewed as a necessary evil, a troublemaker who had to be tolerated because of his influence on the field of play. His outspoken opposition to those who restricted his freedom of speech was worrying to those who might see that freedom used against them. In his twenty years as a journalist, he'd become renowned for the acerbity of his attacks on those who ran football, the lunatics who ran the asylum. Giving him a position of real power was just too frightening for some administrators to contemplate. After all, God forbid, he might actually succeed. Then there'd be no stopping him. The Spurs directors were afraid of appointing him manager in case he took over their club.

Typically, Danny tried to shrug off the disappointment: 'I would have gone to White Hart Lane because Nick asked me to do so. I owed him some respect and I thought he was asking me on behalf of the Tottenham club. No, I was not disappointed when I found out that the Spurs directors did not want me there. They had the right to appoint whoever they wanted and I respect that right. Would you want to work for people who did not really want you? Not me. I could find no real satisfaction in a job where I was looking over my shoulder most of the time.' This was a stoic approach, but hardly a completely honest one. He was genuinely looking forward to taking over at Tottenham. His comments to Brian James had not been grudging. He was clearly excited by the idea of stamping his imprint on the club, his every word saying, 'Won't it be wonderful to take over a club and bring back real football?'

Why the change of heart regarding management? Tottenham obviously provided a huge sentimental attraction, their traditions close to his heart, but there was more to it than that. Although he had enjoyed what amounted to his semi-retirement, Danny was still an ambitious man. After a decade writing for the *Sunday Express*, he had proved himself in that field. Away from his beloved game, he was beginning to feel its pull once more. Had he dodged the challenge of management? Had it been a failure of nerve as much as a rational judgement that kept him out of the game? These were questions that perhaps not even he could answer truthfully. The only way to resolve them was to give management a go. His powerful ego may also have demanded that he try to return to the game and teach it a lesson. In his self-imposed exile, football had lost much of its sparkle. The glorious free-flowing game of the 1950s and 1960s had reached its peak with the epochal Brazilian side of 1970. In the years since then the game had lost whatever traces of innocence that remained. The West German World Cup of 1974 had been quite dismal. Apart from the Cruyff-inspired Dutch, it had been run on the lines of strict tactics and defensive ideals, all the sides showing a blanket refusal to allow the opposition any freedom to play, generally at the expense of their own invention. Even those great Brazilians were superseded by a side that wanted to play like the most brutally disciplined of European sides, perhaps recalling the nightmare of European intimidation they had faced in England in 1966. Having seen all that, maybe Danny felt he could turn back the tide by building a club side in the image of the Double team, one which played its way to titles. That belief was surely heightened by the appointment of Don Revie as England manager. The football bug was back in Danny's system and while he did not actively seek employment, it was apparent that if the right job came along, he would be willing to give it a go. Within a couple of years, that opportunity arose.

It came from a rather unexpected quarter, the Irish Football Association. Just as the Tottenham job seemed an obvious one for Danny, so too did that of manager of Northern Ireland. Since they had reached the summit in 1958, the national side had been in almost terminal decline. Many had worked long and hard to rectify the situation, but it was a thankless task. Former manager Bertie Peacock puts the problem into perspective: 'The pool's just not big enough. It's all right being a manager, but if you've not got the personnel you're in trouble. Ron Pickering was once asked what made a good coach, and he said, "A damn good pupil." And he was right!' In fifteen years, Danny had been regularly passed over for the role, Derek Dougan explaining: 'I don't think he wanted to manage the side initially but, as important, I don't think Harry Cavan at the FA would have allowed him to do the job!' Once again, Danny and the administrators were unable to find a way of working together for the greater good.

By 1976, Northern Ireland's fortunes were at a very low ebb, their plight underlined by a dreadful Home International series – unable to manage a goal in 270 minutes, they conceded three at Hampden, four at Wembley and one in Swansea. Such dispiriting results were the more baffling since the Northern Irish team contained some very good players: Pat Jennings, Pat Rice, Sammy Nelson, Chris Nicholl, Brian Hamilton, Sammy McIlroy and David McCreery were all top performers in the English First Division and should have been at least able to hold their own against the other home nations. Dave Clements, the Irish player-manager, was coming under fire, the more so since he operated from a New York base, having gone to play there for the Cosmos in the NASL. The Irish Football Association came to the perfectly understandable conclusion that it was impossible to do the job from that distance. In the midst of that Home International series, a poll in the *Belfast Telegraph* suggested that the Northern Irish public wanted to bring Danny back as manager. As a symbol of that golden team of 1958 and as a close confidant of Peter Doherty, many saw him as not just a footballing professor but as a talisman, a lucky charm that might transform Irish fortunes. Pat Jennings confirms that 'they had Danny in because he was such a magical name in our football'.

By 15 June, he was installed in the part-time position of national team manager, with a contract which ran through to the end of June in 1978, taking in the World Cup qualification tournament, one which would pit them against the Dutch, Belgium and Iceland. In view of that opposition, it's fortunate indeed that his motives were altruistic: 'When I first got our squad together, they talked to me about bonuses and I told them not to be stupid: "We have no cash, and in any case you never win anything so don't let's waste time theorizing." And since they know I'm not in the job for material rewards, I have their respect and with it a healthy new spirit.' Pat Jennings agrees: 'Danny was such a nice bloke, a real charmer and he was so committed to Northern Irish football, wanting us to do well. Money didn't interest him, he did the job to help out the national side, and we wanted to respond to that.' Pat Rice, another Northern Irish stalwart, adds: 'Before Danny came in, we didn't really know what direction we were going in. Danny arrived with some very clear ideas and principles about how he wanted to attack, to try to give the players at his disposal the freedom to play. From an outfield player's point of view it was exciting to have the shackles taken off and be given the opportunity to express yourself.'

Danny's approach to his latest job was straightforward: 'I know I am putting my head on the chopping block. I won't gain anything financially or in reputation by doing this job. I don't know if I can cope but I must try. My first priority is to get the players together and tell them what I feel is needed and the way we can go about it. I want to explain my attitudes to playing for your country and towards football. I want to explain also the reasons behind those attitudes. I will tell them too that we cannot expect to win everything. This is not logical with our limited resources but I will hammer home the point – and this is vital – that I would expect them to do their best within their own terms. Let's be honest, there is nothing but difficulties in the path of Northern Ireland. We have got to accept that. It takes time to change habits and many of these players will be loath to do this. Still, we must do something if we are to get better, to get out of the rut.'

In truth, he was in a 'no-lose' situation. Northern Irish sights had been so systematically lowered in the preceding fifteen years that just to win a few games would be a major achievement. Given the World Cup group they found themselves in, there was never any realistic hope of qualification, and so there was no expectation to be fulfilled. If Danny simply presided over a further succession of 4–0 defeats, none would think the worse of him for having a go. If a game or two was won, he could only be a hero. That was the most alluring aspect of the job, not necessarily for selfish reasons, but because he had absolute freedom to do the job his way. If the side had had realistic hopes for the future, if he'd been in charge of England, for example, he'd have been expected to carefully shepherd the side through its matches, introducing a greater air of caution than he would have liked in order to get the required results. Instead, Northern Ireland could play without any such obligation – indeed, Danny saw it as his duty to at least give the public something to enjoy in defeat, to alleviate the harsh lives that many were living amid the terrorist campaigns and high unemployment that disfigured the face of the province. 'At least let's give the people some hope' was his motto. Northern Ireland provided a laboratory for him to experiment with his footballing ideals – he still didn't enjoy defeat and wanted to avoid it if at all possible, but avoid it in the right manner: 'If we go out with dignity, knowing that we have attempted to put up a fight, then I'm satisfied. The players have been too defensively minded when I've watched them. They are ingrained in defensive habits and I've got to attempt to introduce an attacking flair. I want to urge them to go forward. They might not like that, might not be able to do it, but it will be an exercise.'

As the manager hoped to entertain, even in defeat if necessary, he saw his most important job as laying a framework for the future. One of the great attractions of the Northern Ireland job, alongside the powerful sense of honour, was that there was every prospect it would be his for a long time should he so wish, giving time for his methods to work, just as Peter Doherty had taken years to build his initially youthful team. In his first interview on the very day he was given the job, Danny was already talking of his youth squad with enthusiasm: 'It's impossible to put the youngsters into the full team. What I would hope to do is get them together some weekends on Sunday and Monday along with the senior squad. It is a practice which has to be attempted despite the Football League fixtures and the demands of the club. Nothing beats a try.' Immediately, he appointed a liaison officer to help him cover the emerging new talent within the Irish League. This was wholly consistent with his career-long preoccupation with helping youngsters make their way in the game, be they players or supporters. So great was his affinity with them and their untainted romance with football that he would go out of his way to assist them, hoping that perhaps some of his ideals about the game might rub off along the way, safeguarding the game's future.

For an international manager, one of the greatest difficulties which must be addressed is that of access to players. Even now, in a supposedly more enlightened age, the club versus country debate is as heated as it ever was, but the likes of Hoddle and Hamilton have it comparatively easy. Back in 1976, international managers were lucky to get hold of their players for a couple of days before a match, on just six or seven occasions in the year. Admittedly, given the advances in air travel and the improving finances of the game as a whole, there were more matches than in the days of Doherty, but it was still difficult to build a cohesive team pattern. From the outset, Danny tried to instigate new training methods to combat the problem. Assembling his squad for his first game, against the Dutch in October 1976, he arranged for his team to play Luton Town behind closed doors, building upon an earlier practice game at Coventry. The Irish side won 2–0 at Kenilworth Road and Danny termed it 'A worthwhile exercise – there are still a number of problems to be sorted out in getting players to change from their defensive attitude. It is a long term project.' Bryan Hamilton, whom Danny described as the fulcrum of their attacking plan, was enthused by the new ideas, explaining, 'I'm excited, there is a lot of potential about it. We must get the ball through to the wings to succeed. Admittedly we looked lost in our first practice at Coventry but against Luton things began to drop into place. It will take time to adjust, but we are capable of doing that.'

By that second practice game, Danny had already carried out a gentle revolution of his own, one of both personnel and philosophy. As his assistant he had appointed Tommy Cavanagh, who was working alongside Tommy Docherty at Manchester United. Between them they ran the team. Pat Jennings confirms that 'the training was on skills, total football, not giving the ball away. He and Tommy thought along the same lines.' But if anything was a statement of intent, it was the recall of George Best to international colours for the first time in three years. Pat Rice asks the perfectly reasonable question, 'How could anyone leave George out?' But Pat Jennings saw it as 'typifying Danny and everything he stood for. He wanted that flair, he could see George could still do it for Fulham and wanted it to work for us.' At a stroke, Danny created more optimism around the Irish camp than had existed in years, as captain Allan Hunter admitted: 'Something had to be done and so we have a new manager, a new coach, a freshness about it all. This is the formation we have decided upon and whether or not it fails in Rotterdam, we must adhere to it in future even if there have to be modifications. Danny is lifting us and Tommy Cavanagh is so infectious he can build your morale or tell you off in the nicest way.'

That injection of hope was something Danny saw as being crucial. He knew the demoralizing effect of playing in a national side that saw itself as cannon fodder. Had he not won his first caps in a directionless side a quarter of a century earlier? Small countries with slim resources desperately need an inspirational figurehead to help them realize, then exceed, their potential. Back in the fifties Peter Doherty had fitted the bill. Now the baton had been passed to Danny himself. By bringing in George Best, as great a genius as ever kicked a ball, he hoped to find an on-the-field sprite, a wizard who could do the impossible, who might lead his lesser colleagues to believe in themselves. As Pat Jennings points out: 'George was better on one leg than most players on two.' His inclusion did provide the manager with one problem though: 'George has no tactical awareness. He is such a great player that he must play, but it means that to get the right balance in our 4−2−4 system I must play fourteen players!' Bertie Peacock notes, 'We didn't have the players that we would have liked to have had to play the way he wanted to play – when Billy Bingham took over, he played the percentage game, which was the only way Northern Ireland could have got success; but Danny wouldn't play that way. It's not about managers, it's about players, and he didn't have them. Because of that, Danny had to try to bring George back. When he got George it was really too late, George was having fun – if Danny had got him at the right time, he'd have worshipped him. Best was a man at seventeen, ready for anything, Danny would have loved to have had him then. He would have transformed the team.'

Danny's first game in charge was a genuine baptism of fire. For the match in Rotterdam he needed all the good omens he could find. The return of Best was one such, reminding his players that they had a man to rank with Holland's Cruyff. He took further heart from the fact that the game was to be played at the Feyenoord Stadium, the scene of his most glorious triumph with Spurs in 1963. On that night, an unfancied side had thrashed one of the best teams Europe had to offer. Would history repeat itself? Certainly the spirit in the Irish camp was good, Pat Rice recalling that 'training was always enjoyable, we'd play games and so on. It was much more relaxed than training with Arsenal because Danny was that kind of man, but you also have to remember that it's not like a club with youngsters, this is a squad full of internationals. If they don't know what to do, they shouldn't be there anyway. Danny treated the players well, like grown men, and he got a good response because of that.' He also made it very clear what he expected of his side: 'In the past we have been swamped in our own half. I promised to do something about this. I haven't promised that we are going to win and eliminate the underdog label but we will go forward all the time. I want my players to respect team discipline, and within that general framework, since no one expects us to win, I tell the boys to go out with heads high and attack the opposition. That way we may achieve the unexpected instead of cowering defensively in our own half hoping to scrape a draw. To me that is undignified. It is better to lose by doing this than by negative, boring defence. If we lose then we do so in a determined manner. Players themselves believe they can win but at the end of the day you must be realistic. Obviously the Dutch are favourites but I think they will know they have been in a battle.'

That they did. For manager and players alike, it was one of those rare, magical nights where every plan worked like clockwork, when the team played above all expectations and scarcely put a foot wrong. Pat Rice remembers that 'George was superb. We all played well but Danny was delighted because his tactics and selection had proved right. From our point of view, instead of us being frightened, this time the opposition were, because we had George Best. That alone proved Danny right.' That night in Rotterdam was perhaps the final flourish of Best's career. Although he played well in isolated bursts thereafter, against the Dutch he had dominated from start to finish. 'They had Cruyff, Neeskens – great players,' recalls Pat Jennings. 'But on the night we were as good as they were, mainly thanks to George. Neeskens even went back to mark him but he nutmegged him so many times that Neeskens finished up trying to kick him. Neeskens went down injured himself at one point and while he was lying there, George took the tie off his socks and gave it to him to tie his legs together. We had a nucleus of a decent side so it was always possible for us to have a good game, but the problem was doing that consistently.' The Irish pushed the Dutch masters to the brink, coming away from Rotterdam with a scarcely credible 2–2 draw. Danny was effusive in his praise, telling the Belfast press, 'This is just too crazy, just incredible. We kept pushing, and that gave us the draw. We did not quit against a team which really played better than our side. Holland were very, very good . . . football is a conflict between emotion and logic. I know it was a peak performance and that henceforth they will probably only get worse. My rational judgement tells me we have a 90 per cent chance of failing to qualify for the World Cup but we will have a go. I'll not deny the people their dreams; maybe they need that in their lives. Failure may destroy their dreams of me but all life is about how we respond.'

The Dutch result was always likely to be a high point, the freshness of the honeymoon period translated into renewed vigour on the field. As the high priest of attacking football, Danny was perhaps fortunate that his first game was against like-minded opposition. Certainly Pat Rice felt 'it helped that they were a footballing side rather than a destructive one'. The greatest problem for the Irish was a lack of quality in attack. Had the Dutch simply sat in their own half, soaked up pressure and hit on the break, then the Irish might well have suffered as they surged forward. As it was, the game in Rotterdam flowed from end to end and the Irish gave as good as they got. Emboldened by this early success, the team returned to national service a month later with renewed hope. 'Team spirit was excellent,' according to Pat Rice. 'Danny was great at building that. Obviously we couldn't do much about the resources we had, they were always slim, but when we got together, we knew each other, the way we played; there weren't a lot of people around you didn't know. That helped build the side. We all enjoyed playing under Danny, whatever the results were like. He was a lovely character, great company to be in, so it was something to look forward to.'

Prior to the Belgian qualifier in Liege, Luton provided practice opposition once more. *The Times*'s Norman Fox was on hand at one training session and remarked that Danny's 'outlook is that of a man who has for some time been detached from the everyday work of organizing a team and has brought a refreshingly light approach to the task'. Danny's answer to that was to point out: 'We have none of those long team talks no one understands. I tell them they are all wearing the same coloured shirts so they might as well pass to each other.' It was an approach that found favour with George Best, who admitted that 'It's fun to play for Ireland again under Danny. He says the same things as Sir Matt Busby used to at Old Trafford: "Go out and enjoy yourself on the field." The only difference is he takes twice as long to say it!' Such a refreshing approach was bound to pay dividends in the short term and his side produced another excellent, highly committed performance against the Belgians, before going down 2–0. After the game, Danny pointed out that 'we from our small country played the game almost as well as we know how tonight', while Rob Hughes agreed with his analysis in the *Sunday Times*: 'The 4–2–4 formation took the game to Belgium for thirty minutes until [Northern Ireland] went behind and lost hope.'

In spite of these two early moral victories, most observers could see a day of reckoning coming. Although the purists loved to see a side playing with such freedom and optimism, all over Europe, national coaches were taking notes. The Dutch and Belgians had been caught by surprise by the progressive and open play of the Irish, but Danny's side could depend on that element no more. In that game in Liege, Belgium had taken a look at the Irish tactics, reorganized themselves and had opted for a highly disciplined counter-attacking strategy. Allowing Best the freedom to operate on the flanks, they were secure in the knowledge that any chances he created would not be accepted by the goal-shy forwards. Once the moves had broken down, the Belgians had time to hit the over-committed Irish side on the break. That was to be the perennial problem for Danny as he went off in pursuit of his glorious vision. When his strikers were the likes of Billy Caskey, Terry Cochrane, Trevor Anderson, Derek Spence and Gerry Armstrong, all good honest triers but clearly not of international class, it's little wonder that few goals were registered.

Not only was he let down by the impotence of his strike force, he was also trying to turn back the clock in an age when football was cloaked in cynicism and negativity. It's impossible to overstate how negative many sides throughout Europe had become by the late seventies. As Danny urged his men on, they found themselves running into the massed ranks of the opposition, who simply picked them off. That much was illustrated when they flew out to Cologne in April 1977 for a friendly against the World Cup holders, West Germany. Speaking before the game, Danny had an inkling of the coming storm, repeating his mantra: 'It's better to lose having a go than be defeated concentrating on defence as Ireland has done so often.' There is no side in the world better equipped to dash romantic dreams than the clinically efficient Germans, who demolished the Irish by five goals to nil, though Pat Rice recalls that 'Danny was tremendous at looking on the positive side. All he'd say was, "We were as good as they were for an hour"!'

As goalkeeper, Pat Jennings was stuck in the firing line: 'Danny's ideas were simple – everything was about going forward and, if necessary, losing in style. He'd rather lose 5–4 than 1–0, the only trouble being we weren't capable of scoring four, but were always capable of letting six in. You had to entertain and hope that we might just win. Which wasn't much good for me as a goalkeeper. A lot of the players weren't too keen on that, especially as things went on, because you don't want to keep getting hammered. We wanted to keep it tight, and rely on nicking a goal at a set-piece or a breakaway. We weren't good enough to take the game to the likes of West Germany and I don't think his tactics were right for us. It didn't suit our players. At times, I was picking the ball up and throwing it behind me to the full-backs to start a move from there, whereas later, under Billy Bingham, if I got the ball I had to kick it and drop it on the edge of the other eighteen-yard box, playing route one, keeping the ball as far away from our goal as we could get it! Danny wanted us to play through people, which we couldn't do. To make it worse, in that West Germany game, I'd been out for four or five months and I was just coming back. We were doing all right until the last few minutes. They got a penalty and the roof fell in – I think Danny called Sammy Nelson a cheat because he handled the ball to give away a penalty! The press wrote me off after that game, Malcolm Brodie in the Belfast press was saying that I'd had it, but going to West Germany, a hiding's always on. Danny was very supportive. He said, "You forget the press, I'll talk to them, you just do your best." He was brilliant like that.'

As hardened professionals, men like Pat Jennings wanted to get results – that was their bread and butter in the English game. To have Danny insisting that results didn't matter was a huge culture shock. However much he lifted the pressure from their shoulders by taking whatever flak flew, no professional wants to suffer a humiliation. Danny understood that himself – he'd played in teams that had been heavily beaten or dispatched by inferior sides. The difference lay in the twenty years that had passed since Sweden. Football was no longer a simple, enjoyable pastime, but a job of work. You could not say that you might as well lose by attacking as by defending. That was not enough, it smacked of laziness, defeatism, of not trying hard enough. Whatever your resources, people demanded results. Danny rebutted such accusations by arguing, 'A manager must have foresight and that means having a different opinion to most people. If they cannot see what you are trying to do, then you get criticized.' He had an influential supporter in Malcolm Brodie of the *Belfast Telegraph*, who noted that his first months in the job had been 'highly successful, invigorating and refreshing', while Danny added, 'If we go forward we can give the opposition plenty to think about. Let's get six men in the box if necessary. My attitude and tactics could be wrong. Hang me for it if they are.' This was the problem: in terms of the greater glory of the game, Danny was spot on; in practice, his attacking ideals, implemented by a relatively weak side, were destined to fail. Just as Danny had been called an 'expensive luxury' by Bill Nicholson in a failing team, so too was his expansive philosophy. 'The problem with attacking all the while was that we had some beatings like the West German game and that knocks your confidence,' explains Pat Jennings. 'It takes a while to get that back again and if you keep getting beaten badly, you can't get over it. But Danny wouldn't change the style. We wanted to, because it's no fun standing at the back watching the ball fly past you. I wanted a good defensive unit around me, and to start from there, but he wouldn't change his principles. We had players like Allan Hunter, who was as good as anyone in Britain, and he didn't want to be carrying the ball up to the halfway line while everyone dropped back. He wanted to look for the lads up front to take the pressure off.' Fifteen years earlier forwards did not drop back to defend – they left that to the half- and full-backs. By 1977, everyone had defensive responsibilities, leaving the midfield impenetrable.

For some months, little seemed to be improving. Defeats at the hands of England and Scotland, a draw with Wales and then, most damning of all, a one-goal defeat in Reykjavik, seemed to suggest that Danny's grand plan was doomed to failure. His idiosyncratic approach to management looked like it had come from a bygone age and did, at times, perplex his players. Once, when training, for example, Pat Jennings 'got the ball and threw it from the edge of our box into the path of one of our players in the other half, and Danny stopped the game. He said, "I didn't realize you could throw the ball that far." So I replied, "It's not a problem, Danny." And he said, "We'll use that tomorrow night, that'll surprise 'em." I told him I could kick it another thirty yards with the same accuracy, but he insisted I throw it.' The others sympathized with Jennings' plight in goal, his Arsenal colleague Pat Rice admitting: 'From Pat's point of view I can appreciate his reluctance, he wanted a solid defence. As a defender, I shared a degree of that, because you naturally have to be cautious in the way you play, but Danny was terrific for the attacking players, especially, because he was saying, "You play, I'll take the responsibility." I think his ideal side would have been the Arsenal defence and the Manchester United forward line! Perhaps Danny was a little naïve in the way that European football had developed. Before we went to play West Germany he asked me about what we did at Arsenal. He said, "If they leave one up at a corner, what do you do?" I replied: "We bring two back, one to mark and one spare." So he said, "What about if they leave two up?" "Well, usually, it's two markers and one in front to pick the ball up if it comes short, because with the two markers you don't need a spare man behind." So he said, "Fine. I tell you what we're going to do. If they get a corner, we'll leave four up and they'll have to keep five back." And I thought, Danny, they won't keep five back, they'll outnumber us in the box and get a goal. But that was his philosophy, we'll attack and let them worry.'

Gradually, very gradually, things started to brighten again. In a scrappy encounter, the Irish finally managed to score two goals against Iceland in a World Cup game in Belfast to register their first win under Danny in eight attempts. That game exposed all the differences between his approach and that of the rest of Europe. Iceland was a nation with even less tradition and resources than the Irish, and despite being already out of the competition they came to Belfast purely to defend. Danny was scathing after the match: 'That's not the way I would have played under the circumstances. They only came to save their face, not to entertain, but I suppose that's the name of the game today.' Three weeks later, in George Best's final game, the pure football of the Dutch brought the best out in the Irish in Belfast, who were defeated by a single goal, *The Times* noting that 'Ireland can take comfort from their control of midfield', though Pat Jennings believes that the home results were better because of a change in style: 'At Windsor Park, the crowd dictated the way we played.

If you had a full house in Belfast, they didn't want to see me rolling the ball out to the full-backs, they wanted the ball in the other half, and so we played a more direct game and we had some good results from that.' One such came in November, when Belgium were caned 3–0 in a comprehensive victory that suggested that Danny's ideas might finally be bearing fruit. One idea had been to introduce a number of Irish-based players to the senior squad in the hope they might attract the attention of English clubs. He asked, with some satisfaction, 'Have you ever seen a time when there was so much movement in Irish football? We have brought in a few young players, we have had quite a few transfers, there has been cash for youth, a policy development at this level and there is sponsorship which is going into the local game at a phenomenal rate. We are all working on the right lines.' The only problem with a long-term plan, correct though it may be, is that football is a defiantly short-term business. Again, the Home International series brought defeats against England and Wales and a draw against Argentina-bound Scotland; never mind that the squad was shorn of its Arsenal contingent – Jennings, Rice, Nelson – the results were still not good enough for many observers.

Fresh impetus was given by the approaching qualification group for the European Championships. Again, Northern Ireland were in a tough group alongside England, Bulgaria, Denmark and the Republic of Ireland, but it engendered much comment, not least because of the games against their closest neighbours. Unsurprisingly, Danny asked the key question of the moment: ' "What about a united Irish team?" There is no time for a complex and long-winded answer but here is a quick one. "Terrific! I'm all for it. If they let us play twenty-two players in a united team, I think we will have a chance to beat the world!" ' The Republic provided the opposition in the first game of the series, in Dublin; the first meeting between the two partitioned nations. The build-up was inevitably frenetic and Pat Jennings recalls, 'We got a police escort through Dublin, it flew through there. The security guys had picked us up as soon as we went over the border and took us through to the hotel. I've never driven through Dublin so fast!' In spite of security worries, Pat Rice states, 'There was no ill feeling between the players. We actually had a vote at one time as to whether there should be one team for Ireland, as they do in rugby union, and the players all said that we should, but the actual governing bodies turned that down. When it came to the game though, nobody wanted to lose! It was inevitable that the game was a nil–nil.' Looked at positively, it meant an away point, though Danny was disappointed at the lack of spectacle. Following the game, he announced that he would only stay with the side until the end of the qualification phase – or into the tournament Finals should they qualify – since he felt a younger man should take the team on to the World Cup in 1982.

It was apparent that he was already feeling a degree of disenchantment with the modern game, upset that results mattered above all else, that few could see the possibilities of his long-term planning. Peter McParland believes that, 'By 1976, when he took over, he knew he could get in among his own people, among the players and inspire them. But I think it was always likely to be a brief stay for him.' Simply, Danny was speared on the horns of an insoluble dilemma – should he retain his principles, even if they are shown to be impractical, or should he renege on them to please those whose opinions he didn't respect? For Danny there was only one choice, as Bertie Peacock acknowledges: 'Peter Doherty and Bill Nicholson both had that bit of grit, something stable in the middle of the field, but Danny wouldn't accept that. Danny was a cavalier fella, loved to go forward – Keegan at Newcastle epitomized everything Danny liked.'

Free of the shackles that any long-term obligations might have imposed, the Northern Irish team suddenly flourished. At home to Denmark, *The Times* recorded that 'Two vital substitutions by Danny Blanchflower earned a European Championship win – the Irish had to overcome the setback of a breakaway Danish goal before Derek Spence and Trevor Anderson, both substitutes, scored . . . Northern Ireland pressurized the Danes with a display of ceaseless aggression.' A month later, they overran Bulgaria in Sofia to win 2–0 in appalling conditions – 'We ended up throwing snowballs at one another after the match,' remembers Pat Jennings. By this stage, Northern Ireland had taken 5 points from 3 games to head the group from England, with 3 points from 2 – already it was turning into a straight fight between those two countries. After the Bulgaria game, Danny warned against premature celebration in the *Sunday Express*: 'Our teams have done us proud. We were expected to be at the bottom of the table but we are at the top. We are not afraid of being there. We have worked hard to get there. But we are a small force with limited resources. The further we go the harder it will become. It is not the time for us to boast about what we have done. We must concentrate on what has still to be done and let the others do most of the talking.'

Ironically, since he had announced his impending retirement, Danny's stock had risen sharply, so much so that he was offered, and accepted, the job of managing Chelsea, the two jobs to run concurrently. The job as manager of Northern Ireland was still seen, not least by the Irish FA, as a part-time one, so there was no disquiet in Belfast about Danny taking on another role, such as Venables does now with Australia. Unlike the England manager, Danny had only a very few players on whom he could call, so scouting was a far smaller part of his job. Equally, Northern Ireland were not looking to embrace the method that helped Jack Charlton find success with the Republic, by finding any player in the land with an Irish relation somewhere on the family tree. Just as Doherty's side had been comprised of Ulstermen, so too was Danny's. That was an issue of pride, even though it did restrict the size of the pool. The Chelsea appointment made it obvious that Danny was now once again viewed as the man with the Midas touch, but in Northern Irish terms, would this prove to be a false dawn? The next test was the stiffest. They travelled to Wembley to take on England in February – if the Irishmen could come away with a point, qualification would be a real possibility. At a time where discretion might have been the obvious approach, Danny continued to urge his side on to the offensive. His view was that that had got them to the top of the group, so why lose confidence in it now? Perhaps the answer to that question came in the opposition. Although Northern Ireland had played so well against Belgium and the Dutch, teams that were at least the equal of England, those two had held few fears. England, on the other hand, did – the legacy of an age-old inferiority complex. As Pat Jennings explains, 'It was always on the cards that England might wallop us – you looked at what they had on the bench and what we had on the field, and that set it up for us. They had loads of good players. We knew them and what to expect. Perhaps ignorance was bliss at times – when we played Belgium or Bulgaria, you didn't know what was coming, what their strengths might be, and so you weren't overawed and just played your game, whereas you knew how good Keegan or Clemence or Coppell or Brooking were.' Of the Northern Irish squad, featuring First Division players such as Jimmy and Chris Nicholl, Bryan Hamilton, Pat Rice, Sammy Nelson and Sammy McIlroy, only Pat Jennings would have been in serious contention for an England place.

England went out at Wembley determined to win the physical battle, causing Danny to complain that 'people were coming in with arms and elbows. That is rugby to me, not football'. The purist was defeated by four goals to nil, though even then he found crumbs of comfort: 'We were as good as England in the first half. They got a goal and then straight away they got another. The underdog can't come back from 2–0 down. The other side might come back and win 3–2. But it's like when three of you take on ten. You have to knock a couple down early on to feel there is a chance. If they knock one of you down first, the other two feel like running away. Will this defeat affect the players? Not at all. Come Saturday they'll be off getting hammered somewhere else and this'll go right out of their heads.' Even in the face of this morale-sapping defeat, the Irish managed to rally and in May defeated a poor Bulgarian side, having gone on to the attack from the first whistle. Nevertheless, the bubble had been burst. Danny had managed to do what Doherty had done in the mid-1950s, create an impression of calm confidence around a powerful team spirit. But it was a fragile edifice and one poor result, such as that at Wembley, was enough to bring it tumbling to earth. Faced with a resurgent Denmark in June 1979, their hopes of qualification collapsed after a 4–0 hammering. Pat Jennings remembers, 'In Copenhagen we were lucky to get away with four. They blitzed us. It took me a couple of months to get over that because it could have been eight or ten, to be honest. They were whipping great balls across the six-yard box between me and the defence. They had a class side – the side with Simonsen was emerging. They completely outplayed us.'

Another heavy beating from England, 5–1 in Belfast, showed just how short of quality players they were. For Danny, the adverse reaction to that result was hurtful. Where a few months before the talk had been of trying to persuade him to stay on in the job, now people were only too keen to bring down the curtain on his reign. Privately, he resolved to see Northern Ireland through their final game with the Republic in Belfast and then bow out. Before the match, he made his frustrations crystal clear: 'We need continuity to make progress. You have to suffer to improve sometimes. I don't think this is the match to experiment . . . six of our ten outfield players are attackers and I think this answers the criticism that we are defensively minded . . . I don't know what all the fuss is about. It's just two teams from England playing each other in Belfast.' Pat Jennings recalls, 'We beat the Republic in Belfast. A few of their side were missing but it was a tough game that we nicked 1–0. There was a bit of crowd trouble too. But that was where we could win, if the game became a battle. If it was open, we hadn't the players.' An assessment with which Pat Rice agrees: 'The basic tactics were simple – attack, don't do anything silly at the back, but have a go. There were times when we came unstuck, but at least people couldn't say, as they had in the past, that we didn't give it a go. Let's lose 7–6 rather than 1–0. The only problem there is that the other managers didn't think the same way. European football was very defensively minded at that stage and the goalscoring opportunities weren't there for us. And when George Best finally went, we didn't have the players up front.'

That perhaps is the theme of the Blanchflower reign – he didn't have the players to do what he wanted. Later managers, north and south of the Irish border, took a more worldly view, as Pat Jennings concedes: 'He restored a bit of pride, but it was really Billy Bingham who transformed our fortunes, with the right kind of tactics.' Danny himself wrote, 'I believe a manager can only improve the team he inherits by ten per cent. If you do it with Iceland or Luxembourg or Northern Ireland, the casual observer will hardly notice it . . . the committee were puzzled and their pride hurt by the heavy defeat by England. I sensed that they were in doubt about the future. I knew that a win against the Republic of Ireland might accommodate most of those doubts. It would shove us up into second place behind England in our European Championship qualifying group, and there was more pride than shame in that for such a small country. But that was not the point as far as I was concerned. If they could not show some faith on a bad day then how could we really believe in one another when the good days were so few and far between? It was time to go. I had done my best. I had paid off my debts. I had made some more friends among the players. We could shake hands and behave like sportsmen. I suppose that kind of attitude is suspicious these days but I am sure that Johnny Geary, Cecil Collins, Billy Maxwell and Peter Doherty, the men who encouraged me as a player, the men who were the Irish FA as far as I was concerned, would understand. Management is about fair play. I prefer to think that every elephant is an animal but not every animal is an elephant. I want us to be incorruptible. I will not stand for cheating. It does not matter about winning and losing so long as the Irish spirit of fair play sparks some admiration and affection in others.' Sadly, those were ideals that belonged in part to another, earlier era.

Among the players, there was a degree of inevitability to Danny's demise, but Pat Jennings was still 'sorry to see Danny go because he was such a smashing bloke. If I'd wanted to win for any of the managers I'd played under – and there have been some lovely fellas, like Bertie Peacock, who was a real gentleman – it would have been for Danny. There wasn't an ounce of badness in him, he just wanted what was good for Irish football, but it wasn't to be. I think he just felt he couldn't do any more, he was getting hassle he didn't need from the press and the FA, and he thought it was time to bow out. He wouldn't want to be anywhere he wasn't wanted. It was an enjoyable experience, a privilege and honour to play for his teams, and I wouldn't have wanted to miss out on that.' Pat Rice adds: 'He was a man of great pride in himself and his principles. He wouldn't change those, and rightly so. What he really did was to brighten up Northern Irish football. All of a sudden there was a lot of happiness, joviality about the camp, a great spirit and sense of comradeship among the players, and I think that stood the team in good stead after he'd left.' He would have settled for that.

10 Can't Get There From Here

For somebody so resolutely opposed to the idea of a career in football management, the 1970s proved to be a very odd decade for Danny Blanchflower. There was the disappointment over the Spurs job, then the post with Northern Ireland. All this from a man who had once spoken of football management with the language of disgust: 'Supporters never meet the obstacles. They never know the frustrations of directors and staff who interfere and of players and staff who buck their authority. They never receive the nasty letters of advice or the criticism in the newspapers . . . the doubts and loneliness of the actual job, the long, weary hours of searching for players and the worry of what is going on at their clubs while they're away.' That was not the most enthusiastic of job applications. His interest in the Spurs and Irish jobs was understandable, perhaps: sentiment overwhelming the cautions of his rational mind. But his decision to take on the job of Chelsea manager in December 1978 was a bolt from the blue. There was no emotional pull, as there had been from Windsor Park or White Hart Lane. No, the attraction was football itself, the erratic involvement with his national squad translating itself into a need to test himself at club level, to work with players on a day-to-day basis. The frustration of working with the national squad was threefold: his pool of players was limited and poor in parts, something which he could do nothing about since there is no transfer market between national sides; matches were infrequent, making it tough to maintain any continuity, the more so since when players returned to their clubs they might be asked to do completely different things; and the lack of time available to him to work with players when on international duty – two or three days at best. In December 1978, when the call came from Stamford Bridge, Northern Ireland appeared to have turned a corner, Danny's ideals seemed to be bringing success. They were top of their European Championship group, had beaten

Denmark in some style and had just won convincingly in Sofia. Given that the Irish didn't have a goalscorer worthy of the name and that they could not train effectively, what might Danny be able to achieve when working with players every day of the week? When he might be able to attract new players to the club, whatever their nationality? With Brian Mears, a good friend, installed as Chelsea chairman, Danny could be reasonably sure there would be no misunderstandings as to responsibilities. Buoyed by that, the offer to manage Chelsea was just too flattering to turn down.

Today, Chelsea hold the FA Cup and have an extremely promising future ahead. Their current fortune (and fortunes) could not be more diametrically opposed to that of 1978 – indeed, it is only the recent injection of cash from the late Matthew Harding that has finally stabilized the club and given it the opportunity to search for honours. Ironically, Danny wrote an article about the ailing club two months before he was offered the manager's job: 'Chelsea had built a very good looking stand on one side of the ground. Now they had dreams of a utopian palace – a British astrodome where future Cup Finals would all be played. But before even part of the dream – the present grandstand – had been built, they knew they were in trouble. Materialism fell into a slump and property values dived. And as they had planned to sell some property to finance the dream, it suddenly became a nightmare. They were soon £3 million in debt . . . the team was in a transition time. Old players were fading and new faces were coming in . . . Chelsea have been doing poorly. Who can blame manager Ken Shellito for that? What big-name manager could erase a £3 million debt?'

Chelsea offered a mission impossible to rank with Northern Ireland a couple of years earlier. Why did Danny set himself such seemingly hopeless tasks? Rather than risking his reputation, surely he was protecting it, as again failure was almost inevitable and would bring no shame, while any success would be all the more glorious. But as before, this was not a function of cowardice, merely a rational realization that in the game's safety-first climate, he would only be given freedom to run things his way in a lost cause, where directors would be ready to throw caution to the winds in sheer desperation. His on-going commitment to Northern Ireland indicated that such radical ideas might work and

Chelsea were in a position to give him the autonomy he required since nothing else was working there.

Danny had not been Chelsea's first choice for the job. That had been the Yugoslavian coach Miljan Miljanic, approached while Ken Shellito was still manager, but with the team stuck in the bottom two of the First Division. Danny had pondered on Miljanic's possible appointment in the *Sunday Express* in October 1978: 'He is a decent man with good principles for whom I have much respect. He agreed to come here and take stock of Chelsea's football assets. That is the most sensible action that any would-be coach could possibly take. He is too wise not to realize that the odds at Chelsea are too high for him to risk the gamble. If he were to take on such a high risk it would only be fair if he were rewarded in keeping with the risk. How can Chelsea afford Miljanic, who has been highly paid by Real Madrid? Chelsea's approach could prove an embarrassment for Miljanic. It has been a bigger one for Shellito. His credibility has been undermined. But what can Chelsea do but grasp at straws?'

If Danny's ego was an important part in the equation – his great self-belief leading him to the impression that he could save Chelsea – there was also an element of self-sacrifice in the deal – that much was implied in that article. He was always sensitive to the needs of those only just entering a profession, be it as player or manager. With Chelsea a particularly young side, he must have felt that he would be able to shield those newcomers from the harsher realities of the game, giving them time to grow in stature as he took the flak. At a time when Chelsea were in such dire straits, he also recognized that it would be virtually impossible for them to attract an established big-name manager and would have to bring in another novice, as they had done with Ken Shellito. The job at Stamford Bridge was simply too big for one without experience and would probably wreck a career. In 1978, Danny didn't need the job, he had an income from elsewhere and so was largely immune to the pressures of the job – if all failed, he'd simply go back to journalism. John Junor at the *Sunday Express* told him: 'You must consider the paper as a harbour for you to return to.' Danny could therefore 'sail the stormy seas and return to tranquillity'. From Chelsea's point of view too, it was not good enough to bring in an inexperienced manager. Amid the financial turmoil, Danny understood that the club was in need of good footballing principles, that these values needed to be instilled in the players. It was not a club where the chequebook could solve problems – it had inflicted plenty – so Danny believed the escape route would come from applying basic ideals, good habits. It would take time, but short of a rich fairy godmother descending on the King's Road, this was the only way back.

In his time away from the game Danny's ideals had become increasingly divorced from the realities of modern football. As a writer, depressed by much of what he had to watch, he had become yet more romantic about the beautiful game as tactics continued to suppress invention. Though an idealist, he was no feckless dreamer, had no time for 'wouldn't it be nice if . . .'. Danny persisted in his view that you could win the right way, pointing to Brazil in 1958, 1962 and 1970, Real Madrid, Hungary, Ajax in the early 1970s, Manchester United in the 1950s and 1960s. In that he was also prophetic, because subsequent to Danny's reign, teams have won things the right way – Holland in 1988 or AC Milan through the late 1980s into the 1990s, for example. Even in England, attractive sides have triumphed – Manchester United were an especially thrilling proposition early in their current reign when Giggs and Kanchelskis were in full flight; Newcastle almost made it in 1996, Chelsea did in 1997. Why did they succeed where Danny often failed? Because the circumstances were right. They had the players to do it. There's an old joke about an English tourist lost in the west of Ireland. Asking a man in the local pub how he can get to a particular village, the reply is 'Sure now, but you can't get there from here.' That was the problem with Chelsea. With the players he had and the money he didn't, Chelsea was never going to be transformed into a beautiful and successful team. But it didn't stop him trying. Tactically, he was incredibly stubborn and refused to compromise his ideals. This was to his credit, for the game could do with more coaches willing to play an open game, but to espouse that view from Stamford Bridge, with a lousy side, was untenable. He had either to cut his coat according to the meagre cloth he was given, or stay out of the way. In addition, he had an outmoded view of what 'attractive football' meant on the brink of the 1980s. In the past, most sides went out with a view to entertaining. By 1978, you had to earn the right to play your football. Sides like Liverpool could still be exciting, but in a different fashion to the Double-winning Spurs. Liverpool under Shankly, then Paisley, had developed an incisive passing game played at pace but with purpose, each player having a specific job to do that covered both attacking and defensive duties. Football orthodoxy circa 1978 stated that defenders defended and attackers defended too, attacking when possible. For Danny, attackers attacked at all times, defenders defended when they had to, but attacked if possible. Allied to this quaint eccentricity, as it was now viewed, he had an odd aversion to employing players who could get stuck in – odd in that his greatest successes at Spurs had been alongside the granitelike Mackay, yet as a manager he was reluctant to introduce a similar balance to his sides, fatally undermining them. Perhaps now that he was finally in control of a club, he wanted to take this last chance to find out whether football genuinely could be the beautiful game, if a side could succeed by artistry alone. Chelsea were to prove that they, at least, could not.

Whatever drawbacks Danny's philosophy might have had, once he articulated it all, it was a beautiful vision, one which could sweep others along with him. Brian Mears had been an admirer of Danny's ideals for some time and, as a friend, he clearly hoped that the two might be able to strike up an equally good working relationship to turn around his ailing club. Mears had great faith in Blanchflower – this was the man who had masterminded the Double, a considerable footballing intellect. He appeared to be working miracles with Northern Ireland, a tiny country with no resources, one in a comparable position to Chelsea. The hope was he could do the same job in London. Sadly, that overlooked the fact that though Northern Ireland had a small squad, they did have one or two outstanding players, notably Pat Jennings. If you have a truly great goalkeeper on your side, then you're always in with a chance of doing something. They also had the mercurial Best to lift hopes at the outset of his reign and good solid professionals like Pat Rice, Sammy Nelson, Bryan Hamilton, Jimmy Nicholl and Sammy McIlroy to bolster the side. Chelsea's cupboard was almost bare – the established talent included Ron Harris, Peter Osgood, the injured Mickey Droy and Peter Bonetti, all four of whom were nearing the end of their playing days. Alongside them was Ray Wilkins, carrying the responsibility for the side at the age of twenty-one. Beyond that, Chelsea were a team of kids. Danny loved to point out that 'Brazil won the World Cup in 1970 playing exhilarating football with a manager they'd only had for three weeks. Great teams don't need managers', though at Chelsea he didn't have a great team with which to work. It was a daunting prospect.

Even so, it was one he approached with his characteristic mix of optimism and realism: 'Brian Mears approached me the morning after Ken Shellito had resigned to try to salvage something. Was it fate calling me out to pay my dues? How could I refuse that and keep my self-respect? How can you hide from fate? It is a tough job and I may not be up to it. There is only one way to find out. Good reputation is not built on fear. It can be lost in battle again. Is that worse than keeping it in a cupboard only to open the cupboard one day and find it has gone? If I had wanted it for the money I would have demanded more and a five-year contract. I have a month-to-month agreement to the end of the season. This gives the Chelsea board the opportunity to part with me without expense . . . my golf hasn't been too good lately, so I considered the offer. I felt I couldn't refuse to help because I love football and Chelsea are one of the important clubs and always have been. I don't know if I can save Chelsea from relegation or from anything else. If you spent a million you can still get relegated . . . what you have to do is go your own way, experiment and not be afraid of failure. Eventual success will make it all worthwhile. There are no consequences if I fail. In any case, I would rather fail with a bit of method than with chaos.'

All at the club hoped that the days of chaos might be at an end. Peter Osgood had returned to Chelsea from Philadelphia Furies. 'Ken Shellito got in touch and asked me if I'd come down. It was sad to go back to that environment, because when I left Chelsea we'd had three Finals in three years, won two, and they'd built the stand – it was a progressive club. When I got back five years later they were skint, struggling. I signed for Ken, but within a few weeks he'd gone. Frank Upton, the coach, walked in the day after and said, "Right, it's not Frank any more, you call me boss. I'm taking over until they appoint someone else." Overnight, they appointed Danny, so we went in the next morning and it was back to "Morning, Frank!" It was a crazy week, three managers in four days, but I think we were all relieved that Danny had come in. At least he was a big name, a guy who knew his football, a great player. Everyone was in awe of him. Brian Mears had seen that he'd done well for Northern Ireland and thought he might bring some stability to the club, that people would look up to him and respect him.'

One of his first duties was to reduce expectations at the club. He did that in remarkable fashion, indicating just how far the game had moved since his time as a player. 'I don't care if Chelsea go down as long as they have done their best. I don't like looking at League tables because I don't like negative things . . . running a club is all about unity. Some people think there is no time left for Chelsea. That relegation would be a disaster leading to liquidation. But Chelsea were in the Second Division the season before last in the same circumstances and have survived . . . the good times come out of the bad. Nobody gets to the promised land without the 40 days in the wilderness. Even Cloughie had 44 days at Leeds.' Can you imagine any manager being allowed to make that kind of comment today, now that relegation from the top division is measured in money rather than lost status?

Inevitably, Chelsea was a club riven with dispute and racked by intrigue. Ray Wilkins was at the centre of transfer speculation, but Danny moved to 'kill off the fantasy of a possible move'. The ubiquitous 'player power' was said to be to blame for much behind-the-scenes wrangling. Danny dismissed it at a get-together with the players: 'They were totally demoralized, and one of the reasons for failure was having the club run by insiders, or Chelsea old boys. I said, "I hear you go straight to the chairman with your moans. If you do so from now, you'll be fined. And so will the chairman."' He added: 'I always make jokes that say something serious. This grandstand is not the liability some make out. It's an asset. So long as we get it filled.' That was the task, one not made any easier by his first game in charge. Heading to Ayresome Park with a team selected by Frank Upton, they faced Middlesbrough. Clive Walker was just making his way into the side and remembers that 'Danny just told us to enjoy the game, not to worry about the score and that we had to learn how to lose before we could win.' Peter Osgood recalls, 'I scored after three minutes and then they hammered us 7–2!' Given his first sight of his new charges, Danny admitted, 'There was a lack of understanding in defence . . . I told the players at half-time that they could lie down and be trampled upon or fight back . . . you can't go into the jungle without getting a bite or two . . . it will take two months before I know whether we have a chance of staying up . . . I'll be demanding but I don't want to break their hearts or their spirits. I can only help them help themselves.'

When a team is in trouble, a pall of gloom often settles upon the dressing room. Danny made every attempt to lift that, Walker remembering he 'always had a smile on his face, whatever the result'. But his job was to sort out off-the-field problems as much as those on the pitch. In his first week he arranged meetings with Barclays Bank, to whom Chelsea were so indebted, pointing out 'there has to be an understanding between us so that I don't make rash decisions which can't be carried out'. With Chelsea owing £2.5 million and paying a further £400,000 per annum in interest, the *Daily Mail*'s City Editor Christopher Fildes made the following semi-serious suggestion: 'Barclays could write off the debt and throw in another million to get the club going. In return the team would play in black shirts with gold eagles and change its name to Barclays United.' Making light of the financial situation, Danny 'told the skipper, when the ref tosses the coin, he's to grab it'.

The real hard work got under way in the week leading up to Christmas, his first full week in the job. Following the Middlesbrough debacle – the precise opposite of the way in which Bill Nicholson's Spurs career had started – Danny took some comfort from the fact that things could only get better. He wrote, 'I am changing things and the players think they know why. I doubt it. Old habits die hard. I think they may just be a little confused at first but I believe in doing things quickly, people get caught up in the pace of things.' In a more candid moment, with Patrick Collins, he confessed that the players were at sea with his ideas. One player complained that training was repetitive: 'I told him, "That's because we are after a repetitive performance. A concert pianist sits at the piano and runs his hands up and down the keys. Five hours a day, every day. Very repetitive. Then he goes along to the concert, sits down to play and he's perfect. Every time. That's what I'm after." The lad just stared at me. I don't know if I got through. But it seemed the best way to explain consistency to him.'

He made it clear that he wanted no rough stuff from the outset, introducing Mickey Nutton to his Chelsea side: 'I saw him play in the reserves at centre-half and liked what I saw. I saw Ron Harris there in the first team and didn't like what I saw.' Duncan McKenzie was restored to the team and Peter Osgood installed as captain. Chelsea were going to play themselves out of trouble or perish in the attempt. For a game at home to Bristol City, Danny set his sights low: 'Let's go for goals. Of course I'd like us to win but more important, I want to see the pattern we've been working on start developing. A win would help us begin believing in ourselves again.' A draw lifted them off the bottom, while another at Southampton suggested a corner might have been turned. Ipswich then administered a rude awakening, 5–1. As the year ended, Chelsea seemed set for the drop. Matters were not improved by the big freeze that descended on the British Isles in the early months of 1979. By 20 February, Chelsea had played just two League games in the new year. Peter Osgood recalls, 'That didn't help, but you can still do your work, your patterns, your formations. You can look at the weather and the injuries we had as excuses, but we just didn't play the right system to suit the players and the position. We had our best performances against good teams, because we knew we had to defend. Any side has to have a steady defence – in the 1970s we had a great keeper and four assassins, Webb, Dempsey, McCreadie, Harris – and they were out and out defenders. That was what he should have done week in week out, but we only did it against sides like Liverpool or West Brom, because if we went after them, we knew we'd get beaten. And that discipline came from ourselves more than from Danny, unfortunately. He wasn't up to doing the coaching be-cause coaching is a young man's game. One day at training he said, ''When I blow the whistle once, I want you to get up, pretend there's a ball there and head it. If I blow it twice, I want you to sprint ten yards, if I blow it three times I want you to turn and run five yards.'' All of a sudden we were jumping up to head the ball and there were whistles going, no one knew where they were supposed to be running, big Mickey Droy was running into people, it was chaos! He just didn't have a clue about coaching players who were playing in a different game at a different level. He tried to do the training that he'd have done with great players at Spurs, but he had young kids around him and they just couldn't do it, pass and run, pass and run. We had people like Trevor Aylott and Tommy Langley, good players, but just starting out in the game, and you couldn't work them the way that you could experienced players like they had at Spurs. The coaching let him down, but away from that he had some real strengths. He created a very good atmosphere, the lads were happy enough with him, but we weren't organized. But it's not all down to the manager, there were some good, experienced players at the club that didn't turn it on for him. Everyone has to share the blame.'

While the side were out of action, Danny managed to prise £200,000 from the bank in order to sign Eamonn Bannon from Hearts. A good passer of the ball, he was the archetypal Blanchflower player. Even so, he was reluctant to make the move south: 'I was a part-timer, studying as a physical education student, and when Chelsea came in, it was a big move for me, in terms of security, money and opportunity. I went down there and I was worried about giving up my degree, so I turned it down at first but Hearts were desperate to sell me because they were going down the pan for £200,000 they owed to the bank!' At this point £200,000 was also a lot of money to Chelsea, so Bannon was immediately placed under pressure, something which Danny tried to alleviate. 'Danny was a very thoughtful, articulate man,' says Bannon. 'I was studying for a degree and played football too, which Danny found very interesting. He took me under his wing at first, took me out to Wentworth and introduced me to his friends, and it was such a difference to what I'd been used to: his friends had a wealthy lifestyle. Danny had a green Mercedes and he'd drive me around, eating packets and packets of Murray mints and talking football. I got the impression he was finding it mildly difficult, not just because of the job but because he had a nice little routine before taking over. He enjoyed his golf, writing his column – he liked that life.'

Danny saw Bannon and Ray Wilkins providing the crucial midfield axis that would lift Chelsea to safety, taking the longer-term view that if Wilkins moved on, Bannon might be able to take on much of that responsibility. There were immediate dividends, for in their first game together, Wilkins scored twice as Birmingham were beaten 2–1, yet this was to be a mere blip. It was increasingly apparent that Danny's views were at odds with the way in which some of his players wanted to operate. In an ever more desperate attempt to find a winning blend, Danny went against his cardinal rule of continuity and made regular changes. Peter Osgood was one victim of the policy, and now believes that 'Danny should have played me at the back as a sweeper the way Glenn Hoddle or Ruud Gullit have at Chelsea in the last couple of years – I could have done that, no problem, and been quite comfy with it. We had some kids there and I could have helped talk them through it – my legs had gone, really, but you just needed a bit of experience and that would have been fine. But Danny had his own ideas and put me in midfield, and I hadn't the stamina for it.'

As the freeze came to a close and League duties resumed, a narrow defeat at Bolton was followed by a creditable draw with eventual Champions Liverpool, after which Emlyn Hughes noted that Chelsea had posed Liverpool 'more problems than anyone else this season'. Eleven days later, Chelsea lost 1–0 at West Bromwich Albion to all but seal their fate. Peter Johnson in the *Daily Mail* damned Chelsea with faint praise: 'Danny Blanchflower is gradually remodelling Chelsea on the push and run elegance of the vintage 1950s squad. Unfortunately they were lacking in the game's basics, such as shooting and tackling.' Danny was defiant, pointing out, 'I'm not happy to lose but the way these boys are going we will have a good team in a year's time. This was the fifth successive time we have outplayed the opposition. Our only problem is we can't score goals.' While Danny couldn't score them himself, he had to take some of the blame for that drought, since tactically he was playing into enemy hands. Eamonn Bannon recalls, 'Danny had a different style of training than most of us were used to. We had a full-scale practice match every day in training – it's like getting chocolate cake every day, you get sick of it after a while, which is the biggest criticism that was pointed at him. He was trying to adopt a style of play which involved the full-backs getting it, passing it to midfield, knocking it back, the full-backs play up to the striker; nice, pretty stuff. What would happen is we'd practice all week, but on a Saturday the full-back would get it, make a pass to the midfield, then it would break down and we'd lose a goal. As players, we wanted to get the ball in their half and play from there. We were struggling and we wanted to battle our way out of it, while Danny wanted to pass our way out of it.' Peter Osgood's view was that, 'Danny was out of touch, had been out for too long. I think he felt his knowledge of the game was good enough to get us out of trouble, and by the time he realized it wasn't any more, it was too late. It was a shame because we had the nucleus of a good team, but he wanted to play the wrong sort of football with what he had. No way would he allow the long ball and slogging your way to a draw. You had to pass the ball, support, pass and run. That was all he'd accept. The little money he had, he used it wrongly. Eamonn flattered to deceive a bit – he became a very good player when he went back to Scotland but he wasn't quite ready to play in the First Division, certainly not in a poor side. If he'd been in a good side, he'd have done well, but he suffered with the rest of us. He worked hard, he was a smashing lad but he wasn't the sort of player that could lift the others on his own, which is what we needed from a new player. If we'd had someone else to do that, to play like a Charlie Cooke, then Eamonn would have excelled, because he had the ability. He should have been the second signing, not the first and virtually the only one.'

It was ironic that Danny should suffer as a manager because of the generation gap. That had driven him away from Barnsley and Aston Villa, but then he was the youngster railing against the time-honoured practices of the elder statesmen. At Chelsea things had turned full circle, with players bewildered by his methods also finding it hard to relate to a man who had retired from the game at about the time they were having their first day at school. One 'anonymous source' was quoted as saying, 'He's fascinating to listen to, but half the time we don't know what he's talking about!' Maybe a few of his jokes did go over their heads – his favourite comment on the tactics was: 'We'll play a fast game to get it over with quickly.' In a more serious vein, he would counsel, 'It's better to have lost a game they should have won than win one they should have lost. The first way you have to think about it and learn from it. The other way you say thanks very much and forget it.' Players conditioned to look for win bonuses in their pay packets would seldom agree. Some were confused by his concentration on means rather than ends, and took that to mean that results were unimportant. In short, things were a mess. 'I understood what he was trying to do,' Eamonn Bannon argues. 'He said he bought me because he wanted an intelligent football player, but players by and large aren't the cleverest bunch, a lot have left school as early as they can. Even then, they're still a cross-section of society: you get bright ones and stupid ones, lively ones and dour ones. Bearing that in mind, he probably over-talked the thing. It was complicated, it was involved, technical, and a lot of times on a Saturday you couldn't see what we'd been practising coming through at all on the field. When that's happening, the players lose heart.'

Nine defeats in ten games pushed Chelsea over the precipice, but still Danny retained his ideals. He was clearly hurt by his failure to turn things round quickly, but he'd been under no illusions as to the size of the task. After losing 6–0 at Forest, questions were asked as to his future. His response was, 'I couldn't possibly leave the club when they are in a position like this. If they want me, I shall stay for next season ... when we were reduced to ten men [by injury] after the sixth goal we played some marvellous football for the last twenty minutes and I was proud of the way those youngsters continued to battle.' Those youngsters were at the very heart of the problem. In part, it was down to the difference between young men of his generation and those that were now playing under him. Danny's peers had been to war or had expected to take part in active service, they'd lived through the deprivations of pre-war depression and post-war austerity and, as such, were harder, more mature people than the twenty-year-olds under Danny's charge. Look now at the way young players like Ryan Giggs have been wrapped in cotton wool by clubs – there's nothing wrong in that for it recognizes changing times and demands on the players – but would men like Finney, Wright, Edwards or Mannion have needed it? The young players at Chelsea weren't expected to be able to cope with the pressure and so it became a self-fulfilling prophecy. Equally, there was not always the same dedication to the game that Danny had been used to as a player. In exasperation, he was finally forced to say of this new crop, 'They need time and they need discipline. Discipline is about doing things you do not like doing. If it were easy and comfortable everybody would do it naturally and there would be no special rewards for it.'

Danny remained sensitive to their needs and made it clear that 'Chelsea need a long-term policy. There is a lack of experience here but the club haven't the money for an immediate remedy. Even if they were allowed to increase the debt it would be wrong to do so until they have found out what the present young players are really like. Things may have to get worse before they get better.

If you play a little football and lose, you still have something. If you play the other way and lose, you have nothing . . . in many ways, this is a very good football club, I would like to develop it from there.' Danny was not so naïve as to think that time would be on his side, especially after such an ignominious start to his tenure, yet he seemed not to care. As the season finally ended, he declared, 'We weren't good enough for the First Division. Now we must build, bring in young players and find a level somewhere in the Second. You can't find a level when you're out of your depth like we have been this season. Of course I want us to come up again next year but only if we're good enough. Failure should please nobody. But if you fear it too much, does that not help it feed upon itself? Given the choice, would you not prefer failure near the beginning of the road rather than the end? Chelsea's first priority is to reduce that debt and we will have to severely limit ourselves. I'm resigned to the fact that the club has got to get back money to pay off the debt. I've tried selling some of our liabilities without any luck so now the only way is to sell an asset, Ray Wilkins. But the fans approach me and ask about a replacement for him. When I try to explain to them that Chelsea are £2 million in debt they shrug their shoulders as if that were totally irrelevant.'

It was as Danny began to plan for the new season that he came face to face with the new realities which ruled the game. His erstwhile Barnsley colleague Steve Griffiths recalls speaking to Danny at the time: 'When we played the game, we signed contracts for a year at a time, but now he said the Chelsea players had two-and three-year contracts, and so he couldn't get rid of the ones who were no good! He was boxed in.' Eamonn Bannon agrees, pointing out, 'At Chelsea you got loyalty bonuses, something like £2000 per season just for staying. So if you had a three-year deal, you got £6000 on top of what you'd agreed – just to say, "Well done, you stayed with us!" There is a problem with London clubs, because if you move there from elsewhere it's an expensive business buying property and so on, so perhaps that was necessary to attract players to London, but it's not an incentive to play well.'

As one who was always looking to change the game for the better, Danny could scarcely complain that things had moved on. He had come to see that his days in control on the training pitch were pretty much numbered, and wanted to appoint an assistant with a view to the future. Having tried to bring in Brentford's Bill Dodgin, he then decided to approach Geoff Hurst: 'He approached me during the Home Internationals in 1979, having broached the idea via a newspaperman, as is often the case. I was delighted – I was serving an apprenticeship at Telford and felt I was ready for a bigger club under Danny. It was an easy decision to make to come back to London, especially since Danny had such a great track record in the game. Obviously, I knew what I was getting into – a difficult time for the club with those debts, the managing director was in control on behalf of the bank, they'd just been relegated – but then again they were the kind of club that if you got it right, there was huge potential there. That was exciting for me. He saw me primarily as a tracksuited coach, which suited me fine. Over the years at West Ham, Stoke and West Bromwich Albion, and with England, I'd worked under a number of managers and gleaned a lot of knowledge from them. They had been playing full-scale practice matches. I wasn't keen on that, I think it's the kind of thing you do now and then, but a lot of coaching can be done sectionally with small groups or individuals, which is what I'd learned from Ron Greenwood at West Ham. Danny was happy to let me get on with that, because obviously I'd come in to do different things with the coaching. I think in part my appointment came about because he hoped the young players would relate better to me because I was fifteen years younger than him – that was how I'd come into the coaching scene with England too: Ron Greenwood felt he needed someone to bridge the gap between him and the players. I think Danny felt I could talk their language, to convey the tactics. We had an awful lot of young players and the difficulty was that they couldn't always gasp what Danny wanted. Danny had vision, but as a coach or manager you have to strike a balance – if you can't be clear in what you want, you can't teach them anything. I know as a youngster at West Ham, some of the things that Ron Greenwood wanted I didn't always fully appreciate until later on.'

The youngsters certainly did take to Hurst – for young men of twenty in 1979, Hurst's World Cup hat-trick would be a cherished childhood memory. Hurst was still a great hero to them and, seen in this light, it was an apparently intelligent appointment, providing an essential lift to the spirits. But for Danny it was merely storing up trouble, for the star-struck kids responded far better to Hurst's blandishments than they did to Danny's. Eamonn Bannon certainly felt that, 'When Geoff Hurst arrived, training improved dramatically, more of a mixture with five-a-sides and so on.' There was greater optimism about the place than there had been for a year or more, but Danny regularly struck a note of caution, stressing that promotion should be gained the right way, with a team that could survive: 'The priority this season has got to be to get our house in order. I don't feel we can get into the big race until we clear most of the debt. The other important thing is to keep pulling in the crowds . . . if we have a mediocre season, the debt would escalate. I've always felt that football is a bit like tribal warfare. The strength of a club depends to a certain extent on the strength of its tribe.'

It had been short-termism that had driven Chelsea to the brink. To continue with that methodology was suicidal. Danny was also keen that someone should accept the specific, and unique, difficulties that Chelsea faced, and then address them. In many ways, Chelsea is a rootless club, one which doesn't have the same solid local support of a Liverpool, Manchester United or Arsenal. In the glory days of the 1960s and early 1970s, Chelsea was the most glamorous club in the country, reinforcing the impression that when the club is doing well, it really can thrive. When success faded, so did much of the glitter and it was left with a considerably smaller hard-core support than similar clubs. Danny accepted that fact, adding, 'It's so near to the West End that it's influenced by its environment. Sometimes the social side is better than the football. You have to try to balance things out without destroying either. Chelsea is a sort of social club as well as a football club. People came in for a drink and a chat, a bit of gossip. Perhaps there are more rumours coming out of Chelsea than from any other football club in the country. The social club is in conflict with good football discipline. To change that might seem a simple answer but can you really change a club's environment and tradition without doing harm? And why had it not been done before? If you chop away the social atmosphere at Chelsea you might chop away a lot of friends. You might chop away support you badly need. I gave all this some thought. Team discipline could only be improved gradually by changing habits and we would need a permanent training facility elsewhere to do that. A great opportunity to start this has been sadly neglected.' Geoff Hurst also admits: 'Chelsea was a very difficult club to manage. The financial problems were serious, but a lot of difficulty comes from where the ground is situated, in the heart of the West End, with the sort of support they got. It wasn't a ground conducive to getting good results at home. It was vast, poorly designed, the Shed was a long way away. Stamford Bridge is part of a vicious circle. You need to have lots of people there to create an atmosphere, but if you don't get the results, you don't get the crowds, and if you don't get the crowds, you don't get the atmosphere that helps get results. If you look at clubs like Liverpool or Manchester United, Spurs, West Ham, they're tight, enclosed grounds with a good atmosphere, and that gives you a start. Also with Chelsea, it wasn't too long after the glory days of the 1960s and 1970s and the players were living in the shadow of that too, without having the quality.'

In retrospect, it's obvious that Danny was living on borrowed time right from the start of the 1979–80 season. As he ruefully admitted later, 'Skill is a rare blossom, you have to encourage it, wait for it. My methods take four or five years to develop. Who, in our football, dares to allow that?' His unease extended beyond the general, however. Specifically, 'I smelt things about the place. You are working with players who have grown up with greater financial rewards than we knew as players. Their values aren't my values and I'm not changing my values. I'm not a cheat. Because it's become so common to get round the rules it's no longer looked on as cheating. You hear rumours of players who are wanting £40,000 free of tax. I wouldn't get involved in that. In my day we had the maximum wage, which was unfair, but the pendulum has now swung too far the other way. There was a time in football when the player had a bad deal . . . the winds of socialism have changed all that. Now the player has freedom of contract. He is free to deal with another club as soon as his present contract expires. Nobody could begrudge him that if the dealings are fair and above board. But there are doubts about some of that . . . Managers tell each other, "So and so asked so and so for £20,000 in cash in his hand as a payment before he would even talk about astronomical wages." Do the players tell each other the secrets too? It is not the growing demands and the big payments that worry me. If they are all honest there is nothing wrong with them. It is the talk of underhand payments that bothers me.' If Danny lost people with his tactical briefings, he utterly bewildered them with talk of integrity. That belonged to yesterday's world – Thatcher had just won her first election victory, after all.

In spite of this unpromising background, Chelsea got off to a good start, holding Sunderland at home, then winning at West Ham. Danny remarked: 'We'll get promotion the Irish way, win away, draw at home.' Things quickly turned sour though, with defeat at Newcastle and a disappointing League Cup exit at the hands of Plymouth Argyle. Geoff Hurst believes: 'He had these ideals about how the game should be played and perhaps he lost sight of the practicalities. When you're in the Second Division, as it was then, probably the hardest to get out of, you have to get results. You need to strike a balance between the two, as Liverpool had. If they had the opportunity to play, they did so, but if they had to grind out a 1–0, then they would. Even so, half a dozen games in was too early to talk of crisis, farcically so, but people do. The papers are on your back, but then look at the way the press reacted when Manchester United lost the first game of the Double-Double season. It's stupid but you cannot escape it, it stirs the supporters up; in business, you have the chance to take a quiet look at your problems and work your way out of it, but a football club is in the papers day after day and you're not given the time, especially if you're a big club.' Chelsea also laboured under the particular handicap of a news media willing them to fall apart – a club like that going to the wall made for a great story. None had gone that way since Accrington Stanley or Bradford Park Avenue, but they were nowhere near Chelsea's stature. Chelsea were back page *and* front page news.

The final straw came in defeat at home to Birmingham City in front of 17,182 paying customers. The following day, a newspaper article appeared under Peter Osgood's name: 'I said that Geoff should take charge because he was closer to the players' age, and it got a bit lost that I also said Danny should become general manager. I got some of the blame for Danny leaving because of that, which wasn't the case – he knew it was coming. I went to see him. I told him I thought he could do a great job still at the club, we all respected him, but that he should have involved Geoff more. But he just said, "Ossie, I made a big mistake, I should never have come back," which was sad. He knew he didn't have it any longer. What would have worked better was to have Danny as the general manager to talk things through with the players. He was easy to talk to, a lovely, reassuring fellow – with me it was all, ''You've had your time, Ossie, but we still need you at the club, there's plenty for you to do here,'' which was fine. Danny was a lovely man, a calming influence, he'd won things and players like to work for men like that because he'd done what they want to do. But he'd been away too long and the game had changed dramatically in those fifteen years.'

On 12 September 1979, Danny offered his resignation, an offer which was accepted by Brian Mears. Geoff Hurst 'got the impression that he knew he'd been out of the game too long. Coming back full-time, with so many young players around, was a difficult transition for him. He recognized the problem, which was why he involved me, but it was too hard for him to come to terms with the changes over fifteen years.' Eamonn Bannon agrees, and adds: 'After the article came out, he felt it was time to go. He was a proud man and he came in on the Monday and just felt he didn't need all the problems any more. A lot of managers would have torn a strip off Peter or sold him, but instead Danny just left the club. In truth, his methods were quite old-fashioned, they were certainly repetitive. Any manager is bound by his results, so whatever he'd done on the training field, if Chelsea had won on a Saturday, he'd have been the manager for as long as he wanted. He was trying his best but he could see it wasn't working, and I think the Osgood thing gave him an excuse. He had the luxury of going back to the life he'd had before, and I think he was happy to do so. Even so, when he gathered us round and told us he was going, it was a bolt from the blue for us.'

In the end, it had been impossible for Danny to turn back the clock to another era, though whether any manager could have salvaged anything from the Chelsea wreckage is highly debatable. It was not failure that pushed him over the edge, but a realization that he simply could not work under the new conditions in which football had begun to operate. Big money deals were becoming increasingly commonplace, hugely inflated transfer fees were destabilizing the game's finances, players and their representatives were taking short cuts and looking for extra financial inducements before they'd sign any contracts. In short, those days were the father of the bastard child that is modern football. Danny wanted no part in them: 'Big money may not be the root of all evil but it is the bait for most evil. The bigger the money gets in football the less morality there will be. Some managers are in it just for the money. You can't really blame them. Many of them are wrongfully sacked, a fair amount are wrongfully employed. It's precarious so they grab it while they can. And players get obsessed with it too . . . one has to recognize evolution and make certain adjustments to survive. But the changes are too wild and weird for me. I don't really trust them and I could not commit myself to them. It was time for me to leave the Bridge. I think the team will be good enough to hold its own in the Second Division. A couple of good signings might help it to promotion. But about three years of careful building and sound economy could see the club back in a good position in the First Division where, when the debt is cleared, it really belongs.'

Two months after Danny walked out of Stamford Bridge, he relinquished his hold on affairs with Northern Ireland. His brief and perhaps ill-judged dalliance with football management was finally at an end. How good a job did he do, or, more interestingly, might he have done in the right circumstances? Peter Osgood believes, 'Danny could have been a great manager – if he'd come to Chelsea ten or twelve years before, when we had good players and a stable club, he would have been great. The football he tried to play . . . players like myself and Ron Harris could see what he was trying to do, and agreed with it, I was 100 per cent behind it, but the kids couldn't grasp it. They worked hard, they were fit and willing, but they hadn't had the great footballing education we'd had with a coach like Dave Sexton. I learned from Dave Sexton and I saw what Danny wanted to do, making the game easy. But the funny thing is it can be hard to do the simple things and the lads couldn't grasp it. He also proved that you can't be a successful manager if you haven't got the resources.' Bertie Peacock agrees, pointing to the example of another mid-field genius: 'Danny would have liked Ruud Gullit, the way he's playing at Chelsea. Gullit loves flair too, but he's got that bit of savvy to get it nailed down at the back, though he basically goes forward. He's got the money and the players to do it with. Danny had neither.' Perennial supporter Hunter Davies suspects, 'He was too intelligent, too sensitive to succeed as a manager. It takes low cunning, not high thinking to do that, pig ignorance of what goes on in the rest of the world is an asset if you choose to live in the isolated, lop-sided, hot-house, mad-house atmosphere of football management.' There's a lot in that, for Danny saw football as a game not a war, and nor was he a natural hirer and firer of men. Twenty years earlier, he had told Ron Reynolds at Tottenham that he could never be a manager because it would force him to do things to players that he would have hated to have had done to him. Danny wanted to be loved by his players, wanted football to be a beautiful affair, a paradise for like-minded spirits. He didn't want to upset the youngsters in his care, did not want to dash their hopes and dreams. Clive Walker says that Danny always had a smile on his face around the club – how many great managers can that be applied to? Certainly the likes of Clough, Dalglish, Stein, Shankly and Ferguson seem to have a permanent scowl etched on their faces. They had the players' respect, certainly, but they had more than Danny had – the players' fear, fear of a rollocking, a spell in the reserves or on the bench away from the lights, the glamour, the money. In the highly charged modern game, fear is a vital tool in the manager's armoury, but Danny didn't want to break any hearts. Ally that to his footballing principles, and, sadly, you have a recipe for failure.

So what is a decent man to do when faced with a game that has sold off most of its virtues and abandoned the rest? In December 1964, Danny wrote a piece about the plight of Benny Fenton, manager of Leyton Orient. Fenton was mercilessly attacked for his negative tactics, tactics which didn't get results. Inevitably, he was sacked. As one whose ideals insisted on attacking football at all times, one would expect Danny to have rejoiced, berating Fenton in the process. But he was too intelligent a man to simply follow the herd. Instead, he looked to the root of the problem: 'Benny Fenton was caught up in the mood of the game around him. He believed he had to tighten up his teamwork to survive. He believed that if he played attacking football without the players really capable to do it then the defensively minded opposition would have had a field day against them. Who is to say he was wrong? Yet if he had played attacking football would he have done any worse? Who is to say? The point is, if he had, would his directors have been satisfied with the same results as they have now? Would the fans? Benny is gone but the dilemma still remains.' That dilemma also did for Danny in the end. He left Chelsea and Northern Ireland before he was pushed. Football lost one of its most radical servants, Danny lost his game. But since the glory game had become the money game, whose was the greater loss?

11   The Beautiful and the Damned

So Danny's career as a manager ended in some ignominy. Perhaps he should have trusted his instincts and let football management pass him by. However, he was at least fortunate in having a career to go back to, returning to his regular berth at the *Sunday Express*, his golf at Wentworth and his close circle of friends. At the very least, he had given management a try and would not be prey to those darkest of thoughts, 'What if . . .'

As a writer, he continued to produce articles of flair and imagination, but some of the fire had gone from his pen, inevitable, perhaps, given that he had been shown to be yesterday's man. That's not to say that his values were wrong, merely outdated. Throughout the 1980s, though he remained an entertaining and insightful pundit, his columns tended to lack some of their early pungency and he had a tendency to write nostalgic rather than forward-looking pieces. It's not unusual for older people to recall their youth with fondness, but for Danny this was not just a period for reflection, but a search for a better, naïve game that had long been forgotten.

In 1988, he contributed his last column to the *Sunday Express*, leaving that august organ at around the same time as its editor, John Junor. From there, Danny's final years were disfigured by ill health. Chronic arthritis rendered him unable to play his beloved golf. Never preoccupied by money in his life, the loss of his job in Fleet Street brought a measure of hardship, a problem alleviated to some degree by a testimonial held at White Hart Lane in May 1990, which brought in £40,000. From there, Danny suffered the awful descent into oblivion that characterizes Alzheimer's Disease, Cliff Jones explaining: 'It was awful to see such a sparkling personality with so much presence just disappear. But when I remember him, it's with a smile. He used to play that way too. He'd say, "Football's a beautiful game," and it was the way he played it, the way he lived his life.' When the end finally came, in Cobham Nursing Home in Surrey on 9 December 1993, it was almost a relief for those around him, people whom he could no longer recognize. On St Valentine's Day 1994, a service of thanksgiving was held in the Cathedral Church of St Anne, Belfast. The service closed with the Cup Final hymn, 'Abide With Me'.

So what can we conclude of Robert Dennis Blanchflower? It's safe to say that football has rarely found a character to match him for wit or invention, for idiosyncrasies or eccentricities, for self-belief or wider belief in the greater glory of the game. He was a paradoxical mix of the self-centred and the kindly, a hard man to get to know but a close and loyal friend, one who would not suffer fools but who would try to educate the inexperienced, a visionary trapped by the methods of yesteryear, an outspoken writer who kept himself to himself. It's true that Danny was a footballing genius, not in the sense of Best or Pele, but as a philosophical giant amid intellectual dwarves, one of very few who could give football a broader perspective. Football was beautiful in itself, but it reflected a wider world. All human life could be found in a game of football, the world's preoccupations embodied in the conflict between twenty-two players, each of whom had a part to play in the subtle unfolding of the drama. The great Caribbean writer C. L. R. James once wrote of the game of cricket, 'What do they know of cricket who only cricket know?' It was a dictum that Danny applied to football. It is not the sum of goals scored, points won, passes successfully made, replica shirts sold, executive boxes filled. That is but a part of the game; it's also about supporters who may have received a bonus at work or may have been laid off, it's about a pervading climate of sleaze or of rejuvenation, it's about ordinary people celebrating life or being frozen out of their favourite pastime, it's about leadership or stagnation, entertainment or gloom, life in the round.

Seen from one end of his existence his life was a triumphal procession, at the other end a faltering tragedy. Blanchflower's life had to have that mix to make it a complete, compelling whole. As with one of his favourite authors, F. Scott Fitzgerald, Danny's life revolved around a great theme, the need for beauty and romance, the elusive, illusory and ephemeral nature of that beauty, and the tragedy that followed in the wake of its inevitable demise. His career with Tottenham and Northern Ireland was a thing of rare beauty, of courage, leadership, intelligence and ability. His spell with Chelsea and as manager of Northern Ireland gave life the opportunity to administer a harsh reminder of its more brutal realities.

In the wake of those comparative reverses, the football world forgot the lessons Danny had helped teach at Tottenham, banished him to the margins of the game, as though it were afraid that his perceived deficiencies might be contagious. No one looked at him for answers any longer since the powers that be branded him a failure. Yet is an idealist ever really a failure? Was Kevin Keegan a failure at Newcastle United? To give people hope, to give them something of rare elegance to cherish, albeit fleetingly, is that a failure? It's a poor, soulless game that can only measure itself in league tables and trophies. It's a worse one that measures itself in money; football doesn't only miss Danny's flair, it misses his principles of honesty and integrity. At the end of each season, of the ninety-two clubs that set out on a campaign, only a dozen will have achieved something concrete – a Cup, promotion, a place in Europe. The rest will have simply played another forty or fifty-odd games of football. The better ones, those most sensibly led, will have given their supporters something to remember, a reason to renew their season tickets. A game without joy, without hope, without ideals is bankrupt, morally and spiritually. British football needs a Danny Blanchflower, now more than ever. The pity of it is, it wouldn't know what to do with him.

CAREER RECORD

PLAYER

BARNSLEY:

	FL	g	FA	g
1948–9	1	0	0	0
1949–50	36	1	1	0
1950–1	31	1	1	0
TOTAL	**68**	**2**	**2**	**0**

ASTON VILLA:

	FL	g	FA	g
1950–1	11	0	0	0
1951–2	42	0	1	0
1952–3	41	4	5	0
1953–4	40	4	1	0
1954–5	14	2	0	0
TOTAL	**148**	**10**	**7**	**0**

TOTTENHAM HOTSPUR:

	FL	g	FA	g	EU	g	
1954–5	22	0	3	0	0	0	
1955–6	40	0	6	0	0	0	
1956–7	39	1	3	1	0	0	
1957–8	40	0	2	0	0	0	
1958–9	36	1	1	0	0	0	
1959–60	40	2	4	1	0	0	
1960–1	42	6	7	0	0	0	Won League & FA Cup
1961–2	39	2	7	2	8	2	Won FA Cup
1962–3	24	3	0	0	4	0	Won Cup Winners Cup
1963–4	15	0	0	0	0	0	
TOTAL	**337**	**15**	**33**	**4**	**12**	**2**	
CAREER	**553**	**27**	**42**	**4**	**12**	**2**	

NORTHERN IRELAND:

1/10/49	Scotland	Belfast	2–8	WCQ
8/3/50	Wales	Wrexham	0–0	WCQ
7/10/50	England	Belfast	1–4	
1/11/50	Scotland	Hampden	1–6	
12/5/51	France	Belfast	2–2	
19/3/52	Wales	Swansea	0–3	
4/10/52	England	Belfast	2–2	
5/11/52	Scotland	Hampden	1–1	
11/11/52	France	Paris	1–3	
15/4/53	Wales	Belfast	2–3	
3/10/53	Scotland	Belfast	1–3	WCQ
11/11/53	England	Everton	1–3	WCQ
31/3/54	Wales	Wrexham	2–1	WCQ
2/10/54	England	Belfast	0–2	
3/11/54	Scotland	Hampden	2–2	
20/4/55	Wales	Belfast	2–3	
8/10/55	Scotland	Belfast	2–1	
2/11/55	England	Wembley	0–3	
11/4/56	Wales	Cardiff	1–1	
6/10/56	England	Belfast	1–1	
7/11/56	Scotland	Hampden	0–1	
16/1/57	Portugal	Lisbon	1–1	WCQ
10/4/57	Wales	Belfast	0–0	
25/4/57	Italy	Rome	0–1	WCQ
1/5/57	Portugal	Belfast	3–0	WCQ
5/10/57	Scotland	Belfast	1–1	
6/11/57	England	Wembley	3–2	
4/12/57	Italy	Belfast	2–2	
15/1/58	Italy	Belfast	2–1	WCQ
16/4/58	Wales	Cardiff	1–1	
8/6/58	Cz'slovakia	Halmstad	1–0	WC
11/6/58	Argentina	Halmstad	1–3	WC
15/6/58	W. Germany	Malmo	2–2	WC
17/6/58	Cz'slovakia	Malmo	2–1	WC
19/6/58	France	Norrkoping	0–4	WC
4/10/58	England	Belfast	3–3	
15/10/58	Spain	Madrid	2–6	
5/11/58	Scotland	Hampden	2–2	
22/4/59	Wales	Belfast	4–1	
3/10/59	Scotland	Belfast	0–4	
18/11/59	England	Wembley	1–2	
6/4/60	Wales	Wrexham	2–3	(1 goal)
8/10/60	England	Belfast	2–5	

26/10/60	W. Germany	Belfast	3–4	WCQ
9/11/60	Scotland	Hampden	2–5	(1 goal)
12/4/61	Wales	Belfast	1–5	
10/5/61	W. Germany	Berlin	1–2	WCQ
7/10/61	Scotland	Belfast	1–6	
17/10/61	Greece	Belfast	2–0	WCQ
22/11/61	England	Wembley	1–1	
11/4/62	Wales	Cardiff	0–4	
9/5/62	Netherlands	Rotterdam	0–4	
10/10/62	Poland	Katowice	2–0	ENC
20/10/62	England	Belfast	1–3	
7/11/62	Scotland	Hampden	1–5	
28/11/62	Poland	Belfast	2–0	ENC

Played 56, won 11, drawn 16, lost 29.

MANAGER

CHELSEA

Division One:

16/12/78	Middlesbrough	A		2–7
23/12/78	Bristol City	H		0–0
26/12/78	Southampton	A		0–0
30/12/78	Ipswich Town	A		1–5
20/1/79	Manchester City	A		3–2
3/2/79	Birmingham City	H		2–1
21/2/79	Coventry City	H		1–3
24/2/79	Bolton Wanderers	A		1–2
3/3/79	Liverpool	H		0–0
10/3/79	Norwich City	A		0–2
14/3/79	WBA	A		0–1
17/3/79	QPR	H		1–3
24/3/79	Wolverhampton W.	H		1–2
28/3/79	Nottingham Forest	A		0–6
4/4/79	Derby County	H		1–1
7/4/79	Nottingham Forest	H		1–3
10/4/79	Bristol City	A		1–3
14/4/79	Southampton	H		1–2
16/4/79	Arsenal	A		2–5
21/4/79	Middlesbrough	H		2–1
28/4/79	Aston Villa	A		1–2
5/5/79	Ipswich Town	H		2–3
14/5/79	Arsenal	H		1–1
16/5/79	Manchester United	A		1–1

FA Cup:

15/1/79	Manchester United	A		0–3

Division Two:

18/8/79	Sunderland	H	0–0
20/8/79	West Ham United	A	1–0
25/8/79	Wrexham	H	3–1
1/9/79	Newcastle United	A	1–2
8/9/79	Birmingham City	H	1–2

Football League Cup:

28/8/79	Plymouth Argyle	A	2–2
4/9/79	Plymouth Argyle	H	1–2

Played 32, won 5, drawn 8, lost 19.

NORTHERN IRELAND:

13/10/76	Netherlands	Rotterdam	2–2
10/11/76	Belgium	Liege	0–2
27/4/77	W. Germany	Cologne	0–5
28/5/77	England	Belfast	1–2
1/6/77	Scotland	Hampden	0–3
3/6/77	Wales	Belfast	1–1
11/6/77	Iceland	Reykjavik	0–1
21/9/77	Iceland	Belfast	2–0
12/10/77	Netherlands	Belfast	0–1
16/11/77	Belgium	Belfast	3–0
13/5/78	Scotland	Hampden	1–1
16/5/78	England	Wembley	0–1
19/5/78	Wales	Wrexham	0–1
20/9/78	Rep. Ireland	Dublin	0–0
25/10/78	Denmark	Belfast	2–1
29/11/78	Bulgaria	Sofia	2–0
7/2/79	England	Wembley	0–4
2/5/79	Bulgaria	Belfast	2–0
19/5/79	England	Belfast	0–2
22/5/79	Scotland	Hampden	0–1
25/5/79	Wales	Belfast	1–1
6/6/79	Denmark	Copenhagen	0–4
17/10/79	England	Belfast	1–5
21/11/79	Rep. Ireland	Belfast	1–0

Played 24, won 6, drawn 5, lost 13.

Bibliography

Blanchflower, Danny, *Danny Blanchflower's Soccer Book* (Muller 1959)

Blanchflower, Danny, *The Double and Before* ... (Nicholas Kaye 1961)

Butler, Bryon & Ron Greenwood, *Soccer Choice* (Pelham, 1979)

Camkin, John, *World Cup 1958* (Hart-Davis, 1958)

Collins, Patrick, *The Sportswriter* (Virgin, 1996)

Davies, Hunter, *The Glory Game* (Weidenfeld and Nicolson, 1972)

Dennis, Brian, *The Definitive Barnsley FC* (Association of Football Statisticians, 1996)

Ferris, Ken, *The Double* (Two Heads, 1996)

Finn, Ralph L., *Spurs Go Marching On* (Robert Hale, 1963)

Finn, Ralph L., *The Official History of Tottenham Hotspur FC 1882–1972* (Robert Hale, 1972)

Goodwin, Bob, *The Spurs Alphabet* (ACL & Polar, 1992)

Goodyear, David & Tony Matthews, *Aston Villa: A Complete Record* (Breedon, 1988)

Harris, Harry, *Tottenham Hotspur Greats* (Sportsprint, 1990)

Holland, Julian, *Spurs – The Double* (Heinemann, 1961)

Jennings, Pat, *An Autobiography* (Collins Willow, 1983)

Lodge, Keith, *Oakwell Saints Go Marching On!* (Barnsley FC, 1987)

Matthews, Tony, *Aston Villa Who's Who* (Paper Plane, 1990)

Morris, Peter, *Aston Villa – The History Of A Great Football Club* (Naldrett, 1960)

Parkinson, Michael, *Sporting Profiles* (Pavilion, 1995)

Rogan, Johnny, *The Football Managers* (Queen Anne, 1989)

Soar, Phil, *And the Spurs Go Marching On* ... (Hamlyn, 1982)

Taylor, Rogan & Andrew Ward, *Kicking and Screaming* (Robson, 1995)

Tottenham Hotspur FC, *The Glory, Glory Nights* (Cockerel Books, 1986)

Walvin, James, *The People's Game* (Mainstream, 1994)

Aston Villa Football Club Official Handbook
Birmingham Sports Argus Football Annual
Rothmans Football Yearbook

Barnsley Chronicle
Belfast Telegraph
Birmingham Evening Mail
Birmingham Sports Argus
Daily Mail
London Evening News
Observer
Sunday Express
The Times

New Statesman
When Saturday Comes

Index